Pillars

of Joy in

Marriage

Looking at Marriage in Heaven's Eyes

Dr. Nozipho N. Nxumalo

WESTBOW
P R E S S°
A DIVISION OF THOMAS NELSON
& ZONDERVAN

Scripture quotations marked (NIV) are taken from the Holy Bible, New International Version®, NIV®. Copyright © 1973, 1978, 1984, 2011 by Biblica, Inc.™ Used by permission of Zondervan. All rights reserved worldwide. www. zondervan.com The "NIV" and "New International Version" are trademarks registered in the United States Patent and Trademark Office by Biblica, Inc.™

Scripture taken from the New King James Version®. Copyright © 1982 by Thomas Nelson. Used by permission. All rights reserved.

"KJV": Taken from the King James Bible.

Scripture quotations are taken from the Holy Bible, New Living Translation, copyright ©1996, 2004, 2007, 2013, 2015 by Tyndale House Foundation. Used by permission of Tyndale House Publishers, Inc., Carol Stream, Illinois 60188. All rights reserved.

WestBow Press books may be ordered through booksellers or by contacting:

WestBow Press
A Division of Thomas Nelson & Zondervan
1663 Liberty Drive
Bloomington, IN 47403
www.westbowpress.com
1 (866) 928-1240

Because of the dynamic nature of the Internet, any web addresses or links contained in this book may have changed since publication and may no longer be valid. The views expressed in this work are solely those of the author and do not necessarily reflect the views of the publisher, and the publisher hereby disclaims any responsibility for them.

Any people depicted in stock imagery provided by Getty Images are models, and such images are being used for illustrative purposes only.
Certain stock imagery © Getty Images.

ISBN: 978-1-9736-2548-3 (sc)
ISBN: 978-1-9736-2549-0 (hc)
ISBN: 978-1-9736-2547-6 (e)

Library of Congress Control Number: 2018904302

Print information available on the last page.

WestBow Press rev. date: 09/28/2018

To my husband, Godwin L. S. Nxumalo, the love of my life.

Your patience, support, calm, and peaceful demeanor are unprecedented!
We have experienced immense joy in our marriage of over four decades.

I would not have written this book without your unconditional love,
understanding, and encouragement. In your quiet way, and through
it all, you have always been a pillar of joy and a tower of strength.

I am blessed to have a God-fearing man such as you by my side as
a spouse and as my running mate in this marriage marathon.

Without a doubt, I could not have married a better man.

I am truly honored to be your wife.

Happiness is circumstantial, euphoric, externally driven, and short lived; but joy is an attitude, a state of mind and is internally motivated regardless of prevailing circumstances.

—Dr. Frank W. Hale Jr.

Contents

Special Acknowledgments

To preliminary reader Kimberley Upchurch and editor Dr. Donald Vanterpool, a special thank-you for your professionalism and expertise in ensuring this piece is biblically and scholarly presentable.
To Keith Manungo, who was responsible for the graphic design of most of the illustrative diagrams in this book. Thank you, Keith. I am highly indebted to you.
To Rebeca Legarde for designing an attention-catching cover for this book. I am grateful for your artistry.
To Raka and Sesethu Pilane, Johannesburg, South Africa, and Ben and Dr. Michele Oyortey, Columbus, Ohio, USA, for providing me with a comfortable and serene environment in which to complete this book. I could not have done it without you. Thank you! May God bless your homes.
And to my South African homeboy Trevor Noah of Comedy Central. Your humor kept me sane through it all. Thank you for unleashing my sense of humor and inspiring me to use it when I communicate truth with power!

Acknowledgments

To God be the glory! It is He who gave me knowledge and wisdom to write this book; the God of peace who sheltered me in perfect storms; my one and only Ranger who guided my marriage through the maze and intricacies of life; my secret code and password to access blessings, peace, and joy in my marriage of fifty years.

In memory of my beloved parents, Killion and Mildred Tenyane, who were my number one role model of a joyous couple, and who instilled in me unconditional love, imparted their moral values rooted in the fear of God, and exposed me to Christian values of education and parenthood.

To my son, Sekie Nxumalo Sr., who kept me
real and firmly grounded on my knees!

In memory of my dear friend and mentor Dr. Frank W.
Hale Jr., former vice provost, Ohio State University.

A special thank-you to my colleague and friend Dr. Valerie B.
Lee, interim chair, Department of African American and African
Studies, College of Arts and Sciences, Ohio State University,
for her honest critique and peer review of the manuscript.

Last but not least, I take the liberty to express my heartfelt gratitude particularly to the following scholars, speakers, and writers whose wisdom has in part, directly or indirectly influenced the undergirding themes shaping the pillars of joy expressed in this book, with permission where applicable.

Dr. Barry Black, sixty-second chaplain of the United States Senate, and author of *The Blessings of Adversity: Finding Your God-Given Purpose in Life's Troubles*.

Dr. Calvin B. Rock, former president of Oakwood University, vice president of the General Conference of the Seventh-day Adventist Church, and author of *Something Better: God's Gracious Provisions for Our Daily Decisions*.

Dr. Jim Sharps, ND, HD, NSC, PhD, International Institute of Original Medicine, author of *Course Study Guide: Fundamentals of Nutrition and Hierarchy of Nutrients* and *Basic Principles of Total Health*.

Dr. Ravi C. Zacharias, renowned public speaker and author of *Why Jesus? Discovering His Truth in an Age of Mass Market Spirituality*.

Introduction

Marriage Disposition

(Pre-Sin vs. Post-Sin Condition and Eternal Condition)

To put the marriage outlook or disposition into proper perspective before embarking on the journey of *Pillars of Joy in Marriage*, it is necessary that the reader review in brief the condition of humanity before humans sinned and compare it to what the human condition is now. In so doing, the reader will appreciate why it is necessary for a couple to build a healthy and mutually fulfilling marriage that looks forward to the coming of the true "Prince Charming," Jesus Christ, when the pre-sin experience will be renewed.

Pre-Sin Condition

Let us roll back the imaginary clock to the time of the garden of Eden to conceptualize what marriage was like before our first parents on earth, Adam and Eve, sinned or broke the law of God. The man and his wife were both naked, but they felt no shame (Genesis 2:25). God made man perfectly holy and happy; and the fair earth, as it came from the Creator's hand, bore no blight of decay or shadow of the curse. It was transgression of God's law, the law of love, that brought woe and death (E. G. White, *Steps to Christ*, p. 10). Therefore, the marriage union was perfectly holy, a relationship in perfect unity. The first couple were perfectly happy and carefree, with no shame or guilt whatsoever. If the first couple had remained connected and obedient to the divine injunctions, then they, and all subsequent couples on earth, would have experienced a completely carefree and sinless environment without strife, guilt, or shame for eternity.

God made humans to be perfectly holy and happy moral beings in all respects. God saw that it was not good for man to be alone. He said, "I will make him a helper who is just right for him" (Genesis 2:18 NLT).

The zebras and elephants could not appeal to Adam's emotional and physical intimacy. Hence, God established the institution of marriage as a mutually fulfilling relationship for both the husband and wife. He Himself performed the very first holy marriage. God joined Adam and Eve in a perfectly happy union and sealed the marriage with a sacred covenant predicated on the vow of permanence. He then blessed the couple to "be fruitful and multiply; fill the earth and subdue it" (Genesis 1:28 NKJV). God invented sex for the couple to cleave together and consummate the *sacred bond* with each other for the purpose of deriving immense pleasure as well as procreation.

For the perfect dowry, God gave the newlyweds everything and fullness thereof in the garden of Eden. For physical development and exercise, He instructed the couple to tend the garden and eat of every fruit therein, including that of the tree of life, to perpetuate their longevity for eternity. For moral discipline and character, God forbade the couple from eating the fruit of just one tree in the garden, the tree of the knowledge of good and evil, which God deemed in His divine wisdom would be detrimental to the couple's existence and usher in the propensity to sin, the preponderance of evil, and death. God said to the first couple: "You may freely eat of every three in the garden except the tree of knowledge and evil. If you eat its fruit, you are sure to die" (Genesis 2:17 NLT), thereby testing the couple's allegiance to Him as their God, Creator, and eternal Father. For supreme mental capacity, the couple enjoyed face-to-face class sessions under God's tutorage in the cool of the morning every single day. For spiritual development, God instituted the Sabbath for the couple to set aside time, come together, and experience an intense true fellowship that glorified their Maker and heavenly Father, as well as provided true rest from their daily activities. For their heavenly inheritance, God unveiled His contingency plan of salvation, just in case humankind were to lose their allegiance to God. Thus, God made a sacred and eternal commitment to save, reconcile, and restore humankind to its original holy image and perfectly happy disposition by incorporating a plan to reclaim the earth and restore it to the garden of Eden's sinless environment.

What needs to be emphasized here is that during the pre-sin era, marriage was far different from what it is today. The first married couple, Adam and Eve, completely enjoyed the following benefits.

- immense happiness in an environment devoid of evil society,
- complete presence of the company of God, their divine heavenly Father,
- perfect holiness and a perfectly happy relationship,
- organic allegiance to God and total submission to the divine order and moral injunction, and
- true connection to God and to each other.

Post-Sin Condition

It is important to note that before Adam and Eve sinned, God clothed them with His own robe of righteousness. Their physical stature was flawless. Their ability and intelligence were unlimited. Satan, the fallen angel and archenemy of humankind, disguised himself as a snake and deceived the first couple into eating of the forbidden fruit, which God had commanded them not to eat. Satan, the devil, promised the first couple a better spiritual life, transcendence to the level of "gods," and immortality, contrary to the divine instruction they had received from God Himself. In their quest for meaning and their search for a better life, the couple fell into the snake's trap, not realizing that the devil had used the same technique that put him at loggerheads with God in heaven in the first place, when Satan wanted to put his throne above that of the Most High God (Genesis 3:1,4; Isaiah 14:12–14), and thus had distorted the truth and broken their allegiance to the Creator. The first couple was deceived in the presence of a prewarning, the abundance of knowledge and divine instruction they had received from God Himself. It is important to emphasize that Satan deceived the first couple in exchange for the following things:

- empty promises and
- loss of covering of God's own righteousness (*Shekinah glory*), in exchange for
  - physical nakedness,
  - spiritual emptiness,
  - experience of guilt and shame,
  - devastating sickness, pain, and death, and
  - potential loss of eternal life.

Once the venomous poison of the devil, the old serpent, took effect, the couple instantaneously changed for the worse. For the first time, the cover of righteousness, the Shekinah glory, and perfect holiness left them. Thus, they felt naked, guilty, miserable, and pathetic, engaging in blame assignment to the extent of blaming God for their existence. Eve blamed the snake, while Adam, who had been thrilled when God gave him the woman, did not hesitate to blame God for marrying them, saying, "It was the woman you gave me who gave me the fruit" (Genesis 3:12 NLT).

Thus, sin altered the gene pool of human beings for all future generations, hardwiring and destining their offspring to a death sentence. Sin has a moral right to kill all sinners. As Dr. Calvin Rock puts it, "We are experiencing dying on arrival (DOA)." Before Adam and Eve sinned, they did not know that they were naked, because the Shekinah glory covered them. After they sinned, the cover of righteousness and perfect holiness left them for the first time. How ironic that contemporary society still struggles with issues of accountability for actions and still grapples with the virtue of obedience to the divine moral injunction and allegiance to God. People have become spiritually schizophrenic, choosing God's divine moral imperatives to govern their existence and simultaneously choosing to follow the dictates of their own moral prerogative, part of which is the autonomy to worship other gods or be self-worshipping.

Simply put, when the first couple, Adam and Eve, disobeyed God's divine injunction, they sinned. Disobedience opened the gateway for Satan, the fallen angel, to distort their allegiance to God; and God was not pleased. God cursed the ground for Adam's sake, proclaiming that future generations would now engage in hard labor, struggling, sweating, and scrambling for sustenance. Eve's disobedience changed the fate and sexual pleasure of women, as now they were doomed to bear their offspring in pain and suffering. Hence, havoc broke loose, and the gene pool of human beings for all future generations was forever altered. Pain, evil, and death became part of human existence (Genesis 3:16–19). It is obvious that the devil's notion that humans are "gods" and are getting better is a fallacy! This quest of human beings to discover their own divinity is what Dr. Ravi Zacharias has coined in his book *Why Jesus?* "the mass-marketed spirituality of the new age." Hence, modern society has allowed itself to continue believing the same old lie Satan told the first couple in the garden of Eden.

The fact is that nowadays the human lifespan is shorter than that of the first couple. For instance, Adam lived for 930 years (Genesis 5:5); Seth, 912 years (Genesis 5:8); Enosh, 905 years (Genesis 5:11); Methuselah, 969 years (Genesis 5:27); Lamech, 777 years (Genesis 5:31); and Noah, 950 years (Genesis 9:29). Now check out what God promised the present generation, you and me: a mere seventy years of life. "The days of our lives are seventy years; and if because of strength, they are eighty years, yet their boast is only labor and sorrow" (Psalm 90:10 NKJV). So, if the truth be told, the human condition is no better now in any aspect of our existence, although the devil promised it would be. Instead, since humankind sinned, men and women have been at war within themselves on issues of allegiance to God and in defining the locus of morality.

It is important to note that the devil's ultimate delusion lies in promising human beings what the devil himself could not attain. Do you remember why he was kicked out of heaven? He had tried to put himself as equal to or above the Almighty God through disobedience to the divine order. It should be noted that the devil's tactics are constant in that the old serpent succeeded in tainting and distorting people's views of eternal life. Satan is still promising to give humanity what we already have (namely, the image of God) and promising to give us what he himself has no power over and cannot give us (namely, eternal life). It's a no-brainer that this pattern of deceit and chasing the mirage has been evidently replicated and is reflective of any sin we commit or adverse behaviors we engage in now and through time immemorial.

God designed human beings to reflect His image and character. However, He made humans free moral agents, not robots, who may choose to serve Him or not. Without connection with God, a vacuum or void is created, a space to worship someone or something else (gods) other than the Supreme God, the Creator of all things. Since humans are free moral agents, they can choose their own destiny, and they have the prerogative to make choices about whom they will worship, how they will conduct themselves, and how they will view the marriage relationship. Thus, it is important to emphasize that it is not only the distortion of who is worshipped, God or gods, and how and when, facing the post-sin era but also the choice of how today's society views marriage relationships and how it conceptualizes, approaches, and builds the holy marriage institution.

Eternal Condition

The explanation of how the general mood or disposition toward marriage in the pre-sin and post-sin condition is not complete without touching on the hope of the second advent of our true Prince Charming, Jesus Christ. He promised He would come back again to take His bride, the church, to be with Him in the land of glory, where we will enjoy perfect holiness and happiness within a sinless world order for eternity (John 14:1–3; Revelation 21:2–4; 1 Corinthians 2:9). Can you imagine a carefree society without sin, greed, guilt, shame, pain, sickness, or graveyards? This biblical narrative of eternal life is not a gimmick or bluff by any means. However, we have the prerogative to choose eternal life or not. Where the first couple, Adam and Eve, failed, the eternal condition (what will be) now provides today's families a second chance or hope to experience the pre-sin condition (what was before) and escape the potential condemnation presented by the post-sin condition (reality of what is now). God did not make us robots but made us intelligent moral beings with the ability to choose what we consider important and what we value. Once the first couple was kicked out of Eden, innocence, holiness, perfect happiness, and a carefree life was no longer possible. From that point, humans had to be deliberate in searching for the pre-sin nature, consciously desire to attain an intimate connection with God, and be intentional about cultivating an organic intimate spiritual relationship with each other. Without inviting and embracing God into the marriage relationship, all these things are unattainable.

Given the discourse above, about the interaction among (a) imagining the pre-sin condition, (b) the reality of coexisting with others given the current condition of humankind, and (c) anticipating the promise of a sinless world order, any human attempts to build, shape, or govern marriage relationships without God are futile and predicated on choosing one of the three following options to guide one's existence and destiny:

1. Building the marriage relationship under the divine moral imperative guided by God's principles to reflect His character through eternity; or
2. Taking the prerogative to model the marriage union after the moral directive of someone other than God; or
3. Leveraging one's individual moral autonomy to build the marriage relationship for the purpose of self-worship, which is propelled by the disposition to please "me, myself, and I."

Looking at divorce statistics of the twenty-first century, we find that one out of every two first marriages ends in divorce. For second and third marriages, the divorce rate is even higher, 60–64 percent and 70–74 percent, respectively. It is alarming that such an old institution as marriage, which predates the church institution, is so mishandled and misunderstood. Maybe some people marry for the wrong reason or expect more than what marriage can offer. Dr. Gary Thomas, in his book *The Sacred Marriage*, has noted that marriage makes us achieve holiness more than happiness. When marriage does not make us happy, how then do married couples derive happiness in matrimonial union? There seems to be a distinct difference between happiness and joy. The late Dr. Frank W. Hale expressed the notion that "happiness is circumstantial and euphoric, but 'joy' is as an attitude or state of mind." Thus, there is a need to find ways for married couples to generate joyous and mutually fulfilling marriage relationships, even in the absence of happiness and amid imperfection, while still striving to attain holiness. *Pillars of Joy in Marriage*, therefore, will explore ways that God-fearing couples may experience the joy of a mutually fulfilling marriage relationship in the absence of true happiness; in the presence of imperfection, which we inherited from our first parents; and amid the escalating presence of evil. Particularly the question is, since humankind lost the perfect happiness in marriage that prevailed in the pre-sin condition, how do couples achieve joy in the context of living in the post-sin era? *Pillars of Joy in Marriage* seeks to examine pillars that can generate joy in a marriage even in the face of imperfection and elusive real happiness, while striving for holiness and gearing up for the coming of Jesus Christ our Savior and Lord. The emphasis here is experiencing *joy* in marriage, not happiness or a euphoric feeling.

Organization

Pillars of Joy in Marriage explores twenty-two pillars of joy. Each subsequent chapter is an analysis of a specific pillar of joy organized into four sections, as follows:

(a) Foundation—Each section starts by establishing a biblical and philosophical foundation for the pillar, based on the psalmist's declaration, "Unless the Lord builds the house, the builders labor in vain. Unless the Lord watches over the city, the guards stand watch in vain" (Psalm 127:1 NIV).

(b) Song—A song appearing within each section expresses how humming hymns along the way of the marriage marathon can help an individual derive internal joy in all seasons of marriage and throughout life's experiences. The apostle James inquires: "Is any among you suffering? Let him pray. Is anyone cheerful? Let him sing psalms" (James 5:13 NKJV).

(c) My Story—I share some of my personal experiences, and some experiences of others, to make each pillar real and relevant.

(d) Last Word—This is a reflective summation of each pillar, including final thoughts and general impressions.

Questionnaire and Action Plan

Please note that at the end of *Pillars of Joy in Marriage*, I have provided a self-assessment exercise to enable the reader to evaluate and take the temperature of his or her own marriage relationship. Following the questionnaire, a framework is provided to give the married couple an opportunity to develop an individualized corrective action plan for revitalizing the marriage, if the reader so desires.

Pillar #1
Perspective on the Marriage Union

Foundation

We walk on the same marital path, but we
do not step on the same stones!

—Anonymous

Perspective in Heaven's Eyes

This pillar examines the joy of having a healthy perspective in times of trial in marriage by asking the reader to look at his or her own marriage through the eyes of heaven. Primarily, the art of having perspective on your marriage is facilitated by perceiving your marriage through God's lens. Looking at your marriage through God's eyes is the basis of a mature marriage. Start by acknowledging the fact that God is the author of your union (as expressed in the introduction of *Pillars of Joy in Marriage*). The perspective that God is your Father, and your spouse's Father as well, will change your marriage trajectory and influence how you interact with your spouse. Just think about it for a moment: if each couple could perceive God literally as a Father and Father-in-Law to whom to answer and be accountable for every action, good or bad, married folks would think twice before treating each other in a hurtful way or saying something hurtful to each other. I have taken and embraced God as my Father and Father-in-Law. This approach in my own marriage has paid great dividends of joy through the years. The idea of answering to God as my Father-in-Law for my mistreatment of His precious child (my spouse) is a sobering thought that sends a chill down my spine. Similarly, the thought of my spouse being accountable to God, my Daddy as well, for treating His child (me) badly takes away the gloom, spares me from picking petty fights with my spouse, and mitigates the temptation to retaliate. In fact, this is how God

1

perceives any marriage union. "For you are all children of God through faith in Christ Jesus" (Galatians 3:26 NLT).

Thus, this model of having God as our mutual Daddy and taking an impartial view of equal accountability forms a strong foundation for the pillars of joy in a marriage. It takes away the sting and gloom when my spouse acts up, is ungrateful, is critical, does not appreciative my needs, and so forth. But at the same time, it brings immense joy to my soul to know that God sees and records it all impartially. Rest assured that when you as a spouse have done all that you need to do in terms of treating your spouse as God expects you to, God, your Father-in-Law, is exceptionally pleased. Conversely, the sentiment applies to your spouse and how he or she relates to you, whether well or poorly. It is reasonable, therefore, to believe that if couples would genuinely embrace the marriage model, the disposition predicated on the dual notion of God as a common Dad and Father-in-Law, then they would never look at their spouses the same way again, even when the spouse gets on their very last nerve. See, they would constantly remind themselves that "indeed my spouse is family."

Who Taught You How to Be Married?
It is unbelievable to me that marriage, an old institution, remains misunderstood by many. Perhaps it is because some books written on marital relations tend to romanticize physical intimacy and say little of the real-life curriculum needed to teach those planning to enter into holy matrimony. For example, if one were to ask the married couples in attendance at a wedding ceremony how many had been taught how to be married, the answer would likely be zero. Even for some who have had premarital counseling by a clergy member, the duration of instruction ranges from one to three months at best. In many cases, the couple is fantasizing about the preparation of the ceremony and honeymoon, instead of synthesizing and internalizing the message at hand. Yet the real marriage starts after the honeymoon is over, and at a critical time the real *welding* of the union begins. Unfortunately, some are traumatized by the sparks and heat given off by the welding of the two different lives together. So, it is my desire that through the twenty-two pillars of joy in marriage as explored in *Pillars of Joy in Marriage*, couples will gain some perspective

and learn the building blocks for creating and maintaining a mutually enjoyable marriage.

Joy or Gloom Is a Choice

Joy should be viewed as depression marinated in hope. Life's challenges in marriage are inevitable, but gloom is optional, and joy is a matter of choice. Both constructs depend on the lens through which we perceive marriage as an institution and the prevailing circumstances or trials that life throws at us. This writer argues that perspective is the DNA of joy in a marriage. Perspective determines what is important and prioritizes and arrives at sound solutions to the problems we face at any given time. Most importantly, perspective determines what we present at the altar in prayer and gives us the right attitude and the patience we need while waiting for direction from the Lord—and the strength to deal with the aftermath when things don't go our way. For example, perspective can generate joy or gloom in times of challenge within a marriage, when Prince Charming or Ladylove starts acting up in the face of the problems of life. Perspective gives you discernment, focus, and decisiveness at crossroads or detours along the marriage journey. One may choose to react, be moody, fuss around, and be gloomy; alternatively, one may choose to rehearse the promises of God and sing songs: "Speaking to yourselves in psalms, and hymns and spiritual songs, singing and making melody in your heart and the Lord" (Ephesians 5:19 KJV).

Perspective Changes Focus

Let's examine a tale of two prisoners. Two inmates at a state penitentiary are on death row. Both are looking through the bars in the window one night. One prisoner looks up and focuses on the stars, while the other looks down and focuses on the mud and gloomy surroundings. The latter exclaims in disgust, "Oh, what an ugly scene! Look at all that mud!" The other, gazing at the sky in awe, exclaims, "Oh, look at the stars! What a beautiful evening!" Here are two individuals, both with similar conditions and circumstances but with different perspectives. One chooses to focus on the gloomy environment, while the other focuses on the stars and the promising hope of a bright sky. God created us as free moral beings with an innate urge to be free and construct our own reality based on what resonates with our view of life. It is not the circumstances that shape us but our attitude toward and perspective on the situations we are in.

The above story is a classic example of the function of perspective in embracing joy or projecting misery. It demonstrates how powerful perception can be in governing or determining joy or gloom when confronting the challenges of a marriage. What breaks one couple may build another, based on their perception, their reaction, and how they deal with the situation facing them. So, it may not be a bad idea to suggest that when couples are faced with challenging situations, they should use this powerful tool called *perspective* and adjust their vision to see an alternative to gloom.

Perspective Changes Fear to Faith

Based on biblical narratives, the presence of doom and death can lead to a resurgence of hope, wellness, and victory. There are many biblical accounts that illustrate this paradigm, but a classic one is recorded in 1 Samuel 17, where the entire army of Israel was intimidated by Goliath, the Philistine giant who growled and taunted, uttering demeaning slurs day and night, causing the Israelite army to be afraid. However, David, a young shepherd, was not intimidated by the huge stature of Goliath and his heavy armor and weaponry. Instead, with courage and resolve to kill the giant, David perceived Goliath as an already defeated foe—an "uncircumcised Gentile" whose fate was in the hands of God, like the lion and bear that attempted to attack David's sheep. The rest is history. With a sling and five smooth stones, the giant came tumbling down. What made the difference here between David and the entire army of men? The perspective toward the enemy, of course.

What needs to be stressed here is that a Goliath does not change from being a giant. But your individual perception of "the giant" could be different from that of the rest of the "fearful army" of family, friends, and associates in your life, including your spouse. A preacher once said that if you focus on the size of the giant in your life, on how massive and scary your life situation is, then you will stumble. But if you focus on God, your giant will tumble! So, we need not entertain fear in the presence of a giant God. Simply take the Goliath in your marriage to the big God. Boldly declare to your Goliath how big your God is, instead of rehearsing to God the magnitude of your situation and how big your problem is.

Perspective Controls Impulses

There is no better story illustrating the phenomenon of impulse control in the face of temptation to sin than the saga of Joseph, a young Hebrew slave, in the seductive claws of Potiphar's wife (Genesis 39:7–13). Imagine Joseph in the prime of his youth, seemingly at a physiological stage when the male hormones are running wild. But Joseph was in a predicament like that of the first couple, Adam and Eve, in the garden of Eden; he too was faced with choosing between two opposing allegiances. Joseph's challenge was either (a) to succumb to Potiphar's wife's illicit sexual advances and enjoy the physical push to satisfy his own libido or (b) to choose to deny the seducer and himself to please God. Thus, Joseph refused to fall into the snare of the devil (Potiphar's wife in this case). Joseph quickly adjusted his perspective. Before damage was done, he removed himself from the scene and took off and ran, blurting out, "How then can I do this great wickedness, and sin against God" (Genesis 39:9 NKJV)?

What separates Joseph from the rest of us when the moment and setting is appealing is the ability to pull away from the snare of the devil (fornication in this case). The key is in having the right perspective, a sharper focus, and the deliberate resolve to please God at all costs. In the context of this pillar, the emphases for married couples are (1) choosing to pay homage to the Supreme God over pleasing and fearing a spouse (or anyone else for that matter) and (2) embracing the idea of not disappointing our common Daddy—God—and Father-in-Law in our marriage journey. Once this perspective is in place, the rest will take care of itself. Joseph taught us just that! The narrative account tells us that Joseph was later imprisoned unfairly, but God was with Joseph and elevated him from a prisoner to prime minister of Egypt. Oh, let's all dare to adopt Joseph's perspective in times of competing allegiances.

Perspective Promotes the Desire for Eternity

The ultimate joy is founded on establishing a marriage disposition that looks forward to the restoration of the pre-sin condition articulated in the introduction of *Pillars of Joy in Marriage*. That is, while enjoying marriage, raising a family, and engaging in productive work to support that family (i.e., occupying oneself until Jesus comes, as discussed in Luke 19:13, couples must keep a sharp perspective focused on the original plan of our existence: to reflect the character of God. Because we are primarily God's children designed to reflect His image, our existence is incomplete without an organic and intimate relationship with Him. It is important to view the marital relationship through heaven's eyes, as God sees it and expects it to be. Keeping humankind's existence in its proper perspective helps couples to develop an unshaken desire and longing for spending eternity with their beloved Daddy, God, in a carefree environment completely devoid of sin, pain, suffering, decay, and death, which are part of the world order in which couples and families exist now. A biblical narrative to demonstrate the perspective of eternal focus is found in the parable of the ten virgins, as recorded in Matthew 25:1–13 NKJV. In this parable, several themes are highlighted, as follows:

1. *Purity*—All ten women are virgins.
2. *Purpose*—All ten virgins are awaiting the coming of the bridegroom.
3. *Human condition*—All ten grow tired of waiting and thus fall asleep.
4. *Defining character*—Five are wise and five are foolish.
5. *Preparedness*—All appear to have oil in their lamps, but such is not the case. The wise virgins had filled their vessels with oil.
6. *Presumptuousness*—The foolish virgins leave their fate to chance by deceiving themselves in thinking that there is no significant difference between being prepared or not. They presume that they will meet the bridegroom anyway.
7. *Perspective*—All are waiting for the arrival of the bridegroom, but not all are fully ready to meet and welcome him. The foolish, having neglected the call of duty, are preoccupied with other things than what is important (filling the lamps with oil). Thus, they are condemned for life.

Likewise, as married couples living in the post-sin condition, we find ourselves exhausted by and overwhelmed with battling life's problems and because of this, lose the focus of preparing for Jesus, the Bridegroom, to come. The parable of the ten virgins reminds us of the importance of our existence and God's original purpose for humanity. We cannot afford to lose sight of the reason for our existence: to reflect the character of God. Our perspective should be clear and our resolve unshaken to one day meet our true Prince Charming and Bridegroom, Jesus Christ. This biblical narrative of the ten virgins fortifies my own belief that the ultimate crown for our existence as married couples and family members is to achieve eternity. We may even fall into the sleep of death, but the hope of resurrection and of meeting our ultimate true Prince Charming and Bridegroom, Jesus Christ our Savior, must be undaunted. Thus, in light of this discourse, individuals should reflect on the following:

1) Am I really waiting for the Bridegroom?
2) Which group of five virgins do I fall into?
3) Is my lamp filled up with the Holy Spirit (oil) and the joy of longing to spend eternity with my Daddy God and Father-in-Law in an environment untainted by sin, betrayal, suffering, and death?
4) Is my perspective clear and my focus undaunted that heaven is my goal?
5) As expressed in Hebrews 11:10, am I determined to search for that city whose builder is God?
6) If Jesus, the Bridegroom, were to come today, would I be ready for Him or would I hide from Him?
7) The Bridegroom has said, "Look, I am coming soon, bringing my reward with me to repay all people according to their deeds" (Revelation 22:12 NLT).

As you ponder on these provocative questions, be mindful that whether you are ready or not, the Bridegroom will come. Which of the following would you want the Bridegroom to say to you?

a. "Well done good and faithful servant; you were faithful over a few things, enter unto the joy of your Lord" (Matthew 25:21 NKJV).
b. "I never knew you; depart from Me, ye that work iniquity" (Matthew 7:23 KJV).
c. "Not everyone who says to me Lord, Lord shall enter the kingdom of heaven, but he who does the will of my Father in heaven" (Matthew 7:21 NKJV).

    d. "Many shall say to Me in that day, Lord, Lord, have we not prophesied in Your name, cast out demons in Your name and done many wonders in Your name? I will declare to them I never knew you; Depart from me who practice lawlessness" (Matthew 7:22–23 NKJV).

    e. "Believe me, I don't know you" (Matthew 25:12 NLT)!

    f. "Outside the city (of God) are the .... sorcerers, sexually immoral, the murders, the idol worshipers, and all who love to live a lie" (Revelation 22:15 NLT).

Note that the decisions we make, the road we take, and the place we land in life are all predicated on individual choices we make today, so please choose wisely in life!

Perspective Keeps Us Vigilant

As a Christian family, we are all commissioned to be vigilant watchmen. "Watch therefore, for you know neither the day nor the hour in which the Son of Man is coming" (Matthew 25:13 NKJV).

Song

We know not the hour of the Master's appearing;
Yet signs all foretell that the moment is nearing
When He shall return—'tis a promise most cheering—
But we know not the hour.

<u>Chorus:</u>

He will come, let us watch and be ready;
He will come, halleluiah! halleluiah!
He will come in the clouds of His Father's bright glory—
But we know not the hour.

—F. E. Belden

My Story

In the early years of our marriage, my husband, Godwin, and I sought to establish a closer relationship with God. First, we both agreed to be children of God, personally grounded and plugged in to the power of Jesus Christ. Second, we both acknowledged Him as the central absolute authority and guide of our union, where both of us could mutually and spiritually meet to connect in times of trouble or foolishness, or when we were fussing or carrying on. This created common ground for us. Especially when we do not agree about something or are facing uncertainty and challenges, we know whom to turn to for wisdom, arbitration, and guidance. Second, we had the insight to establish a four-dimensional perspective for viewing our horizontal relationship, enabling us to accept, see, and relate to each other in several dimensions as (a) lovers, (b) family, (c) best friends, and (d) roommates. I have no doubt in my mind that the longevity of our marriage is predicated on our understanding and embracing of our duty to God first and to each other second. Even today, fifty years later, we are still holding on to these values—the aforementioned four-dimensional perspective. We are still the best of friends, true kinsmen, and lovers. I remember that my son once remarked, "You and Dad are cut from the same cloth! You are just like two peas in a pod." Well, whatever that means, it sounded good and affirming to us.

Perceiving your mate as a roommate is the *least understood* and most loosely defined of the four-dimensional perspectives. Some have interpreted being roommates as entailing a lack of physical intimacy. Wrong! The idea of being a roommate, if taken lightly or misunderstood, can break a marriage. For me, being my spouse's roommate presents more challenges than does being a friend or family member. In my own experience, I have discovered that our challenges come from this segment of the multidimensional perspective, that of being a responsible roommate. Sometimes Prince Charming or Ladylove takes the other for granted and assumes it is the other person's responsibility to tidy the house, hang up the clothes, make the bed, and pick up after the other. You know how that goes! Well, there are many stories I could share about this topic, but one decision that I think was life-changing, and that presented a turning point for me, was when my husband, Godwin, used humor to help me redirect my focus.

My job required that I travel a lot, and sometimes I made back-to-back trips within the same week. I was rushing one morning. I could not find my favorite belt in my wardrobe. Those who know me intimately know that I really love belts, and it is important to me that any belt I wear matches my outfit. Do you feel me now? Frantic, I asked my husband, "Love, have you seen my [such-and-such] belt?" I suppose he thought, *Why don't you wear any one of your many belts?* But he was wise enough not to say what was in his heart. He just said, "Love, why don't you check your website?" I asked, "What are you talking about?" He responded, "Log on to www.yourbedroomchairpile.com" (referring to the clothes piled on my bedroom chair). Indeed, there on my chair was my belt, among other items that should not have been left there in the first place. I got the picture and started laughing. Trust me, Godwin drove the point home—and that did it for me. From that point forward, no matter how physically or emotionally tired I felt, I avoided piling up my clothes on that chair. There were three simple options: hang them, fold them and place them in drawers, or drop them into the washing basket. I am proud to say that my bedroom chair website is now closed and no longer in service. The chair is certainly no longer a place for dropping clothes. Thanks, love, for your humor!

Likewise, my husband knows what is important to me, such as having my bed made up no matter what. If my husband wakes up later than I, he now makes the bed. Even when I was still traveling I would find the bed made as if it were in a hotel suite, with decorative pillows and all, just the way Godwin's roommate (me) likes it.

Through the years, we have striven to relate to each other by considering the various perspectives, especially as "responsible roommates." This perspective should not be taken lightly, because it can make or break a love relationship.

What area of the four-dimensional perspective poses the greatest challenge for your mate? What about for you; what area is your greatest challenge?

In sum, there are times and situations that demand a lover's response, whereas in other times they demand a family perspective or an appeal to the friendship aspect of the relationship. But in some cases, the situation requires a spouse to appeal to the aspect of being a responsible roommate, as in my case. I encourage married couples to try this model. It may work for you too, especially if you pair it with humor. Unfortunately, the concept of referring to your spouse as a roommate is misunderstood by society and is mostly construed as being a condition where there is no physical intimacy. Wrong! Try to squeeze the toothpaste tube in a wrong way or leave the toilet seat up; then you will realize that the protocol for sharing a room with Prince Charming or Ladylove is as serious as a heart attack.

Last Word

Marriage is a serious institution. Primarily, it was intended for couples to reveal the character of God's love through ministry to each other's needs in all respects. Couples may create a joyful marriage while still striving to attain holiness and waiting for the Lord to come and restore the world to the pre-sin condition. Marriage calls us to be faithful stewards, asks us to be vigilant watchmen, and is tied or paired up with ministry in that it reflects the image of God despite our own imperfections and the flaws of our spouses. It is patterned after the relationship of the Lamb, Jesus Christ, with His church. A question that has been bothering me and which prompted me to write *Pillars of Joy in Marriage* is why such an old social institution like marriage, which dates back to Eden at the beginning of humankind, and which was instituted by God Himself prior even to establishing the church, is so misunderstood and mismanaged. What is the missing piece? There seems to be something drastically amiss or wrong somewhere. Some answers to this question, in my view, are that (a) we have in some way or other succumbed to Satan's "distortion of our allegiance to God" as articulated in the introduction of *Pillars of Joy in Marriage*, and (b) we have lost perspective and failed to heed the commission that we be vigilant watchmen for the coming Bridegroom, Jesus Christ, our ultimate true Prince Charming! Both views seem to illuminate this puzzle for me. Thus, in the context of marriage, the missing ingredient may be our human failure to grasp, understand, and accept the fatherhood of God in its four dimensions, as indicated below:

1. *Divine heavenly Father*, the author of the marriage union and the sustainer of our relationship's existence.
2. *Intimate Father*, who created us to love us and spoil us. He loves us so much that He emptied heaven to redeem us. Pastor Ty Gibson

expressed this viewpoint well: "Calvary proves that God would rather die forever than live without you and me!" Indeed, Brenda Walsh affirms that "Jesus loves us so much that He can't imagine Heaven without us" (p. 201).

3. *Common Dad and Father-in-Law*—a dual perspective. Embrace Him as both your Dad and your Father-in-Law simultaneously, the one to whom you are accountable for the way you treat His other kids (your mate in this case, a precious gift God gave you).

4. *Supreme Counselor*, an absolute guide, a consultant, and the center of peace and joy in the marriage journey. Jesus assured us, "The words that I speak to you are spirit and they are life" (John 6:63 NKJV).

These themes and much more will be explored and discussed at length in the forthcoming pillars in *Pillars of Joy in Marriage*. Keep reading!

Pillar # 2
In-His-Time Virtue

The Foundation

I have learned, in whatever state I am, therewith to be content.

—Philippians 4:11 (KJV)

Joy in marriage can be derived from understanding God's agenda or timeline and accepting His divine plan over our own agenda because He knows the future and we do not. In His timeline, phenomena foster understanding of the virtue of patience in waiting and being at peace amid whatever circumstances we find ourselves in while waiting for God to come through for us in His own time. Waiting is a discipline in our microwave age and a challenge to the instant-gratification attitude of the modern generation. If truth be told, life forces us to wait in line at places like the airport, the bank, the post office, and the doctor's office. We wait for the seed we planted to germinate like all other living organisms. Then we wait for it to grow, develop, and mature before we can harvest it. Otherwise, there would be no reference to the concept of dwarfed or stunted growth or premature birth, or to an unstable frame of mind, miscalculated moves or choices, impromptu decisions, aborted plans, or underdeveloped relationships. The virtue of being patient, thinking through our options and processing potential consequences before we act, is a discipline that sometimes goes against our human nature. The ability to wait patiently helps us to pray, stand firm, and hope that things will be all right in heaven's timeline. Thus, the perspective of embracing the virtue of His timeline helps us to do the following:

1. Remain joyful amid uncertainty, when we have more questions than answers.
2. Remain joyful even when God says no.

3. Remain joyful amid God's silence.
4. Remain joyful when God does not make sense to us.
5. Encourage ourselves in the Lord.

Remain Joyful When You Have More Questions Than Answers

I am sure that at one time or another you, like the rest of us, have been at a crossroads of adversity, where you find yourself faced with more questions than answers. Seeking to understand the Lord's agenda as it unfolds in His time is a test of our spiritual maturity and character, and key to worshipping God even when there is no apparent reason to praise Him at that moment. In my experience, God has His own agenda for your life, and He gives you the answers in His time, sometimes long after you have forgotten the questions you asked Him in the first place. But one thing is certain: when He comes through for you, you will realize without a doubt that you were not prepared to handle the information at the time you wanted it. Instead of fussing, trust His heart and wisdom. You will begin to praise Him anyhow, even when you do not understand His purpose for you.

The narrative recorded in the book of Job is a profound reminder and illustration of this phenomenon. I can only imagine what crossed Job's mind when he received news of the sudden death of his ten children and the disappearance of all his possessions on the same day. In my sanctified imagination, I can hear Job saying, *Why me?! My neighbor lost one camel. Did I have to lose all of mine on the same day? I have heard that my friend lost a child, but why did I have to lose all of mine on the same day? To add insult to injury, I have sores and stinking boils, and I smell like a skunk. My wife won't even hug or kiss me!* Even God had enough of this Job's asking why. Why, why, why. He said the following to His servant Job:

Where were you when I laid the foundations of the earth? Tell me, if you have understanding. Who determined its measurement? Surely you know! Or who stretched the line upon it? To what were its foundations fastened? Or who laid its cornerstone, when morning stars sang together, and all the sons of God shouted for joy? Or who shut in the sea with doors, when it bursts forth and issued from the womb; when I made the clouds its garment, and thick darkness its swaddling band; when I fixed my limits for it and set bars and doors; when I said this far you may come, but no further? (Job 38:4–11 NKJV)

There are several lessons that can be learned from Job's situation, as follows.

1. God answered Job by questioning Job. God asked Job, "Do you still want to argue with the Almighty? You are God's critic, but do you have the answers" (Job 40:2 NLT)?

2. It seems that God had more questions for Job than Job could ever answer. Job replied to the Lord, "I am nothing—how could I ever find the answers" (Job 40:1–2 NLT)?

3. God answered Job by restoring his losses twofold, after Job had prayed and interceded for his friends (Job 42:10), not when Job was still complaining.

4. Instead of engaging in questioning or complaining about our circumstances, we should focus on intercessory prayer on behalf of others. Someone once said, "If you need a blessing, bless others first. If you need a friend, be a friend. If you want God to hear your prayers, pray for others first." Wow!

5. Job recognized and acknowledged who was in control and who was the driver of his existence. Listen to what he said: "For I know my redeemer liveth; … and though after my skin worms destroy this body, yet in my flesh I shall see God" (Job 19:25–26 KJV).

6. God will restore what you lost in time. He says that He will give you back what you lost (Joel 2:25) and supply your needs, not based on your need analysis but according to His unlimited supply. "And the same God who takes of me will supply all your needs from his glorious riches, which have been given to us in Christ Jesus" (Philippians 4:19 NLT). "God is able to do exceedingly above all that we ask or even think, according to the power that works in us" (Ephesians 3:20 NKJV)—in time!

Remain Joyful Even When God Says No
Most of us enjoy God's yesses. But even for a Christian it is difficult to face and accept His nos. Yet our faith should shine through especially when God says no. To enjoy the ride when the going gets tough, the key is to remember

He who is the driver of our existence and who sits in the control tower of our lives. In this way we will understand how Jesus "rolls." His works, thoughts, and ways are far different from ours (Isaiah 55:8–9). Dr. Barry Black, the author of *The Blessing of Adversity*, stresses the importance of trusting God and praising Him, even for unanswered prayers. If we believe this, we will be very grateful and praise Him for those unanswered prayers, once we come to our senses and realize that Jesus's no was the best thing that could have happened to us at the time. So why stress and make yourself sick, when you have a Father God who is all-knowing, all-present, all-powerful, and all-loving, who stands ready to apportion a fresh supply of blessings every day?

Remain Joyful through God's Silence

Dealing with God's silence over a long stretch of time is one of the most difficult Christian challenges. In my experience, there are several principles to remember in such a situation, as follows:

1. *Wait.* Patiently wait for the Lord and murmur not for Him to come through. He will, in time.
2. *Walk.* Exercise your daily walk of faith and trust in His assurance that He will solve your situation, whether great or small, in time.
3. *Talk.* Call on Him in prayer and listen to Him talking back to you.
4. *Remember.* Rehearse His promises made in His Word. (We get discouraged when we forget how God led us in the past.)
5. *Count.* Take stock of His blessings bestowed upon you. Name them one by one, and you will be amazed how good God has been to you. You will begin to celebrate and praise Him for his endless mercies.
6. *Trust.* Believe in His presence. Even when you cannot trace Him, trust His heart, love, and providence. Jesus said that He will send the Holy Spirit to dwell among us, to guide us and teach us how to live.
7. *Sing.* Sing and pray at the crossroads of life, especially when He seems silent to you. He is not silent; He hears.
8. *Invite.* Invite the Lord of Peace and Tower of Strength in times of stress to tabernacle with you and to quiet your anxieties. He will give you the peace that passeth understanding and enable you to endure until He comes through for you.

Remain Joyful When God Does Not Make Sense to You

The beginning of wisdom and understanding is anchored in trusting God, especially when He takes us out of our comfort zone and we do not understand where He is leading us or why. Barry Black in one of his sermons suggests that we should brace ourselves to enjoy the journey and leave the destination and outcome in the hands of God. To illustrate Dr. Black's wisdom, let us examine the story of Abraham and his barren wife Sarah. God had promised Abraham that he would be the father of nations and had blessed him with countless children like the sands of the sea and the stars in the sky. He told him that his wife Sarah would bear him a son. Despite their lack of faith and their failure to wait, God fulfilled His promise to Abraham and Sarah. Isaac was born. Note the delay of the blessing. Abraham and Sarah's lack of faith in waiting for God to show up did not alter God's promise. The fulfillment of the promise occurred in God's heavenly timeline. Isaac was conceived when all the vital signs of childbearing were gone. God fulfilled His purpose in His timeline even though, in desperation, the couple had taken the matter into their hands and manipulated God's promise, putting a spare wheel, Hagar, into the mix of the heavenly promise, to the detriment and dysfunction of the household.

Later, when Isaac was a young man, God instructed Abraham to take the lad and to sacrifice him on Mt. Moriah. Abraham was obedient and followed God's instructions despite his fears and what he might have been thinking. Would Sarah perhaps understand or think that senility had set in and possessed her aged husband? We will never know the answer because God intervened. The hand of God, Jehovah-Jireh Himself, provided a ram caught in the thicket for Abraham to sacrifice instead of his beloved son Isaac. Oh, what a God we serve. Even in our foolishness, He loves us. He is the same yesterday, today, and tomorrow. He will always provide for us if we wait for His ordained will to manifest in our lives. In the meantime, let us do His bidding, even if it does not make sense to us. Our part is just to obey and let God be God, knowing that He will intervene, show up, and provide, not based on our need but predicated on His riches and glory. Our responsibility is to relax, connect with Him, and trust His heart, even if we cannot trace Him. In any event, we must trust His love for us. God is all-knowing, and His ignorance supersedes our earthly wisdom:

"Because the foolishness of God is wiser than men; and the weakness of God is stronger than men" (1 Corinthians 1:25 KJV).

Encourage Yourself in the Lord

Encouraging yourself has its time and place. When King David, the great psalmist, was very depressed, he encouraged himself. The enemy had taken his two wives and children captive, and his own men had risen against him. David was now in great danger. All his men were very bitter about having lost their sons and daughters. They began to talk of stoning him. But David found strength in the Lord his God (1 Samuel 30:6). The only thing he could do was to start praising the Lord while amid his hopeless circumstances. He snapped out of his "pity party," picked up his harp, retreated to a place of solitude, and began to hum tunes of praise to his Almighty God, who had fought his battles and won in the past. Surely, David did not want to sing, but the more he sang, the more he recovered from depression, regaining his strength and courage. Hence, David wrote many psalms to encourage all of us in our walk of life.

In the context of marriage, seek to encourage yourself even when your spouse and friends are against you. Job had a similar encounter with the death of his children and the loss of his possessions in one day. Job's bosom buddies blamed him for his adversities. Even the love of his life, his dear wife, was cynical and indifferent to him. In disgust, she looked at Job, whose devastating sickness had left him covered him with smelly septic boils, and blurted out: "Why don't you curse God and die?" Pretty discouraging! Yet unbeknown to all of them, God was in control of Job's situation, dark and gloomy as it appeared. No doubt Job felt empty and alone, but he encouraged himself in the Lord. What a lesson for us as married couples!

When I am going through difficult things myself, and after engaging in serious introspection to determine where I may have contributed to the situation and why the devil is on my trail, I relax and find peace and joy in knowing that perhaps my Father God was bragging about me as His child, as He did with His servant Job, to prove to the devil that my allegiance is grounded in the Lord. I begin to quote the scriptures and promises of God and to realize His ability to restore all that the devil has stolen from me, not according to my agenda but in His time. He affirms, "I will restore to you the years that the swarming locust has eaten; the crawling locust, the swarming locust, the consuming locust and the chewing locust. … Then you shall know that I am the Lord your God and there is no other. My people shall never be put to shame" (Joel 2:25–27 NKJV). Oh, what an assurance.

Keeping a song in your heart is another way of encouraging yourself and refilling your tank of joy, even in the face of marital trials, hardship, and depressing circumstances.

Song

Blessed assurance, Jesus is mine!
O, what a foretaste of glory divine!
Heir of salvation, purchase of God,
Born of His Spirit, washed in His blood.

<u>Chorus</u>:

This is my story, this is my song,
Praising my Savior all the day long.

—Fanny J. Crosby, 1873

My Story

There are things in life that are worth waiting for, no matter how long they take to happen. The delay of God's blessing can solidify the joy of waiting in anticipation if both you and your spouse are in tune with and connected to the heavenly lifeline. Listen, Godwin and I waited for our son, our only child, whom God gave us after seven long years of waiting. Like Hannah, whose story is recorded in 1 Samuel 2:1–17, we waited and prayed intensely before the dream was realized. In the seventh year of our marriage, our son, Sekie, was born. It was one of the happiest moments of my life. His middle name is Samuel, a name that was given to him by my late father, who did not witness his birth. Dad passed away few years before my son was born. He gave the name to my son in anticipation of his birth. Indeed, Godwin and I made sure that he carried that name, as his story bore a parallel to that of Hannah and Samuel. The name affirmed my dad's prophetic promise that God had seen my tears, honored my faith, and would give me a son.

On the other hand, waiting for a child can present a challenge that tests the very core of the marriage relationship if you and your spouse are not grafted to and firmly grounded in the Word of God. In African society, not bearing children is a taboo, and not looked upon kindly. Just like Hannah, my family-in-law became restless for a grandchild. I heard some innuendos, witnessed some overt actions, and observed subtle things that tested my faith. But I hung in there because of the consistent, assuring love and unfailing support my husband showed me during this difficult time, just as Elkanah showed to Hannah (1 Samuel 1:8).

I remember, as though it was yesterday, when my father-in-law gathered his courage and confronted my mother with his concerns. He suggested that it was due time that his son, my husband, should consider getting a second wife to bear him a child. Alternatively, my family could choose to provide a maiden from my side of the family to bear Godwin a child. Both are acceptable practices in traditional African society. The dilemma was that my husband and I embraced a different culture, that of Christ, who was the model of our morality. My mother's response to my father-in-law was, "You should address your concerns with your son, not me. It is up to your son, certainly not me, or you, to make the judgment call and to consent to this custom!"

I am pleased to let you know that when this incident took place, I was already pregnant, but I had not made the news public yet. So, when Mom shared this encounter with me, I just laughed and recited my favorite Bible verse: "Before they call, I will answer" (Isaiah 65:24 NIV). The good that came out of this experience is that I have never forgotten how my husband stood firm, displayed integrity, upheld his principles, and never caved in to ill-advised suggestions that could have threatened our union. Through the years, we have bonded and grown together to be the best of friends and soul mates, as we've been for fifty years now, because of this incident. God's delay is not a denial. If you and your spouse stick together in hard times, you will grow old together as well.

Last Word

Surely, there can be no dull moment, no anxiety or fear of the unknown, when one is truly connected to the True Vine and waiting for God's blessings to unfold in time. No matter how long the wait is, it is worth it! Elder Henry Wright made a profound statement in his sermon entitled "Here Comes Jesus!": "I have a God as my father above, Jesus as my brother beside me, and the angels watching my back, as my personal bodyguards. I have nothing to worry about. I am somebody." This applies to you and me, of course. Oh wow, what an assurance!

Pillar # 3
Loving Unconditionally

The Foundation

The opposite of love is not hate but indifference!

—Carol Spaulding Colbum

The word *love*, both as a noun and verb, has been used and overused to mean many different things, to the point that some people, perhaps, do not grasp or have a real concept or clear understanding of what really love is and means. We are all familiar with statements of love for generic objects, such as "I love my car" (or blue sweater, red shoes, hot dogs, pizza, ice cream, lasagna, macaroni and cheese, roses, or carnations), as well as statements expressing love for endearing subjects, such as "I love my dog" (or wife, husband, parents, boss, doctor, or teacher). Thus, *love* has become loosely defined and is used to express a feeling toward different objects and situations equally.

Before discussing unconditional love, it is first crucial to address what love is and what love is not. Thereafter, we will differentiate between love and unconditional love.

What Is Love?

Biblically, *love* is defined as the fruit of the Spirit and is paired with qualities such as peace, joy, long-suffering, gentleness, goodness, and faith (Galatians 5:22 KJV). Generally, *love,* as applied to close friends or kinship, has been defined by *Merriam-Webster* as "a feeling of attachment induced by that which delights or commands admiration; preeminent kindness, or devotion to another; profound tenderness and passionate affection for another person; as the love of brothers and sisters." Biblical scholars have separated love into four categories, *agape*, *philia*, *Eros*, and *storge*, which collectively can apply to spousal relationships.

1. *Agape*

    Agape is pronounced "uh-GAH-pay" and denotes a selfless, sacrificial, unconditional love. It is the ultimate form of love, the immeasurable and incomparable love our Father God has for all of us (humankind). Such love propelled Him to die for us so as to save sinners like you and me so that we may be saved from eternal death. There may be good people or prophets out there, but none came to die for sinners so that the latter could be saved. No religion other than the Christian faith can attest to this selfless love of Christ, who chose to die and be crucified on a rugged cross on Calvary, to redeem and give undeserving sinners like you and me a chance to one day inherit eternal life with the pre-sin condition restored (where there is no death or sorrow). This is matchless love that no human being can emulate. Still, we are called to be Christlike. In the context of marriage, a spouse can choose to develop a culture of unconditional love by looking beyond a mate's faults and addressing his or her needs.

2. *Philia* or *Phileo*

    Philia describes benevolent, kindly brotherly love and affection. Both *philia* and *phileo* are pronounced "FILL-ee-uh," originate from the Greek term *phílos*, and are characterized by tender, heartfelt consideration and kinship. Or the terms can refer to a friend, a confidant, someone dearly loved in a personal and intimate way, or a trusted confidant who is held dear in a close bond of personal affection. This sentiment could easily apply to spousal love when the spouse is considered as being a best friend. (This last point will be explored further under pillar #9.)

3. *Eros*

    Eros is pronounced "AIR-ose." This love is characterized by the intense physical, sensual intimacy between a husband and wife.

Within marriage, sex is used for emotional and spiritual bonding and reproduction. Eros is characterized by a romantic or erotic loving that occurs between married couples in a bed undefiled. God invented sex to be enjoyed, only within the undefiled matrimonial bed. If Eros occurs outside the marital boundary, it, having been forbidden, violates God's law of "thou shalt not commit adultery" (Exodus 20:7 KJV). When it occurs between unmarried platonic friends, it is considered to be fornication. God admonishes us to flee from fornication, to run from sexual sin. No other sin so clearly affects the body as this one does. Sexual immorality is a sin against your body (1 Corinthians 6:18). Furthermore, when Eros occurs between parents and their children or between siblings, it is incest—work of the flesh—and equally offensive in the eyes of God (Galatians 5:19–21).

That being said, Eros alone between married couples is not adequate to provide mutually fulfilling spiritual intimacy, without the presence of the other ingredients of love, namely, agape, philia, and storge. (This will be further explored under pillar #7.)

4. *Storge*

Storge, pronounced "STOR-jay," describes the love that is found among family members. *The Enhanced Strong's Lexicon* defines *storge* as "cherishing one's kindred, especially parents or children; the mutual love of parents and children and wives and husbands; loving affection; prone to love; loving tenderly; chiefly of the reciprocal tenderness of parents and children."[1] A compound form of *storge* is found in Romans 12:10 (ESV): "Love one another with brotherly affection. Outdo one another in showing honor." In this verse, the Greek word for "love" is *philostorgos*, a conflation of *philos* and *storge*. It means "loving dearly, being devoted, very affectionate, and loving in a way exhibited between husband and wife, mother and child, father and son." In Romans 1:31 (ESV), unrighteous people are described as "foolish, faithless, heartless

---

[1] James Strong, *Strong's Expanded Exhaustive Concordance of the Bible* (Nashville: Thomas Nelson, 2009), s.v. "storge."

or ruthless." Thus, in a marriage relationship, couples are called to embrace storge not *astorgos* which means "heartless" in Greek.

Power of Love

Love is a powerful principle and not a feeling. Love is both an action verb and a command. It is not a feeling; instead, it is a doing. Look at God's commanding imperatives to His children: "Love your neighbor." "Love your enemies." Love and loving comes from God. Love, morals, and ethical principles cannot be legislated by lawmakers of this world; they can only be legislated by God. Love is powerful when put under the influence of divine directive. It cuts across religious persuasions, social strata, and political and racial divides. There is no other story that embodies and demonstrates all these assertions than the story told by Jesus Christ of the Good Samaritan, as chronicled in Luke 10:25–36. The Samaritan risked his own life when he stopped to help a badly injured victim of robbery, who was a Jew. Others who passed by, a priest and a Levite, would not help. The Samaritan put the injured man on his donkey and checked him in to a hotel to be taken care of. He paid the cost and promised to come back later to check on the man and pay whatever additional costs might have been incurred. There are several principles of love that couples can draw from this story, as follows:

1. Love is God's provision. It can come from an unexpected source.
2. Love cuts across racial and cultural divides.
3. Love is not static; it is dynamic, as expressed in doing, in active action.
4. Love costs less than hate or indifference.
5. Love goes all out, even to the point of impelling you to risk your own life.
6. Love is not boisterous; it does not expect accolades, pomp and circumstance, or reward.
7. Love is not a "one-shot deal"; it follows its duty to the end.

What Is Unconditional Love?

Love forms the base and the *foundation* of the marital relationship. However, unconditional love is the *nourishment*, the bread and butter of joy, in the marital relationship, even when your spouse does not act right or is unlovable. Unconditional love means continuing to love when you do not feel like loving or during times when it feels like your spouse does not deserve your love. In a dynamic marital relationship, all these conditions can easily manifest themselves. This is where and when unconditional love kicks in and can be a viable form of nourishment to an ailing marriage. The Bible paints a clear portrait and provides an operational definition of unconditional love, as follows:

Love suffers long and is kind; love does not envy;

Love does not parade itself, is not puffed up;

Does not behave rudely, does not seek its own,

Is not provoked, thinks no evil;

Does not rejoice in iniquity, but rejoices in truth;

Bears all things, believes all things,

Hopes all things, endures all things.

—1 Corinthians 13:4–7 (NKJV)

True love is predicated on meeting the need of unconditional love, and God is at the center of unconditional love. I once heard a preacher saying that unconditional love is "hate that is showered by the blood of Jesus Christ and sanctified by the Holy Ghost." Thus, unconditional love starts with God, and when embraced by couples it is a powerful tool and can change lives, including that of your mate. In a 2000 study conducted by Dr. Gary and Barbara Rosberg on hundreds of couples across the United States to determine the primary love needs of men and women, the Rosbergs discovered that unconditional love is viewed by men and women alike as the number one need. To put it succinctly, without unconditional love, marital bliss can dwindle, dry up, and ultimately die.

This section seeks to explicate the essence of unconditional love and to substantiate the assertion that if unconditional love rules, joy in marriage can still be attained in the face of an unloving spouse, with the loving spouse experiencing an undaunted commitment to the marriage, even in the face of being mocked and rejected by his or her mate. Thus, the essence of unconditional love is experiencing joy from loving that overrules hate or indifference. If unconditional love rules, joy in marriage can still be attained in the face of an unresponsive mate. There are many different scenarios or patterns of loving that could be discussed, but I elect to examine only four of these:

1. Loving when loving does not make sense.
2. Loving when love is rejected or unreciprocated.
3. Loving when love is betrayed.
4. Loving without expectations.

Loving When Loving Does Not Make Sense

The story of the prophet Hosea and his harlot wife Gomer, recorded in Hosea 1:2–3, blows my mind each time I read it. It is a classic example of how love rolls when loving does not make sense. Hosea's behavior of showing love to Gomer despite her past is symbolic of the stance God has taken toward building an authentic and organic intimate spiritual relationship with His church, despite tendencies that include apostasy, idolatry, and paying homage to or honoring other gods. This story confirms that God is love and that God is the greatest lover and the giver of the many blessings and gifts we enjoy, including the gift of our mate. "Love of the Lord never ends! His mercies never cease. Great is his faithfulness; his mercies begin afresh each morning" (Lamentations 3:22–23 NLT). How much more would we be given if we would willingly connect with Him genuinely and willingly acknowledge Him as our God with contrite hearts? He has assured us that all good things come from Him and that His grace is sufficient for us. If we acknowledge Him as the driver of all things in our marriage, He will direct our steps because the steps of a good person are directed by the Lord (Psalm 37:23). Your job is just to connect, sit back, and enjoy the ride!

Loving When Love Is Unreciprocated

The only way to pass the test of loving when your love is not reciprocated is to look upon Jesus and try to emulate His pattern of love and loving.

Jesus loved us before we loved Him, yet He knew that we may choose not to love Him back, as it turns out to be in most cases. Even when it comes to doing the Lord's work, there is no goodness in us, and the seemingly righteous acts we purport to do or think we possess "are nothing but filthy rags" to Him (Isaiah 64:6 NLT). God loves us unconditionally with all our wrinkles and deformities. He blesses us despite ourselves and when we do not love Him back. Brenda Walsh sums it up well when she writes, "God does not choose us because we are perfect for the job. He chooses us because His plan is perfect" (p. 66). Likewise, we can continue to do good to our mates because it's the right thing to do, even when they do not act right or our love is unreciprocated.

Loving When Love Is Betrayed

Loving your mate unconditionally is like the skeletal system, the thing upon which all aspects of the marriage relationship are built. Marriage is the only relationship that is compared to the relationship between Christ and the church. Jesus came to this earth to save sinners, knowing that they would betray and kill Him. He died anyhow, so we all can have a chance of being redeemed and reconciled to the Father. Without Christ coming to die for us, we would be lost for eternity. In Luke 15, the father of the prodigal son embraces his wayward son and welcomes him back home although he had left his family and squandered all his inheritance in a faraway country. Dr. E. E. Cleveland once said, "Unconditional love is loving someone not because he or she is lovable or deserve your love or even wants your love but loving that person because he or she needs it." Sometimes pride gets in the way of our accepting love because we do not want to appear needy or because we feel ashamed of being vulnerable and admitting our wrongdoing. We act out, or stay closed off and bottled up inside, rather than show our willingness to communicate our need.

Loving without Expectations

In our selfish capitalistic society, it is hard to fathom the concept of giving unconditionally, that is, without getting something in return. "What's in it for me?" (WIIFM) is the usual driver for many people. None of us is immune to this feeling, unless of course Christ is the ruler of our lives. Unfortunately, when the WIIFM spirit is manifest in a marriage relationship, it can spell disaster. That is where unconditional love kicks in. Unconditional love is a form of disinterested benevolence, like the love spoken of in the parable of the Good Samaritan. The Good Samaritan did not expect a thank-you, accolades, or a monetary payback of any kind. He was moved only by the need or suffering at hand and was motivated purely by compassion. In the Xhosa language, we call this phenomenon *Ubuntu*, which entails humaneness and selflessness combined. Problems in marriage start when selfishness gets in the way of reasoning.

In sum, we should love unconditionally as Jesus loved us. God is love! He demonstrated His profound love by sending His only begotten Son to die in our place. He loved us unconditionally even before we loved Him and were yet sinners. Christ acquiesced to God's plan of salvation to redeem humankind from sin and committed to be the sacrificial lamb and be crucified for our iniquity so that we could be saved. We are by all accounts undeserving, and there is nothing we can do or could have done to prompt Him to die for wretched sinners like us. Only pure love could have prompted Him. Thus, the Lord looked beyond our faults and saw our need for salvation. What touches me most is that Jesus could have come to die for one lost sinner, me and me alone, just to save me! Therefore, let us practice unconditional love toward our spouses despite each other's ineptness. As children of the King, we can take clues from our Father. I believe we can do it one step at a time, one little kindness at a time, yielding to His will and guidance. Refer to the lyrics of the Dottie Rambo song, as follows, when you meditate on God's love for you. These words will keep you humble, as they often do for me. They force me to remember that we are all human and have faults. They will make you more tolerant of your spouse's weaknesses, preventing you from entertaining an unforgiving spirit or sitting on a judgment pedestal.

Song

> Amazing grace ... Will always be my song of praise.
> For it was grace that brought my liberty,
> I do not know, just how He came to love me so.
> He looked beyond my faults and saw my need.

<u>Chorus (instrumental)</u>:

I shall forever lift my eyes to Calvary,
To view the cross, where Jesus died for me
How marvelous, His grace that caught my falling soul
He looked beyond my faults and saw my need.

—Dottie Rambo

My Story

It is amazing how God works sometimes. He gives you a challenge, and if you could have your way, you would unequivocally say: "No, Lord, not me, not now. I am not ready for this!" The year 2016, two years ago, was one of those years when I felt tempted to say just that. But God the Almighty, knowing me very well, prepared me to meet the challenge I will be discussing in this pillar, as follows:

1. My husband and I chose to read Dr. Barry Black's book entitled *The Blessing of Adversity* as our morning devotion. Little did we know that this book would fortify my resolve to commit an unthinkable act.

2. My pastor, Elder Noah Washington, prior to the incident described below, preached a sermon that impacted me for life. He said, among other things, "If God would show you your blessing and what He is preparing you for, it would blow your mind and you would say, 'Really, Father, you are going to do [this and that], just for me?' 'Yes, but you must go through some stuff first.'" He continued by saying that if God chose to show me what I must go through to get to my blessing, I would scream and say, "Oh no, Lord, I pass!"

3. I kept on rehearsing God's promise that He will not give us anything we cannot handle, and that He provides us with the strength we need to endure the trials and with a way of escape (1 Corinthians 10:13). It is ours just for the asking.

Well, one morning Godwin and I were reading Dr. Barry Black's book, where he related an account of his painful childhood. He mentioned that his mother had to deal with eviction several times. He shared the pain of coming home from school, only to find that the family's belongings were scatted all around the apartment complex. Tears started streaming down my face. I could feel the pain as if it were my own family. I remember thinking something like, *Lord, if I had been there in that complex, I would have invited the young mother and her children to come and live with me until she was on her feet. I would do all in my power to bring smiles of joy in the children's faces.* Right then, a voice within me whispered, *Really, would you do all that?*

Hardly a week later, the Lord gave me an opportunity to make good on my promise. To cut a long story short, my husband and I found ourselves hosting a homeless young woman who'd been sleeping with her two kids in her SUV for almost a month. She came and stayed with us for a month or so. Meanwhile, with the help of two of my Christian friends, she navigated the intricacies of the social welfare system, created a resume, found a job, and found a place to stay. We donated money, a stove, furniture, curtains, and the like. But there was yet another major challenge. She needed a babysitter to take care of her toddler, who could not be integrated in a regular day-care center because of health challenges, including a compromised immune system. She could not afford to pay for special home-care services. The Holy Spirit impressed me to talk to one of my friends, Ms. H., and ask her to keep the child for no charge while the young woman was at work and the other kids were at school. I said, "Lord, please help me on this. I am not comfortable asking Ms. H. to do this free of charge. Please, could You talk to her for me, Lord?" God has a sense of humor! He understands our idiosyncrasies and knows that we mean well.

As I was coming out the church door one Sabbath morning, Ms. H. called my name and beckoned me to come to her. I did. She told me that she had heard through the grapevine of my assignment from the Lord and said that she wanted to help. Before I said a word, she told me that the Lord had impressed on her to keep the child for the young woman until he was cleared by his physician to be integrated into the regular day-care system. She added, "I can pick up the child and keep him at my house, or I can go to the young woman's home and babysit at no charge, for as long as it takes." Oh, I started crying. The deacons came over to ask what Mrs.

H. had done to me. I smiled and said, "Nothing. I am just overwhelmed with joy, that's all."

Following this incident, God has given my family breakthroughs we did not deserve. It would take another book just to recount His goodness and mercies. All I can say is that doing good for others is not in vain, even if it is an inconvenience at the time. Serving others is not doing them a favor by any means. Instead, it is an opportunity to serve and give back to society in your own way and to save one person at a time.

Last Word

Loving unconditionally as described in this chapter, in the context of couples in a marital relationship, is *not* winking at the shortcomings of others, including your mate, but looking beyond your mate's faults and accepting and loving him or her despite the shortcomings. Someone once said, "A good husband should be *deaf*, and a good wife should be *blind*." We fare better in our relationship with our spouses by focusing on and accentuating the good we find in them, not their faults, as confirmed by Philippians: "Fix your thoughts on what is true, and honorable, and right, and pure, and lovely, and admirable. Think about things that are excellent and worthy of praise" (Philippians 4:8 NLT). Adopting this attitude and practicing these things will pay many dividends in your relationship with your spouse. The two of you will be friends, soul mates, responsible roommates, and spiritual partners in your marriage journey, in His time! May the Lord "fill you with *joy*, be like minded, having the same love, being of one accord of the mind" (Philippians 2:2, emphasis added). The safest place to put your marriage is in the arms of God. This requires looking at your spouse as God sees him or her, as a work in progress. It calls for listening for what is not being verbalized so that you may identify and respond to the needs of your spouse beyond what you see and hear.

Pillar # 4
Laughs and Laughter

The Foundation

Laughter is an amnesia of the mind!

—Trevor Noah

Let's look at the virtues or benefits of laughter and laughing when it comes to enriching an individual's life and even improving the health of a marriage. A sense of humor should be considered a gift from God. The ability to laugh and make others laugh must not be taken lightly, viewed in negative terms, or deemed to be the result of a lack of seriousness. Rather, it should be viewed as a virtue and an inherent asset. Besides doing our family devotion, before my husband and I turn in to bed every night, we watch our favorite South African homeboy Trevor Noah on Comedy Central and have a good time laughing and giggling like teenagers. I have no doubt that good nutrition, a prayerful lifestyle, and humor have all added to our longevity. Those who know us well can attest to how much fun we have together. Someone once said that frowning uses more muscles than smiling and that being grouchy adds more wrinkles to your face. Many people marvel at my husband and me when we disclose our ages. "Get out of here!" They just cannot believe it. Try humor; it works. Now let's hear what others have to say on the matter:

1. *Humor is a gift from God.* Humor is good for a relationship. It is a sign of intelligence and keeps us in a joyful mood (Adrian Rodgers).
2. *Humor is good for the soul and medicine for the body.* The Bible states: "A cheerful heart is good medicine, but a broken spirit saps a person's strength dries up the bones" (Proverbs 17:22 NLT).

3. *Humor strengthens our immune system*, helping us to fight illnesses and experience healing. Thus, laughter keeps the doctor away (Charles and Frances Hunter).

4. *Humor is a tranquilizer for problems.* When we laugh, we relieve stressful situations, which can potentially damage our bodies. Also, humor is a matter of survival, especially for women (Nancy Van Pelt).

5. *Humor has emotional benefits.* When we laugh, we build self-confidence, renew hope, increase resilience, and enhance our coping skills to overcome adverse situations. We may even find light within cancer's shadow (Lyn Eib).

6. *Humor has an Rx benefit.* A sense of humor is one of the strongest pieces of psychological armor at one's disposal. A hearty laugh is like a daily dose of vitamins to the system; it is "one medicine that seem to provide physical, psychological, social and quality of life benefits for virtually everyone," practically with no adverse effects (Whole Health Insider).

Laughter Has Healing Properties

It is not surprising that some hospitals invite clowns to perform for sick children. Nancy Van Pelt shared a story related by a physician that supports the notion of the positive effects of humor on seriously ill children. She gives an account of a sick girl who snapped out of her unresponsive catatonic state because of laughter. Thus, humor creates a conducive climate for socialization as well as improving the immune system. This does not mean that people who have joyous relationships will not get sick, but their condition is likely to improve faster when humor is thrown into the mix. It is not surprising that social relationships have the potential to make or break the individuals who are part of them if not handled properly. Thus, it is beneficial for couples to build their marriages on Christ. They should strive to develop and embrace a culture of humor, fun, and togetherness, which is especially helpful when trying to resolve conflict. This is discussed in the following section.

Using Humor to Resolve Conflict

Every relationship has its moments. In each marriage walk, there is a time for everything. There are times when difficult topics must be addressed. This is where humor is a plus. I have found that humor relaxes stressful situations, easing the mood when you are tackling controversial issues and resolving conflict. My husband and I have different personalities and temperaments. I am a go-getter, whereas he is a cool, laid-back dude. But we are doing all we can to build a culture of humor and fun. We strive to use humor when tackling sensitive matters, resolving conflict, or dealing with challenging situations. We have found that humor tends to lighten up a tense situation and smooth out our differences.

For example, recently we were facing a potentially volatile situation that involved my in-laws. Godwin wanted to dig up the dirt and address the situation with his blood relatives. Normally, I would have supported him in this, since we both believe in not keeping things in or holding stuff back, and in ironing out grievances, burying the past, and moving on. But in this case, I was convinced that dealing with the issue was not a wise idea, although it was high on his agenda. After I laid out my reasons and prayed about it, I could see that my husband was still adamant about going through with his plan. Well, my last resort was to use the humor strategy. Drawing from Godwin's favorite scene in *My Cousin Vinny*, I said, "Honey, I see my honorable cousin Vinny is adamant about pursuing the matter and presenting it before the judge, but may I warn you, sir, my honorable counsel, that I will not stand with you on this one. Your star witness, Miss Vito, is a hostile witness." He looked at me, and we both burst out laughing so hard that he never brought up the matter again. He got the point. I am sure he pictured Vinny dragging Miss Vito, his star witness, to the stand as she kicked and fussed before the judge. That did it for him! I agree with Trevor Noah's notion that "comedy exposes the truth, but helps you speak truth to power in a delightful way."

Embrace Personality Differences to Create a Positive Atmosphere

Know your spouse, including what makes him or her tick, as well as his or her shortcomings. But please, do not use his or her shortcomings or different personality traits or weaknesses as put-downs. Instead, take them as strengths to complement your traits and your personality. I know this is easier said than done. But take it from me, if you make a conscious effort to identify your mate's strengths and the places where he or she excels, though these may be opposite from yours, you will begin to see these traits as a bonus, a supplement for your weak side. Likewise, your strengths will complement your spouse's weak areas. In other words, your weaknesses are your mate's strengths, and his or her weaknesses are your points of strength. So, both of you are even. This perspective will make you more tolerant of each other as partners in the marriage marathon, instead of harping on each other's weaknesses until Jesus returns.

Let's examine the four temperament types, sanguine, choleric, melancholic, and phlegmatic, that are used widely in the counseling realm. These were originally developed by Hippocrates, an ancient Greek philosopher and physician. He believed that the four personality traits were represented by body fluids, with blood indicating a lovely temperament, yellow bile indicating an active temperament, black bile indicating a dark temperament, and phlegm indicating a slow temperament, respectively. In time, these personality types were given another spin by noted psychologists Hans J. Eysenck and M. W. Eysenck to explain biological differences leading to different personalities. Eysenck's typology identifies the sanguine personality type as being people oriented, the choleric personality type as being aggressive, the melancholic personality type as being rigid, and the phlegmatic personality type as being even-tempered. In the context of embracing strength-based relationships, I am particularly impressed by Dr. Tim La Haye's integrated biblical approach to addressing these personality traits. In the book *Your Temperament: Discover Its Potential*, La Haye emphasizes the understanding of oneself and discovering strengths and weaknesses to achieve positive relationships across the board and to enhance the godly marital relationship.

Given the fact that each personality trait involves qualities that are viewed as strengths or weaknesses, and also as positive or negative, this section focuses on accentuating strengths and helping couples to celebrate their differences instead of focusing on each other's shortcomings. Married people can reconcile their mate's differences by drawing from the partner's strengths to achieve productive communication and amicable solutions, which are crucial to determining marital success. By maximizing strengths rather than focusing on weaknesses, couples can create a positive environment within which humor and understanding can thrive while they manage conflict and solve problems. To illustrate this view, I have created an example of how this may be achieved. The following exercise demonstrates (1) how each temperament can be used to complement the opposite traits and add value to the relationship, (2) how the different personalities can contribute to a successful interaction, and (3) how conflict can be managed and become productive when the couple is aiming to reach mutually agreeable solutions.

Exercise

Scenario or Framework

Let us assume that (a) there is an important project or task to be done, (b) the team of spouses involved in the project represent the four temperaments cited under the team dynamics below, (c) the focus is on applying a strength-based positive view of the temperaments at play, (d) the input of each party is considered in the analysis of the problem, (e) each personality is complementary to the others, and (f) the spouses are trying to arrive at a mutually satisfactory solution, one that reflects their opposite sets of strengths.

Team Dynamics

There are two couples with the following personality traits: (1) choleric (impulsive), (2) sanguine (sociable), (3) phlegmatic (careful), and (4) melancholic (controlled).

Here we go! The process might look like this:

Action

The *choleric* spouse will spearhead the process and assume a position of leadership in managing the project. The people-oriented *sanguine* mate will make sure the integrity of the process is maintained in an amicable and friendly way, without compromise or disregard of people's feelings. The expressive and methodical *melancholic* spouse, on one hand, will question the veracity or legitimacy of the process and call for an extensive analysis of the root cause of the problem before leaping forward. This will ensure that things are not done in a haphazard way or without thought, so as to avoid having things come back to haunt the participants after the fact.

The *phlegmatic* mate, on the other hand, may want to guard against the tendency of the process to get stuck in a rut or become bogged down by too many details or by paralysis of analysis, which is a side effect inherent to any methodological approach. Thus, each of the four temperaments has character strengths, and although different, they are complementary to one another. Note that all the different personalities add value to the integrity of the process. Like with a car, all four wheels are in motion and doing their part. If one wheel is flat, the car stalls and cannot move forward. Similarly, the input from every personality in this exercise shines through to achieve a common purpose. Let's emulate this behavior in our own marriages.

Celebrate Personality Differences as Strengths

Difference is not spelled b-a-d. Instead, it means, "I am me. I am fine, cool, and comfortable in my own skin." God covers all temperaments with His love and mercy. No one is better than the other; we are just different. My husband and I are very different, but our relationship has, after being tested, lasted for fifty years. We are living proof that couples can have productive communication and a mutually satisfying relationship despite differences and opposite personality traits. But we must be deliberate and intentional in perceiving and utilizing the differences as strengths, not weaknesses. We each depend on the other to pick us up when we stumble. Regardless of what your temperament type is, God loves and treats you the same as anyone else. "For if a man think himself to be something, when he is nothing, he deceives himself" (Galatians 6:3 KJV). So, let us be kind to and tolerant of each other, and create an environment wherein laughter can thrive. Things to bear in mind are as follows:

1. Establish a propensity for resolving conflict. Conflict is a naturally occurring phenomenon in a dynamic relationship with two persons who have opposite traits and temperaments.
2. Embrace differences and capitalize on strengths.
3. Use the protocol for addressing conflict, as follows:

   a. *Identify the problem.* There is a popular expression that a problem identified is a problem half solved. Identifying the root cause leads to open, unadulterated analysis and the reaching of appropriate solutions to address the issue at hand.

b. *Describe the facts.* In describing the facts of the matter, it is crucial for the couple to be upfront, vulnerable, and without hidden agendas, and to facilitate or ensure the integrity of the process.

c. *Analyze and diagnose the conflict.* Seek to address what is wrong and not who is wrong; this attitude allows both parties to focus on their common *interest* instead of on each other's *position.*

d. *Consider alternatives.* Listening to each other's viewpoint and what is best for the collective *us*, rather than for me, myself, and I, or considering "what's in it for me" (WIIFM), should be the focus if you wish to achieve the goal of arriving at a mutually acceptable solution.

e. *Implement the solution.* Implementing the solution and following up on the matter is crucial. Leaving things hanging can prove to be more detrimental to a relationship than not solving the problem at all. Therefore, couples should be mindful of choosing a doable solution and avoid prescribing a permanent solution to a temporal problem.

f. *Evaluate the solution.* When a solution is doable, it is more likely to facilitate performance measures. Evaluating allows the couple to redirect, reinforce strategies, or maintain what is working and adjust what is not working to improve the situation.

g. *Assess the relationship.* Assessing the aftermath is a vital strategy and by far the most important component of resolving conflict. This step should not be taken lightly. It is important to assess how both parties feel about everything that has been said and done. Listen for dissatisfaction, residual anger, and an unforgiving spirit following a conflict or crisis. The aftermath may require further attention, love, resources, and the like.

h. *Reaffirm the relationship.* Following the addressing of the aftermath, pray, kiss, and make up, thus clearing the stifling air of any residual grudge and animosity. Open the window of the heart and mind, allowing the fresh air of fun and laughter to flow through. The goal of solving conflict is predicated on creating a positive environment that is conducive to embracing each other's love and laughing again, especially following a setback.

Embrace Conflict as a Skills Challenge

Remember that you and your spouse are different *social animals* from different planets, and you will always encounter situations that reveal your different viewpoints. John Gray refers to this phenomenon as "men are from Mars and women are from Venus." Satan's duty is to tempt us to see our differences as a source of discontent and strife. God, however, does not tempt us. Instead, He tests us to see if we are mature enough to marshal the complexities of our personality as strengths. So embrace God's pop quizzes to test your (1) knowledge of the Word, (2) dependence on His promises and assurances, and (3) skill set for resolving conflict daily, and especially before sundown. "Be ye not angry, and sin not. Let not the sun go down upon your wrath" (Ephesians 4:26 KJV). The measure of your character, and of your development and progression toward the next level of spiritual growth, is your ability to give way to anger and resentment. It is also found in the strength of your desire to connect and reconcile with your spouse, getting past pettiness so that you can love and laugh again. Maya Angelou once said, "I don't trust anyone who doesn't laugh!"

Song

I have a Friend so precious,
So very dear to me,
He loves me with such tender love,
He loves so faithfully;
I could not live apart from Him,
I love to feel Him nigh,
And so we dwell together,
My Lord and I.

—Mary Ann Shorey

My Story

My husband and I have fun together. We are the best of friends. We laugh more than we fuss, quarrel, or get on each other's nerves. Please don't get me wrong, though: the ship is not always smooth sailing. There is a time for everything. As previously stated, my husband and I are very different. He is a laid-back cool dude, and I am a fast-driving sister. But we balance this different energy with humor. Literally, I am the clown. My hubby is my willing audience. He laughs very hard as he listens to my unending jokes. But like all other couples, we test each other's patience sometimes. Although my husband is a cool dude, he is also very stubborn, I tell you. So, there are times when we fuss and even have "intense fellowship"; you would think we were ready to kill each other! But in my house, these moments do not last. We have built a culture of fun around us to neutralize any tension.

From time to time will Godwin share a funny story or two with his dry humor, and I find myself assuming the position of spectator. I understand how much it takes for him to be a clown. He enjoys laughing, but humor does not come naturally to him (whereas for me it's a piece of cake). Sometimes when I watch Trevor Noah on Comedy Central, I can't stop asking myself, *Did I miss my calling?* But for my husband, humor is not one of his virtues, not even if his life depended on it. What is funny, though, is that he has the memory of an elephant. He will pull out one of my jokes when a situation demands it. Guess what? In most cases, I had forgotten the joke. We laugh and laugh. It works, you all! We have real fun together and we are best friends, next to Jesus. You can have the same type of relationship too, or better. Trust me!

Last Word

My advice to you is that you and your spouse embrace your differences! Build a culture of fun around the house. All I can say is, please have fun together. It will neutralize the bitter feelings when Prince Charming and Ladylove get on each other's nerves. Be best friends. Laugh more than you quarrel. Use humor before you argue and find a way to turn an argument into a humorous situation. Seek to be of one accord despite your differences. Find unity in your diversity and strive to reach a common goal with the Lord. All this is possible with God at the helm of your marriage. Be intentional about building a positive environment that focuses on accentuating and drawing from each other's strengths to promote productivity and achieve mutually acceptable solutions.

God, who stretched the spangled heavens
Infinite in time and place.
Flung the sun in burning radiance
Great Creator, still creating,
Show us what we may do
Creator give us guidance till our goal and yours are one.

—Eurydice V. Osterman

Pillar # 5
Altar of the Sacred Vow

Foundation

The world should not judge you by how low you fall,
but how high you rise, after you had fallen.

—Nelson Mandela

It's never too late to redirect your energies and cultivate the right attitude, disposition, and perspective in marriage. Dr. Frank W. Hale Jr. would always say "attitude determines your altitude" in understanding and life existence. Thus, our understanding of and attitude toward God, as well as our willingness to be guided by His ordained will of marriage, will shape the height to which we rise. When you fall low, confess your foolishness and repent. God is pleased when you repent and will enable you to reach higher grounds afterward. God winks at those moments or times of ignorance, if we repent (Acts 17:30 KJV). The mistakes of yesterday do not matter when today we redirect, do the right thing, and follow what is wise in the eyes of God to save our marriage. First, holy matrimony is not sealed by a kiss by any means. It is sealed by a *sacred vow*, a promise of marriage permanence, and a prayer to commit to keeping the promise of being on this journey together with the help Almighty God. Prayer in this pillar is referred to as "the altar of the sacred vow," and the altar of the sacred vow seals the portals through which the joy of marriage permanence can escape or ooze over time.

I truly believe that most couples, whether they get into marriage for the right reason or wrong reason, start with a desire for the marriage to be a success, not a failure. Why then does marriage get sour or tasteless with time? There are many answers to this question. One reason lies in the conscious or unintended neglect to pray for the marriage union to thrive. Couples get so caught up in the problems of living that they forget to attend to the one thing that will cement the sacred vow they made at the altar. Thus, married couples should create, nurture, and maintain a viable and sustainable culture of prayer and praying for each other. Bring everything and anything of concern, small or great, including all hopes and fears, and trials and temptations emanating from all spheres of the marriage, to God.

Questions to be addressed in this section are highlighted below:

1. Does prayer really work?
2. Does it matter how we pray?
3. Is there a designated spot where we should pray?
4. Is there a way we should pray?
5. How often should we pray?
6. What should we pray for?
7. Why should we pray?

Does Prayer Really Work?

Yes. All the time when we pray, God hears our prayers and speaks to us in various ways, as follows:

1. *God speaks to us through His Word in the Bible and His promises to His people*, such as the promise that before you call, He will answer (Isaiah 65:24). God has assured that "whatever you ask when you pray, believe that you receive then, and you will have them" (Mark 11:24 NKJV). "God shall supply all your needs according to his riches in glory" (Philippians 4:19 NKJV).

2. *God speaks to us through sermons* that directly touch us and address our concerns. He hears our prayers, He provides a direction in which to go, and He shows us ways to solve our problems.

3. *God speaks to us through other people's testimonies or experiences*, which usually remind us how good God is. In some cases, they give us a new perspective, an epiphany or "wake-up call" about how vulnerable we are and what is important in life.

4. *God speaks to us through impressions of the Holy Spirit*, which give us a clear vision in the face of uncertainty and perplexing

circumstances and points us in the right direction when we are at a crossroads in life.

5. *God speaks to us through prayer and praying.* Prayer is a two-way street whereby we call on God and He, in turn, speaks back to us. I can attest to this phenomenon. I have experienced, while on my knees, the Holy Ghost emailing me from heaven above and giving me a specific word or instant wisdom, showing me the way to solve a problematic situation, and giving me the needed strength and courage to withstand a trying time.

6. *God speaks to us through answered prayers* by touching others to come to our rescue as directed by the Holy Spirit. He can speak through unanswered prayers, for which in time we thank Him because what we had asked for would not have been the best thing for us. So, trusting God's plan and will for us is the key when we pray. He knows the future and what is best for us.

7. God speaks to us through the Holy Spirit which convicts us to repent from our besetting sins. The key is asking God to speak to us, other than telling God to listen to us when we speak.

Does It Matter How We Pray?

Dr. Barry Black in one of his sermons identified prayer as the most powerful tool in the arsenal of a Christian, saying that it is the most underestimated and underused, and suggested several things for developing a prayerful lifestyle, as indicated below:

a. Praying early in the morning.
b. Praying with a *sense of need.*
c. Praying for leaders and those in position of power, so they can make informed decisions and create sound policies impacting our lives.
d. Praying even if God seems silent (He is listening).
e. Praying and singing at a crossroads in life and through stressful times.
f. Praying with faith and holding on to God's promises.
g. Praying for the guidance of the Holy Spirit.

Is There a Designated Spot Where We Should Pray?

We can pray anywhere, but it is good to have a prayer closet or a designated prayer altar or room. Jesus would retreat to a solitary place and pray for intimate spiritual connection with His Father (Matthew 1:35; Luke 6:12). He prayed privately, but sometimes He prayed in a crowded area when prayer was demanded. A story is told of a woman who had many children. In her busy life, she would stop at random, and while standing, she would cover her head with her apron and pray. Her children knew not to disturb their mom's prayer time. So, amid the hustle and bustle of our hectic schedules, whether we are standing, sitting, kneeling, or lying down, we can seize the opportunity for talking to our Father in prayer, and we will be all right. It is crucial for couples to adopt a prayer lifestyle, individually and collectively, and to establish a sacred altar upon which they present their marriage to God daily.

Is There a Way We Should Pray?

The answer is yes, but how do we do this? According to 1 John 5:14–15, John 15:7,2, and 2 Chronicles 7:14, there are things God wants His people to do for the Lord to hear and answer our prayers. When praying, you should do the following things:

- Have *confidence* in Him.
- Ask according to His *will*.
- *Abide* in Him so that His *Word* will abide in you.
- *Humble* yourself before Him.
- *Seek* His face.
- *Turn* from your wicked ways.

When you have done all the above, the outcome will be phenomenal. Whatever you ask or desire, it will be done. His promises are sure. God assures that He will do the following things:

- *Hear* you from heaven.
- *Forgive* you of your sins.
- *Heal* the land you dwell in (that includes your household, your marriage, and everything about you).

Wow! That says it all. What more assurances do we need? None.

How Often Should We Pray?

The answer is that you should pray when you have the need to. If you are experiencing challenges, call in prayer for God to meet you at your point of need. He will do so. Prayer does not change God; it changes us and lifts us up to God. However, we should not pray only when there are needs or challenges in our lives; we should also pray to and praise God anytime for who He is.

What Should We Pray For?

Given the discourse articulated in the introduction to *Pillars of Joy in Marriage*, in the context of a prevailing marriage disposition under the post-sin condition, there are no limits to what we should pray for. One may ask, are there specific things to pray for? Yes, while there are many things and situations we may need to put before the Lord, there are three specific things couples must pray for. All other concerns or issues seem to hang on these three things. They are (1) a spirit of discernment, (2) clarity of purpose, and (3) the wisdom to make right decisions. These three things are explained in depth below:

1. *Pray for a spirit of discernment.*

    The concept of the spirit of discernment tends to provide us with a spiritually and socially dynamic view on life in general. Based on one's sociological orientation, the spirit of discernment offers a twofold perspective, anchored in the emic-conceptualization and etic-conceptualization.

    a. Emic-conceptualization

    This view gives us the ability to engage in sharp introspection and to "smell ourselves." This posture is necessary in the marital relationship because it enables each spouse to look within himself or herself and identify or discern the part he or she has played or how he or she has contributed to each situation that may assail the couple. This posture is crucial and curbs the tendency to shift blame onto someone else. Some people do not see any wrong they have done. It's always the other person, not me, who is the culprit. The first couple, Adam and Eve, went as far as pointing the finger at God Himself (see the introduction to *Pillars of Joy in Marriage*). Blame is usually assigned to things like a health condition, friends, a job, one's boss or colleagues, one's parents, one's neighbors, a developmental phase, or one's nature ("This is who I am," or "That is how men [or women] are"). The list goes on, with people blaming anything and everything on someone else. In so doing, such people refuse to take any responsibility for their actions.

b. Etic-conceptualization

This view gives us insight to interpret the world around us and gives us the ability to come to accurate conclusions about what we observe in others. Thus, a spouse can discern what is wrong and help his or her mate to redirect when necessary. In the marriage dynamic, both the emic and etic perspectives are crucial. Generally, couples tend to be fixated on the etic view of life, pointing out the faults in others and neglecting to look at themselves. In so doing, they find it hard to redirect and address their own shortcomings for lack of introspection or emic-conceptualization. The Word counsels us to first examine our own shortcomings before we go pointing a finger at others. "How can you think of saying to your [mate] let me help you get rid of the speck in your eye, when you can't see past the log in your own eyes. Hypocrite! First get rid of the log in your eye; then you will see well enough to deal with the speck in your [mate]'s eye" (Matthew 7:1–4 NLT).

2. *Pray for clarity of purpose.*

The marriage institution is like the love affair between Jesus and His church. Prayer streamlines our resolve to inherit the kingdom. While Jesus commissioned us to wait until He comes, we should not lose focus of our eternal home. The Lord's Prayer to His disciples reminds us, "Thy Kingdom come, thine will be done on earth as it is in heaven. ... For thine is thy Kingdom, the power and the glory for ever and ever amen" (Matthew 6:10, 13 KJV). Thus, the joy we derive from the institution of marriage is designed to take us ultimately to the marriage celebration with our true Price Charming, Jesus Christ, the Lamb of God, in glory, where we will be perfectly happy for eternity.

3.   *Pray for wisdom to make the right decisions.*

King Solomon, the wisest person who ever lived, prayed for wisdom from God. He prayed not for riches or possessions, nor for mighty strength to annihilate his enemies, but for wisdom! God granted him wisdom and many material possessions he had not even asked for. "Because you have asked for wisdom in governing my people with justice and have not asked for a long life or wealth or the death of your enemies. I will give you what you asked for! I will give you a wise and understanding heart such no one else has had or ever will have! I will also give what did not ask for riches and fame" (1 Kings 3:11–13 NLT). We too can access the gift of wisdom and God will grant us wisdom and all the other gifts that come from God, exceedingly, abundantly, above anything that we may think or ask (Ephesians 3:20 NKJV). It is not fun to go through life literally stupid and repeatedly making foolish mistakes and uncalculated decisions when wisdom is available and readily accessible through prayer. God will give it to you just for the asking!

Why Should We Pray?

Prayer links us to the heavenly throne. Whether we are praying alone in private, with family, or with fellow believers in church amid a corporate setting, prayer connects us with our Father God in an intimate way. Referring to the temple, Jesus said, "My house shall be called the house of prayer" (Matthew 21:13 NKJV). He could have said it would be a house of preaching, teaching, or even singing. While all these activities are essential to worship, the Lord emphasized prayer as His signature by which His house would be identified and which it would be noted for. We pray for God to give us power to withstand the guiles of the wicked enemy, Satan. The old serpent means no good and seeks to destroy the marriage institution. Listen to Jesus's counsel to His disciples in the Lord's Prayer: "Lead us not into temptation but deliver us from evil." We must pray for Satan to stay off our backs. If you are to keep him off your back, then it is crucial that you make a sacred vow to create a prayerful lifestyle for yourself, your mate, and your family at large. This concludes the matter of why we must have an altar of the sacred vow, a covenant of marriage permanence.

Song

Sweet hour of prayer, sweet hour of prayer,
That calls me from a world of care,
And bids me, at my Father's throne,
Make all my wants and wishes known!
In seasons of distress and grief,
My soul has often found relief,
And oft escaped the tempter's snare,
By thy return, sweet hour of prayer.

—William W. Walford

My Story

God our Father created us to reflect His image and to connect with Him for our existence through a prayerful lifestyle. Individual prayers are powerful; however, collective corporate intercessory prayer is even more powerful. To illustrate the powerhouse of corporate intercession, I would like to share just one story that had a great impact on mer. I remember as if it were yesterday, a member of another denomination appeared before our church family, the Ephesus Seventh-day Adventist Church, in Columbus, Ohio, asking the congregation to pray for his hospitalized young wife. She had a heart ailment and was waiting for a heart transplant. Her condition had deteriorated to the point that she had written letters to her little children to be read at each milestone in their lives: graduation, marriage, and so forth.

One Sabbath morning during prayer time, Brother Gibson, who was leading the corporate intercessory prayer that day, said something like this:

"Lord, today we are not asking for the availability of a donor as expected by the medical staff because a donor must die to make a heart available for a successful heart transplant. But we implore You today, Lord, to intervene and perform a miracle. Please, Father, *jump-start* this woman's own heart!" God did it! The young mother snapped out of her condition. The rest is history! Heart specialists and interns alike were shocked and amazed by the instant development. News about the miracle was published in the *Columbus Dispatch*. The young woman was eventually discharged and is still alive, kicking, and going strong. Her grateful husband came back to Ephesus Church to thank the congregation for what God had done for his wife and family. Wow, indeed, God is able and can do exceedingly above all that we ask, according to the power that worketh within us (Ephesians 3:20). God has said "My house shall be a house of prayer," not of preaching, as good and necessary as preaching is. Thus, individual prayer is powerful, but when paired with intercessory prayer in a corporate setting, praying in one accord, it is even more powerful.

Last Word

Frank M. Hasel, the principal contributor to the *Adult Sabbath School Bible Study Guide,* entitled "The Holy Spirit and Spirituality," identifies the Holy Spirit and prayer as inseparable, saying, "True spirituality and prayer go together. There is no real spiritual life without vigorous prayer. The prayer of faith enables us to live in response to the abundance of God's promises" (p. 116).

Prayer is like any intimate conversation. It is a two-way street. When we pray, we should assume a posture of listening to what God is saying to us, instead of rehearsing a long laundry list of wants and not pausing to hear what God is saying back to us. We should not regard prayer as a command or demand for God to listen to us. Figuratively speaking, "Listen, God, I am talking" is the wrong attitude to have. Rather, it should be the other way around. Like Samuel, we should assume a posture of humility and say, "Speak, your servant is listening" (1 Samuel 3:10 NIV). When we do this, we put God at the center of our attention and consciously demonstrate a true and authentic desire to have an intimate conversation with Him, now and through eternity.

This concludes the matter of why we must have an altar of the sacred vow, a covenant of marriage permanence, and longing for our final marriage with the Lamb in the land of glory. God our Father created us to reflect His image. Someone once said that when we pray, we are elevated to God and we intimately kiss the face of God. Prayer changes us; it doesn't change God. Above all, heaven's prayer line is toll-free, on God's account. There are no concerns about a Wi-Fi account. It's free, with unlimited data at your disposal. You can download and stream His promises anytime and anywhere. His emergency lifeline has no voice mail or busy signals. It is available twenty-four hours a day, around the clock. He is just a call away. When you call, His angels run to your rescue. Even before you call, He answers. What a promise!

Pillar # 6
Remembering the Old Times

The Foundation

> If we forget the past, we fall in a trap of repeating
> the same fatal mistakes of the past.
>
> —Leslie Pollard

Remember the beginning of your love relationship. Remembering the old times, look back, turn back the hands of time, scroll back to the time you first met your spouse-to-be. Review the film, feeling the warmth in your heart when you saw him or her approaching. See the smiles and excitement when you chatted and joked with each other. Remember, you could not get enough of each other, walking in the park, sharing a lunch, giggling, and planning the future. Nothing around you seemed to matter. Remember how you used to turn the heads of people around you as if you were from outer space? Do you remember how you used to talk and talk over the phone as if the calls were free? Have you forgotten those days when you were so in love and saw nothing wrong with your Prince Charming or Ladylove, and when whatever words other people were saying to discourage you from marrying your woman or man were like an empty vessel?

If the things I mentioned now seem to be a blur, what do you think happened? What went wrong? Answers to some of these questions will help you to see where you used to be and whether you are still on the right track. Or perhaps you need to reminisce about the old times and try to build on a few things that might trigger the warm feelings. Here are some questions to ponder:

1. What brought you together in the first place?
2. What made you marry your spouse?

3. What qualities made him or her stand out?
4. What made you say, "This is the one"?
5. What did you really like about him or her?
6. If you could do it over, would you still choose the same mate?
7. If your mate had known everything about you then, as he or she intimately knows you now, would he or she have chosen you as a spouse?

When I ponder the past, two competing phenomena or constructs are present: (a) positive selective memory and (b) negative selective amnesia.

Positive Selective Memory

In the Bible, when God says "remember," He gets your attention because He is about to say something very serious and important. Remembering the reason you were attracted to your Prince Charming or Ladylove is a step toward developing a memorable and lasting impression of your mate. Once you put into perspective or bring into full view why you married your spouse in the first place, you will see how far you are from the start of your courtship. You will regroup, if need be. When you lose sight of or forget where you have been together, it is folly. Even with God's providences, when we forget how good God has been to us, how He has led us and fought our battles in the past, we tend to fear the future and our faith fails us. Revisit your blessings. Name and count them one by one. Celebrate the trophies you won because of the Lord. You will regain the strength to rise and fight new challenges. Now, let us examine the opposite scenario.

Negative Selective Amnesia

The flip side of remembering the good old times is the tendency to bring only memories of bad experiences from the back burner to the front. All that matters is rehashing, accentuating, and rehearsing only the unpleasant things that happened during your relationship, even if there is no longer a threat now. This is very destructive and discouraging to your mate. Please do not get me wrong: If there is a reason to bring up old grievances for discussion, it's good to talk about them, clear the air, resolve them, and move on. Otherwise, those skeletons can resurrect, grow muscles and gain blood, and haunt the memories of your marriage for a long time.

I remember counseling a friend who was locked up in bad or unhappy memories of her past. Her spouse had treated her badly, womanizing and carrying on back then, but he had chosen my friend at the end of the day. But she was still caught up in the feelings of what he had done way back then. I said to her, "From what you have shared about your mate now, you have a wonderful marriage. Your spouse loves you and worships the ground you walk on. You should forgive his foolish indiscretions of the past. The guy you are with now is not the same man he used to be. But it looks like you are still married to his ghost. Your marriage is in jeopardy, girlfriend, unless you destroy the old man, entomb the remains, and start learning to love the new man in your life." The rest is history. To date, they have been together, going strong and enjoying each other's company, for about twenty-two years now. So, accentuate the positive and celebrate what the new man or woman has turned out to be, rather than expending quality time and energy beating a ghost.

Rediscover Your Spouse and Reintroduce Yourself to Him or Her
If by some chance you happen to fall into the category of having negative selective amnesia, then use the following twelve-step toolkit to help rediscover your mate.

1. Pray to overcome the indifference harbored and entertained.
2. Reintroduce yourself to the new, changed man or woman.
3. Reconnect. Continue dating again as if you are not married.
4. Receive the gift of the new man or woman.
5. Fall in love and remarry him or her in your mind.
6. Embrace your new man or woman and lock him or her in your mind and your heart.
7. Continue with the sweet talk and doing the things that attracted you to each other in the first place. They were vital then and are even more important now.
8. Tidy up. Clean and groom yourself to look good for your mate. Invest in a healthy lifestyle so that you will be there for each other for the long haul.
9. Refrain from letting yourself get rusty.

10. Try to wear your age well. Please do not allow yourself to sag and bulge out of control, becoming unrecognizable in shape to your Prince Charming or Ladylove. Be intentional and determined not to let your guard down through all the seasons of your marriage. To do so is too risky, both for your health and, even more, your love relationship.

11. Learn to enjoy your mate and spend quality time together. Nothing or no one, not even children, should take the place of your mate in your heart and mind. Oh, children will try to take that place, but keep reminding them of what a friend once told me that he tells his kids: "Hey, guys, I love you dearly, but I am not in love with you. I am in love with your mama." Of course, this view applies to both mates. Surely there is a clear distinction between loving the kids and being in love with their mama or daddy.

My parents had a saying for us: "You guys come second on our list, and even if you turn the list upside down, you stand at number 99, not 100." So, we took that and ran. Mom, especially, would remind us that she and our father were there in this marriage before we came along. She said that one day we would all leave the house and go our separate ways, and when we came back to visit, we would still find them minding their business together. Sure enough, that did happen. Wow, trust me, that really shaped my own marriage trajectory.

Once the children are grown and gone, you do not want to be stuck with a disengaged, estranged, and bitter mate who became that way because he or she felt short-changed in the relationship by playing second fiddle to your children. As a result, you will wonder, *Who is this man [or woman], and what am I supposed to do to bond with this grouchy person? What am I going to do with this?* Before you get to this place, it is necessary to realize from the beginning that you are both in this union together. Create positive impressions and a lasting bond with your mate, the best you know how. Prepare to grow together. Invest in your relationship now so that you may cash in on it in your later years. Thus, you will enjoy smooth and peaceful quality time together later, during your twilight years, when your nerves are fragile, and you have less energy and endurance to start building a marriage bond.

Song

Looking ba-a-ack over my life
I can see where I caused you strife
But I know, oh yes I know
I'd never make that same mistake again

Once my cup was overflowing
I gave nothing in retu-u-urn
Now I can't begin to te-ell you
What a lesson I have learned

—Brook Benton

My Story

God blessed me with a good and faithful husband. During our courtship, he proved to me that he genuinely loved me. Godwin told me that I was the one and promised me that he would be here in this marriage for the long haul. How do I know this? I am glad you asked. My best friend had an eye on my then fiancé, bigtime, but he had no clue. I did not know how to address this. I just prayed about it and waited to see how it played out. The Lord revealed to me that time would tell. *If Godwin wants your friend, then there is nothing you can do about it. Give him a chance to choose.* I did just that. I took a two-week vacation to visit my parents, who lived far from where I was working at the time, to allow my friend the opportunity to intensify her quest and engage in her pursuit uninhibited. But instead of falling for my friend, my fiancé's heart, the farther away I was, grew fonder. He chose me, and the rest is history. As I look back now, remembering those times, I realize that I can trust my husband in any situation without a doubt. I knew then that he would be a faithful husband and be with me for the long haul. I was his girl. Case closed! The confidence he inspired then in my tender years has proven to be an assurance to me, and a *bedrock* that is still strong after decades of being together. He has never betrayed my trust.

Amazingly, I find myself being picky sometimes, fussing and carrying on, complaining about my husband and thinking stuff like, *Oh, I really wish he could be this or that and not this or the other*—whatever the case may be. I realize that he is not a saint, and neither am I. So, I begin to imagine him looking at me and saying, even if he is not verbalizing it himself, *Hey, girl, you are not perfect either!* The epiphany of my own imperfection has really humbled me. It has helped me to realize how blessed I am that God gave me the spouse I have. Furthermore, this introspection has made me wonder, if my husband was as perfect as I wanted him to be, would he have chosen me or someone else? Thus, asking this rhetorical question has had the effect of bridling a wild horse, to say the least. It has kept me real! Hence, engaging in reflection and introspection before jumping on that "pity-party wagon" has helped me to develop a new perspective. Try using the technique yourself before judging your mate's imperfection.

Last Word

The reason it is crucial to remember the old times is that it keeps things in perspective. If we forget the humble beginnings, we are more likely to repeat the errors we made in the past or miss the things we need to maintain. John the Revelator, who sent messages to the seven churches of the Bible, addressed the church of Ephesus in Revelation 2:4 (NKJV): "Nevertheless, I have this against you, that you have left your first love." Likewise, we should constantly remind ourselves of the things that worked on our marriage journey and build upon them. Some people who study the psychology of monkeys know that a monkey does not juggle two things at a time. For example, if it has a banana in its hand and you throw it some peanuts, it throws away the banana and grabs the peanuts. If the monkey grabs a tourist's purse and you want it to release the purse from its hands, just throw it a piece of candy or something. The monkey will release the purse, which then can be recovered by the owner. We can't afford to be like the monkey. We should build on and improve on things that worked. Similarly, if we forget our first love, we might throw away a good woman or man for a new toy. You know what I mean! Even with God's blessings, we cannot forget what He did for us in the past. If we forget His provisions and guidance, our faith will cool down or we will lose the grip of God. This we cannot afford. When doubt crosses your mind, just remember the good old days and the promises you and your spouse made to each other to live by God's grace. His promises are sure, and He delivers to those who trust and depend on Him.

Pillar #7
Spiritual Intimacy

The Foundation

Sex is an icing on a cake!

—Linda Kot

Spiritual intimacy is the cake itself. With all the underlying vital
ingredients, such as intellectual, mental, and emotional connection,
seasoned with authentic and organic commitment to the marriage
union, and blended with positive communication, without which
sensual intimacy, *standing alone*, is void. Thus, if a marriage relationship
is *only* predicated on sensual intimacy, there is no marriage there!

—Nozipho N. Nxumalo, PhD

Before I delve deep into explaining what *spiritual intimacy* is all about, I
would like to take a moment and address *physical intimacy* first so that the
reader may understand the fine line between the two phenomena as well
as discover the common thread binding the interaction between the two,
learning how they jive or dance together to achieve the ultimate goal of a
mutually satisfying intimate marriage relationship. So, what I would like to
stress in this pillar is the existence of a common thread of interdependence
between spiritual and physical intimacy, which are not mutually exclusive
domains. They both need each other if a couple is to arrive at a mutually
fulfilling intimate relationship.

What Is Physical Intimacy?
Physical intimacy includes sex, an intense physical and sensual closeness
that creates a superglue-like bonding experience. Physical intimacy includes

things like the prelude of a romantic candlelight dinner, which sets the stage for passionate lovemaking. The Almighty God created sex as a gift of love for couples to enjoy within the confines of the undefiled marriage bed (Hebrews 13:4). Various metaphors have been used to described sexual intimacy, to express its seriousness and thrill. Some of these are as follows:

- Sex is a "cleaving together," like superglue that binds or bonds the two as one (a biblical metaphor).
- Sex is a "special gift of God," a way for couples to meet each other's deepest need (Steven Cole).
- Sex is the "icing on the cake" (Linda Kot).
- Sex is "an oasis" for your marriage and the "oil" of the relationship engine (Tricia Goyer and others).

Whatever way you choose to describe sexual intimacy, clearly it is a unique and sacred gift for married couples. Our souls crave physical intimacy. We cannot have a healthy marriage without physical intimacy (Steven Cole). It is not surprising that the devil seeks to defile and destroy the marriage bed in many ways, but he is only successful if we allow him to take control of our appetite and violate the boundaries of marriage.

To set the stage for lovemaking, Tricia Goyer counsels, "Before you flip off the light, look at the light in your spouse's eyes and the smile on your spouse's face. … Take note of the peace and contentment in your own soul."

I will not dwell on physical intimacy, because Hollywood, the music and film industries, *Playboy* and *Playgirl* magazines, social media, and the like have spared no details in scripting, projecting, and glorifying the physical aspect of intimacy. Now even a child can figure out what sexual intimacy is. Unfortunately, such instruments have failed to address the spiritual component of intimacy. Instead, they devalue and pervert sex to depict a deplorable attitude toward marriage and the home, thus reducing sex to an "art of seduction," as observed by Charles Willschiebe, author of *God Invented Sex*. Hence, the emphasis of this pillar is on explicating the notion of a profound interaction between the ingredients of spiritual intimacy and physical intimacy and discussing how this reaction can make or break a marriage.

What Is Spiritual Intimacy?

Spiritual intimacy is the connection between the minds of the married couple and the mind of Jesus Christ. "Let this mind be in you which was also in Christ Jesus" (Philippians 2:5 KJV). Spiritual intimacy includes other ingredients, such as a commitment to the marriage union, positive communication, and intellectual and emotional intimacy. When all the cited ingredients are marinated together, they enable mutually fulfilling physical/sexual intimacy. Conversely, if some of the ingredients are missing or are not well mixed and thoroughly baked, physical/sexual intimacy, the icing on the cake, becomes tasteless or may be entirely absent. To illustrate this phenomenon, I remind you of the incident recorded in Matthew 4:4 (KJV). When the devil tempted Jesus to turn stones into bread, after He had fasted for forty days, Jesus answered, "It is written that a man shall not live by bread alone, but by the word of God." Similarly, the pleasure from physical intimacy alone is not sufficient for achieving a sustainable, mutually fulfilling marriage without the core ingredient of spiritual intimacy. In light of this sentiment, therefore, the reader may elect to take a moment to reflect on the intimacy of his or her marriage and complete the questionnaire in appendix C, in an attempt to assess and address the condition of the intimacy in his or her marriage.

The Interaction between Physical and Spiritual Intimacy

In running a race, the most important words are "Get set! Get ready! Go!" This sets the mood of the runners to focus on the race at hand, and to run with all their might until they get to the finish line. At this point, the anticipation of finishing the race and being the first to touch the rope is the only focus. This phenomenon reminds me of physical intimacy, and of the four words that are important in determining the winner. I call these the four P's: posture, prayer, plan, play.

Posture

Attitude and mood are everything when it comes to experiencing an enjoyable intimate relationship with your mate. Get yourself ready and set the mood in anticipation of enjoying what you are about to receive, just as you do when you prepare to enjoy your favorite meal. Your attitude is important. It sets the mood for the lovemaking event. Especially for women, if you are quarrelsome and begrudging, dragging the unresolved issues of the day into the bedroom, thinking things such as, *He did this or did not do that,* and being emotionally jacked up, then your attitude will get in the way of your enjoyment of the lovemaking. See, men are different animals; they are wired differently than women. Intimacy to women is spelled t-a-l-k, whereas for men, intimacy is spelled "s-e-x" (Dr. Gary and Barbara Rosberg). Dr. John Gray's notion that "men are from Mars, and women are from Venus" confirms that men and women are wired differently. To men, sex is *physical* and, to women sex is more than physical; it is emotional and spiritual. This implies that grudge or no grudge, men could care less! They will enjoy lovemaking 100 percent despite your sour attitude. Remember that when you have already made up your mind to enjoy or not to enjoy the intimacy, you have determined the outcome. So, how you view and prepare for intimate times together will determine the outcome of your lovemaking. Simply put, beware of self-fulfilling prophecy!

Pray

Hey, why not pray for the Lord to bless what you are about to receive and give Him thanks for it? We pray over food, at the beginning of a journey, and on many other occasions. Should we assume it is silly or not important to pray for the Holy Ghost to tabernacle with us in this important endeavor? Donna Sigl-Davis, of Worthington Center for the Healing Arts, suggests, among other things, that "exploring how God is part of your lovemaking" improves intimacy for married couples. If you have never practiced praying before lovemaking, try it. You will be surprised at the results. Pray and resolve other marital issues so as not to let them fester and spoil your intimacy. Prayer will loosen you up, get rid of the dross of anger, and allow your spirit to be receptive to your mate's love and lovemaking. See, you cannot pray and be angry at the same time. I see now why God admonishes us in Ephesians 4:26, "Let not the sun goes down on your wrath." Jean Fuller, addressing the topic "What does Shekinah glory have to do with sex?", made the following observations:

1. *There is nothing as intimate and spiritual* as becoming one spiritually, physically, and emotionally with your spouse.

2. *God celebrates lovemaking* within the marriage bed undefiled.
3. The *Shekinah glory of God's presence* hovers over the marriage bed when the husband and wife sexually unite.
4. When Christian couples understand and embrace the beauty and spirituality of sexual intimacy and dispel myths that sex is dirty, only then can they behold the "sexual transcendent moment of ecstasy, where they glimpse the beauty of God!" Thus, when the marriage bed is defiled by infidelity of a spouse, the golden chain or sacred bond that binds the couple is violated or breached beyond measure.

Humankind did not just stumble on physical intimacy. It is God who invented sex. God intended sex to be inclusive, to go above and beyond the duty of procreation to include enjoyment and bonding or cleaving of the married couple. Remember this principle before you are tempted to have an extramarital affair. Just because some people have run with the gift of sex and polluted it with pornography, illicit sex, fornication, adultery, and all forms of promiscuity does not mean we can do as we please outside the spiritual parameters that God set for physical intimacy.

Plan
Mutually fulfilling lovemaking does not just happen. While sex is a naturally occurring and spontaneous expression of love for couples, it does take some planning, like anything else we do in life. Without denying spontaneity, sometimes lovemaking needs a certain level of preparation and forethought for its success. Yes, of course, we plan and prepare for meals, putting our best efforts into making sure the meal is palatable and tasty. What is wrong with planning the event of lovemaking and anticipating its occurrence? For example, the wife may initiate the encounter by calling her hubby and saying that she needs him to show up tonight! Make sure you put on special bedding with inviting colors, clean your body, brush your teeth, look fresh, smell good, drop those flannel pajamas and put on a slick silky negligee, and dim the lights to a romantic glow. Woo! Hello, here I come!

Play

Sex is beautiful. It is a holy gift from God for couples to enjoy. Through sex, couples bond within the marriage bed undefiled or unpolluted by extramarital affairs. Whether we care to admit it or not, God is in that bed. Otherwise, when the marriage bed is defiled, or when physical intimacy boundaries have been broken, or when the other spouse has been neglected, misused, and abused through sexual indiscretions and sordid affairs outside the confines of holy matrimony, God, our heavenly Father, is displeased. So if we believe this, why not invite God to be part of lovemaking and help us achieve mutually fulfilling intimacy? Well, some may not want to pray and invite God, because the things they practice can drive the angels out through the bedroom window. Okay, I get it! But know this: the angels love to watch couples engaged in lovemaking within the confines of marriage bed. Imagine, God's halleluiah and Shekinah glory covers the married couple when they enjoy the apex or climax of physical intimacy (Jean Fuller). It is ironic that when boundaries are violated, something so good and pure can cause so much strife, pain, and loneliness between a couple. There are numerous books written on the physical play part of intimacy. Left out of these books is the spiritual part of intimacy, which is the essential ingredient for achieving mutually fulfilling intimacy between a married couple. And such intimacy involves the physical, emotional, and intellectual domains.

How Do You Know if You Have Embraced Spiritual Intimacy?
Some of the ingredients and guiding principles that may indicate your level of spiritual intimacy are as follows:

1. You make a practice of clearing the air when issues arise. You do not allow the sun to go down on your anger, and you are not bent over double about things that ticked you off in the daytime.
2. You choose to be forgiving instead of holding a grudge. Thus, you resolve issues and are at peace with your mate before lovemaking.
3. You resist making decisions that may impair or destroy your sex life, such as using silence and sex to punish your mate for whatever reason.

4. You make sound decisions "showered in prayer." You refrain from making important decisions under duress, or when upset, hungry, or sick. (Remember how hunger led Esau to sell his Jacob's birthright over a bowl of lentil soup, as recorded in Genesis 25:19–34?) So, making uncalculated moves may put stress on your relationship and even bring about the demise of your sex life.

5. You surrender and give yourself fully to your mate, forsaking all others and allowing yourself to be vulnerable in your mate's arms. "A husband should fulfill his wife's sexual needs and the wife should fulfill her husband's sexual needs. … Do not deprive each other of sexual relations" (1 Corinthians 7:4–5 NLT).

6. You meet each other's needs, physical, spiritual, emotional, and intellectual, and you do not withhold sex to punish your spouse. Thus, you prevent your mate from being tempted to seek out extramarital affairs so as to fulfill the needs that are being unmet at home.

When the Emotional Side of Intimacy Can Help

The emotional side of spiritual intimacy is delicate and touchy and can be switched off by little upsets. There are times in marriage when especially the female mate is not in the mood for sensual intimacy; she is just out of it and does not want to be touched for whatever reason. Then what? This is where spiritual intimacy kicks in. Spiritual intimacy renews joy in times of emptiness. John Gary describes this Venusian mood as like being in a well. However, he argues that the woman by herself cannot snap out of it; she needs her man to pull her out of the well and provide the missing piece of the puzzle, which is *talk*. The man may talk her out of it through caring *sweet talk* and *romance*. Don't just jump into sexual intercourse at a moment like this. Physical intimacy alone, without any nurturing of the emotional intimacy, is not enough for women. Caring, finding out what is wrong, and apologizing if necessary for things that did not go well can help a great deal. Spiritual intimacy goes beyond the physical domain and kicks in when the sexual side proves limited or is a challenge.

Whose Responsibility Is It?

Both mates have a collective responsibility for promoting a climate wherein spiritual intimacy can thrive. Each spouse is individually accountable to God for building a spiritual relationship with Him that predisposes an intimate environment where the sexual part of the marriage relationship can be fulfilled. However, God has designed it so that the "powerhouse" of sexual desire resides within the male species, which in turn makes the man fully responsibility for fulfilling his mate. A man's duty is to love his wife as he loves his body, and to love her as Christ loves His church (Ephesians 5:25–30). A woman's role is to submit to her husband as he submits to the Lord (Ephesians 5:22). In addition, God wants both husbands and wives to *submit to each other* (Ephesians 6:23). God leaves no stone unturned; all our roles come with responsibility, whether we agree or not.

Core Principles for Striving to Achieve Spiritual Intimacy

There are several specific principles that, among other things, married couples need to embrace and practice that have the potential to enrich their intimacy and build a conducive environment wherein physical and spiritual intimacy can interact and flourish. These principles are as follows:

1. *Commit to Your Vow of Marriage Permanence*

    Joyous intimacy is predicated on commitment, which is the foundation of strong love and a successful marriage (Randy Maxwell). Commitment is like a pledge of marriage permanence made before God. Reassure your mate that you are in this marriage marathon for the long haul, not just in words but also in action. You must be intentional and substantiate your words with your walk, your deeds, the steps you take, the places you choose to visit, how you spend your money, how invest your time and talents, and whom you share these resources. This includes the type of books you read, the programs you choose to watch, and more importantly, the people to whom you give the love that is reserved for your mate and family. Commitment means investing in your marriage relationship and forsaking all others, no matter how cute or seemingly better than your spouse they are. This concept of marriage as an investment will be explored further under pillar #13.

2.   *Commit to Meeting Each Other's Needs*

Establish what your spouse's needs are. Take time to learn everything about your mate so that you become able to fill his or her love tank and meet his or her needs, physically, spiritually, intellectually, and emotionally. This disposition is not a onetime action but a conscious and deliberate commitment to doing the best you can every day. Can you imagine if each one of you had the same commitment? The prevailing notion of having a 50-50 relationship is faulty at best. A strong marriage can be achieved only by having an unwavering commitment to serve each other's needs, unconditionally, until your last breath on earth. Come with the goal of having a 100–100 relationship and you will be rewarded in due season.

3.   *Exorcise the Demon of a Third Party in Your Relationship*

Your spouse is not perfect, and neither are you. Be patient with one another, remembering the adage, "Rome was not built in one day." Keep on doing the right thing and inspire your spouse to dream. There are some men or women who are married to a figment of their imaginations. They wish their mates could be something different than what she or he is, whether skinnier, prettier, taller, darker, lighter, more outgoing, more reserved, or with better hair. The list goes on. These qualities should be considered when a person is searching for a mate, not after the fact of marriage. Instead of bending over double about things that one cannot change or that cannot be reversed, the person should start by dispelling the fantasy lover, the imaginary tall, dark, and handsome man with six-pack abs, or the slim Coca-Cola-bottle-shaped woman who does not exist in reality. The fact is that sharing love with a third-party lover, whether he or she is real or imaginary, is considered cheating. Adultery is a sin before God. One must forsake the fantasy man or woman, bury and mourn him or her, and move on with the reality in mind that he or she is not yours. Learn to love and appreciate the man or woman God gave you. Celebrate differences, draw from each other's strengths, and accentuate the positive qualities your mate has, instead of being fixated on his or her shortcomings or weaknesses.

4. *Learn to Love the Spouse God Gave You*

Learn to love, appreciate, and nurture, the one mate God has given to you. This is easier said than done, but it is important and right in the eyes of God. Needlessly expending energy to serve other people and doing for them what you are not willing to do for your mate is silly, precancerous, and a form of cheating, and is not a good investment of your time. Simply put, invest in your spouse, the one God gave you, period! Forsake futile fantasies and learn to be loving toward your own spouse. Be nice and engaging with your mate. Many people are Mr. Nice Guy or the gracious sweet cookie when out in public but are mean, grouchy, critical, and disengaged at home. This is duplicitous. Anyone who cannot express the same sentiments at home with a spouse and children as he or she expresses when out in public is hypocritical and a sinner in heaven's eyes!

5. *Practice Healthy Communication*

Communication is a broad topic and a complicated phenomenon that cannot be fully addressed in this section. But I will highlight a few working strategies to foster positive communication, as follows:

a. *Commit to being vulnerable.* Be open and truthful when sharing and discussing issues that impact or have the potential to threaten the marriage relationship, especially the issue of intimacy. Openly share with your mate what is working or not working for you. Remember, your spouse is not a mind reader or fortune-teller. Please, talk things out. Be gentle, kind, honest, and vulnerable. Tact is crucial. The tongue is deadly if not guarded. A Greek friend shared this saying: "A tongue does not have bones, but it does break bones!" That is how powerful speech is. Why not use it to break indifference, animosity, jealousy, selfishness, and related vices? Use the tongue to build intimacy, grace, love, and tenderness.

b. *Commit to addressing conflict.* Do not fear addressing conflict. Using silence to punish your spouse is dangerous and is one of the worst things to do. Have an honest desire and be determined to work out problems early, not letting them fester and infect the bedroom. Never withhold sex to punish your spouse. This has serious implications and is destructive to the relationship. If you are sick or have sex-related problems, discuss them openly with your physician or your sex or couples' therapist. Have a mutual mind-set that, regardless of circumstances, divorce is not an option. Avoid using ultimatums such as "I am done with this marriage" or "I want to out of this marriage." These may lead to irreversible consequences that you may regret later. This will be illustrated further under pillar #14.

c. *Be gracious and considerate.* Remember, you do not have the right-of-way all the time. So, you are not always right. Allow your mate to be right. Be gracious and avoid making derogatory statements, hurling insults, making innuendoes, or uttering demeaning remarks that put down your mate, no matter how wrong his or her responses are. Just state what the matter is. It's not what you say that will destroy the relationship, but how you say what needs to be said.

d. *Pray together and for each other daily.* The topic of prayer and developing a of prayer life was discussed under pillar #5. However, I want to mention that nothing else in my marriage experience solidifies my spiritual base and accelerates my spiritual growth and development as does hearing my supportive husband lifting me up in a special way in prayer. Wow, it just does it for me! What I have noticed is that somehow Godwin and I do not feel down at the same time. Thus, each one of us can minister and be a tower of strength and encouragement to each other. One young man shared with me that his wife enjoys beating him down the more he is stressed. I grieved when I heard this because I simply could not imagine such a life. At the same time, it helped me to reflect on my marriage and made me count my blessings. I felt very grateful for and appreciative of my own spouse and thanked God for my marriage.

e. *Focus on what is good for the collective.* Selflessness exponentially builds up a relationship. This fact cannot be overemphasized. I am convinced, without a doubt, that if there is one thing that can tear up a relationship bit by bit, one step at a time, it is the flaw of selfishness. This view is based on my observation of my own marriage walk of fifty years. Looking back, I praise God for blessing both of us with the selflessness we have displayed toward each other through the years. Young couples frequently ask my husband and me to tell them of just one virtue that has sustained our relationship. Our response has been *selflessness*, putting each other's needs before self. Also, lavish your spouse with compliments.

f. *Be intentional about meeting each other's needs.* Any driver needs to be familiar with the type of gasoline the car he or she is driving requires, whether it takes diesel fuel or regular, premium, or high-octane gasoline. These types differ in quality, power, performance, and price. Like cars, men and women have different needs, both physically and psychologically, when it comes to intimacy. To a greater degree, men are stimulated or turned on by what they see and are physically motivated. They see it and want it! Whereas for women physical intimacy is emotionally motivated, according to Dr. Gary and Barbara Rosenberg, authors of *The Five Love Needs of Men and Women*. There are different varieties of love language that each gender speaks, and how the love is expressed and received differs as well. Dr. Gary Chapman, author of *The Five Love Languages*, identifies these primary love languages as (1) quality time, (2) words of affirmation, (3) giving and receiving gifts, (4) acts of service, and (5) physical touch. According to Dr. Chapman, when these things are not fulfilled, the love tank runs low to empty. It is like drawing money from the bank without ever depositing any cash. I think it would not be a bad idea for readers to know what love language their spouse speaks. This way they could better serve the needs of their mates. It works for me and my husband. My primary language is *words of affirmation*; it means a lot what my spouse says and does not say to me. His is *acts of service*; what I do or do not do matters a great deal to him. He loves it when I serve him meals like a king! He enjoys running errands for me and washing my car. One thing he does not like is vacuuming the house. One day I said to him, "Hey, love, you look sexy when you vacuum!" Picture him rolling that baby around the room like there was no tomorrow! It worked.

g. *Avoid spreading the malady.* One mistake couples tend to make when they bump up against a challenge is that they follow the urge to tell a third person about the problem and neglect to tell God. *I simply must tell someone, my friend, my mother, my father, or another family member.* Doing this is like spreading a virus. A third party, or a fifth wheel, is used to get sympathy or is used as a crutch. It is not helpful to a relationship. Rather, it is dangerous in that it complicates the issue and spreads the malady like wildfire. How? I am glad you asked. Check this out. The problem moves from being personal between two lovers to being public, played out with a larger arena. It becomes a "street fight," a friends and family feud. In some cases, it spreads to the "gossip column" of the church corridors, restrooms, dinner table, and fellowship hall, all under the guise of "Please pray for *X* and their situation." It is sad to say that one may catch a glimpse of the news coming from the pulpit. The wounds take longer to heal and longer to mend because the spouse now faces a larger pool of sympathizers, gossipmongers, and paparazzi. Be aware that there is always some John Doe or Lady Needy out there ready for an opportunity to step in and dress the wounds, for his or her own selfish reason or benefit. Remember the adage "One man's thrash is another man's treasure!" Thus, be careful of airing your dirty laundry in the street. Try the gag order and engage with your mate to resolve your problems quietly, together, in prayer and supplication. When appropriate, seek the help of a qualified counselor or a pastor. But the most effective weapon is to take everything to God in prayer. Do this first. Tell the Lord about all your troubles. The Lord is an expert in all matters, and there is nothing that catches Him off guard (Dr. Barry Black). There is no situation He cannot solve, "for nothing is impossible with God" (Luke 1:37 NLT).

h. *Seek intervention early.* Seek to resolve conflict early, before things escalate and get out of hand. Remember the adage "A stich in time saves nine." What I have observed is that a story changes over time, often for the worse. Residual animosity and anger fester, and the wound collects pus. It is better to suffer the pain of removing the pimple than the pain of surgically removing an ulcerated wound. The flip side of this is that a spouse may be overzealous to attack the problem or find premature solutions for a situation that requires time to think through. The danger of this is that the person rushes to treat the symptom but not the disease. At the same time, to underestimate the issue at hand and dismiss or trivialize it as no cause for concern is not wise either. By studying and weighing a situation carefully and prayerfully, using a medical model, you can diagnose the problem and prescribe a treatment to address the root cause. Hence, it takes balance and attentiveness to find the best solution.

i. *Commit to attending marriage enrichment seminars.* Attend seminars to keep yourself informed. Also, attending seminars gives you time to refresh yourself and keep the marriage flame burning. Continual dating and the postcourtship period are crucial. See, men are hunters by nature, and once they catch their prey and make their kill, they are done! They do not feel the impetus to continue chasing the woman, and that is where a problem starts. Big mistake! Dating and spending quality time together are both critical and are as important to maintaining the relationship as they were in the initial phase. Trust me, brother, girlfriend would not have married you if she had known that as soon as she said "I do," it would be the end of your sweet talk and her quality time with you! Continue the quest, and she will continue to respond as she did before. This assures her that even after bearing your babies, she is still appealing to you.

Song

> When I fall in love it will be forever
> Or I'll never fall in love
> In a restless world like this is
> Love ended before it's begun
> And too many moonlight kisses
> Seem to cool in the warmth of the sun.
>
> When I give my heart it will be completely,
> Or I'll never give my heart.

—Nat King Cole

Note: Little did I know when I was a young and naïve bride that my husband was pouring his heart out to me and making a real promise that he would keep fifty years later. Oh, that is so sweet, my love!

My Story

Speaking of spiritual intimacy as the cake and sensual intimacy as the icing, I would like to illustrate this by drawing from one of our successful romantic stories that I have shared with couples at retreats. It involves all the components that make romance vibrant and a mutually satisfying event. To put this in context, imagine our bedroom decor in soft tones of cream and black, from the comforter, to the bed ensemble, to the curtains. It looked good to me and inspired some compliments from a friend who knew my style and taste in color. Well, I was blindsided. I had forgotten my own imperative of viewing my mate in *four-dimensions*, as a friend, lover, family member, and roommate, as discussed under pillar #2.

Since interior design is one of my fortes, and because it is my household responsibility, I ran with the ball without seeking input from my "roommate"! He'd never made an issue of it before, but one day, out of the blue, my husband said to me, "Love, I really do not like all this black in our bedroom. I am not dead yet."

73

Wow! "Where did that come from?" I asked. "You know I like black and white, and I thought you liked this bed ensemble, honey!"

"No, I don't," he said.

"Why did you not tell me this before?" I asked.

"I'm telling you now," he responded.

Here was a conflict of interest that presented me with the opportunity either to attend to my husband's concerns and meet his needs or to be stubborn and engage in a hopeless argument, fussing and carrying on. I decided to choose the former. I promised to attend to his concerns and rectify the situation. At that point, I was just saying I would, and feeling hurt. But God gave me an idea about how to bring sunshine into my bedroom and change the gloom in my husband's mood. To cut a long story short, I took the next day off from work without telling my husband. I went to Macy's and bought a new bed ensemble with beautiful warm tones of rust and cream, with a touch of mint green, along with matching curtains and the like. I put down new throw rugs, and bathroom decor in spring colors. Meanwhile, I cooked his favorite meal. Everything was smelling good and inviting. I took a shower and changed into a silky negligee. I heard his car pulling into the garage. Once he was inside, I opened the bedroom door, grabbed him by his tie, and said, "Welcome, sir, to your mistress's penthouse. Are you ready?"

His eyes lit up. With a silly smile, he said, "Yes, ma'am, I have been ready."

Well, the rest is history! My attitude determined the altitude of our romance. I hate to think what might have happened if I had followed my pride. What is your story?

Last Word
Spiritual intimacy in the context of married couples is more profound and a richer fertilizer of love than we realize. Spiritual intimacy can only be sustained when all four biblical types of love, agape, philia, Eros, and

storge, are present in a marriage and acting of one accord. As I mentioned before, Eros is like the icing on a cake for couples, but the other three types of love make up the vital components of the cake itself. Thus, for Eros, the sensual domain of intimacy, to thrive, and for the married couple to attain mutually satisfying sexual intimacy, spiritual intimacy must be in effect as an underlying active core ingredient. Please note that although it may not have been your intention to go into marriage just to see it fail, things happen with time. Unintentionally, you may have been too busy with your life and neglected to pray and to meet your spouse's need for love, resulting in unfulfilled intimacy. A self-assessment instrument has been provided in appendix C to allow you the opportunity for introspection, time to step back and evaluate your performance in light of intimacy. This will enable you and your spouse to have an open discussion about what needs to be addressed. Remember that the survival of your marriage depends *entirely* on your recognition of what needs to give or change, as well as on your own willingness to change.

Pillar #8
Obeying God's Ordained Will

Foundation

Rejoicing in hope, patient in tribulation, continuing steadfastly in prayer.

—Romans 12:12 NKJV

God's Ordained Will for Marriage

Joy in a marriage comes from *knowing* and *following* God's plan. This section will look at God's ordained will for our lives and the permissive will of God.

A.   *What Is God's Ordained Will?*

The ordained will of God is His ideal original plan that was given to Adam and Eve in the garden of Eden in their pre-sin condition (Genesis 2:24; Matthew 19:4–6a). God intended for the first couple to be holy, to experience full happiness in a carefree environment without sickness and death, and to live their lives be in perfect harmony with His will. All subsequent generations would have experienced the same condition if Adam and Eve had adhered to the ordained plan of God. After the first couple fell (sinned), sin got in the way of God's ideal plan for human existence, a plan that included marriage permanence. God wanted the permanence of the marriage union to continue on earth. "'I hate divorce,' says the Lord" (Malachi 2:16 NLT). Because God created us to be free moral agents with the innate freedom of choice, He did not prevent the first couple from disobeying Him or choosing their own allegiances.

Thus, God's ideal plan for us is what God originally ordained, intended, designed, and orchestrated for each one of us. It is His desire and promise mapped out our lives, whether we believe it or not. If we were to understand that His will brings us joy, we would have no problem adhering to His plan over one of our own choosing. Listen to God's sovereign purpose and assurances: "For I know the plans I have for you; they are plans for good and not for disaster, to give you a future and a hope" (Jeremiah 29:11 NLT). Our plan is always to consult with God and ask for His will for us in every aspect of our lives, including marriage. If we follow this plan, we will not go wrong.

B. *The Permissive Will of God*

Because of the hardness of our hearts (Matthew 19:7–8), God provided allowances to accompany His ideal original plan. These allowances are not sinful, but they are not what He originally ordained for us either. The permissive will of God is reflected in Jesus's response to His disciples after they raised the question of divorce: "Moses permitted you to divorce your wives because your hearts were hard. But it was not this way from the beginning" (Matthew 19:8 NIV). Divorce was thus allowed because of humankind's sinful condition. Furthermore, God allowed Jesus to come and die in our place to save us from our sins and from eternal condemnation, to reveal the love of God, and to lead us back to God's original plan, which provides us with greater joy and hope of eternal life. However, since we are free moral agents, we make an individual choice to accept or reject the sacrifice of Jesus on the cross at Calvary. We can choose or not choose to embrace the true desire to reflect His character and hope of His coming back to take His children or church to be with Him in the world made new for eternity.

C. *Humankind's Choices apart from God's Ideal Plan Are Often Sinful*

There are many biblical narratives one could refer to, to illustrate the ordained will of God; however, let us look at the love triangle between Abraham, Sarah, and Hagar, as recorded in Genesis 16. God had promised Abraham that he would be the father of nations and that his seed would be countless like the sands of the sea and the stars of the sky. Abraham at first, because the promise was delayed, thought his trusted servant Eliezer would be his heir in fulfillment of the promise, but such was not the case. God explicitly told Abraham that the child of promise would come from him and his wife Sarah. However, the couple chose their own plan. With Sarah's collaboration, the old patriarch agreed to take Hagar as his second wife, and they had a son, Ishmael. But that was not what God had planned. This love triangle almost caused irreparable damage. Hence, God's delay does not mean He is denying or defaulting on His word. Hang in there! Stay the course and don't jump ship!

The point I want to put across here is that just because God permits us to go ahead, run with the rope, and do what we want to do, it does not mean He has ordained it. That is our plan, not His plan. Most of our plans are outside the will of God and are driven by our selfish desires, hardheadedness, rebellion, presumptuousness, lack of discipline, stiff-neckedness, impatience, and unbelief. One preacher once said, "It is just like you to tell God what you want to do, regardless of what He wants. God in return replies, 'Okay, go ahead with your plans. Let's see how far you can go.'" Really, is that what we want? The consequences are real and severe. Look at the Israelites' journey to the Promised Land. God intended them to journey for about a month, but because of their lack of faith, their unbelief, and their murmuring and bickering, just at the border of Canaan He condemned them to journey in the desert for four decades, until the entire generation of fighting-age men, including Moses, died. Only Joshua and Caleb survived among the fighting men to enter the Promised Land. Therefore, choose the ordained will of God or else suffer the consequences and backlash of God's permissive will.

Following God's Ordained Will

It is crucial for us to seek to understand, accept, and follow the ordained will of God, even if we do not understand it. When we do this, God will give us peace that passeth understanding. Hence, invite the God of peace into your life and pray for faith to obey His ordained will. "Without faith, it is impossible to please God" (Hebrews 11:6 KJV). Faith defies the laws of common sense. Hebrews 11:1 express an undergirding doctrine of faith. The principle is that faith gives us the capability and assurance to see and accept blessings before they happen. One of the giants of faith, Elder E. E. Cleveland, broke down the definition of faith in one of my religion classes as such: trusting God in the absence of evidence, and still trusting Him in the presence of contrary evidence. The latter is even harder to comprehend and accept than the former. It takes a strong woman or man of faith to accept and trust God despite receiving an answer from Him that is contrary to what you were hoping for. God is sovereign, and His divine wisdom is enough for us to get on board with Him and trust His direction and commands, knowing that He does not sleep or slumber and that nothing catches Him off guard. Although Adam and Eve made a choice that resulted in our inheriting sin, Jesus came to redeem us, adopt us, and reconcile us to His Father, but it is an individual choice to accept this provision or plan and thereby decide where we want to spend eternity.

The following are important building blocks to be learned that may help you in establishing and maintaining a culture of obedience to God's ordained will:

1. Asking through prayer and supplication for God to guide your destiny.
2. Seeking God and asking Him to reveal His divine plan for you.
3. Humbling yourself to follow God's direction for fulfilling your destiny.
4. Accepting His wisdom and choice of circumstances as those that will best shape your destiny, even if you do not understand His logic.
5. Relying on His provisions to underwrite His plan for you.
6. Waiting patiently on Him, according to His timing, to tell you when to do what, and how.
7. Praying for the God of peace to give you the peace that passeth understanding while you wait on His ordained solutions.
8. Beginning to anticipate and praise Him for unseen ends, emanating from His divine architectural design for you.
9. Embracing God's ordained will. Praising Him and celebrating the victories or success stories of your life!

10. Trusting His judgement and glorifying His name for the outcome, even if it is contrary to what you expected, knowing that He never makes a mistake and will reveal His reasons in His time.

Pray for God's Ordained Will

Many times, we find ourselves at a crossroads in life, not being sure where to go or which way to turn. It is at this very moment that we need God's direction the most. If we are not careful, we may gallop and run with our plans, going in the wrong direction, thinking we are guided by God's ordained will yet being driven by our own will. God may just permit us to run away without Him, to our detriment. Why not then seek to inquire of the Lord His purpose for our lives, His agenda for our existence, and His will for our plans? This is where praying for God's will comes in, to help us follow and be completely under the direction of God's will. Hence, we need to understand the attributes of prayer, as outlined below:

a. Prayer *lifts us up* and brings us close to God (it does not bring God to us).
b. Prayer intimately connects us to our heavenly Father (like kissing the face of God).
c. Prayer *changes us* to be in accord with God's will. It does not change God or twist His arm. He already knows what we want to say, as He will answer even before we call on Him.
d. Prayer is a two-way street. We talk to God, and we must tune in to His response and carefully listen to what He says back to us. Clear the air of doubt, arrogance, and presumptuousness.
e. Prayer gives us power to be obedient to His will. God can do exceedingly above all we ask or think (Ephesians 3:20), but we must believe in Him and trust His power to direct us.

Remember, God will not ask us to do anything that He will not enable us to do, and He will guide us to success. He will not force Himself into our life or force us to obey His will. A question we need to ask ourselves is, "Are my lifestyle, dreams, and plans, and my marriage, in line with Your ordained will for my existence in this world?" If not, put your mind and soul in God's care. Do not settle for less when you have the Prince of Peace on your side and the Holy Spirit covering you. Trust me, these things are available to you just for the asking—and at no charge. The bill was settled at Calvary by the blood of Jesus. Just ask!

Song

My hope is built on nothing less
Than Jesus's blood and righteousness;
I dare not trust the sweetest frame,
But wholly lean on Jesus' name.

Chorus:

On Christ, the solid Rock, I stand;
All other ground is sinking sand,
All other ground is sinking sand.

—Edward Mote

My Story

In 1981 my husband and I were impressed to enroll as self-supporting students at Oakwood College (now University) in Huntsville, Alabama. We lived in apartment #4 of the married student complex with our then five-year-old son. My husband pursued a degree in business administration, and I pursued a double major in psychology and social work. This was neither easy nor a bed of roses for us as self-supporting students, but God never left us or forsook us through it all. Both of us strongly believed and practiced the biblical principle of tithing no matter our finances.

We knew if we followed God's ordained will, we would be successful, both academically and in life. As a result, He blessed us with intellect and abilities! We graduated in record time. My husband earned cum laude, and I summa cum laude. We both graduated without owing a dime to the university, defying the odds and the skeptics who told us that no married couple could be in school full time, carrying a full load, and graduate on time together. But we did so through God's grace. We proceeded to complete our master's degrees, and I subsequently went on to complete a doctorate without any debt to any of the institutions we attended. Praise God Almighty!

This experience strengthened our faith and has become one of the pillars of joy in our marriage, knowing that if we follow God's ordained will, we will be all right. Now that we are retired and living on a fixed income, we believe that if we are faithful stewards and obey His ordained will implicitly, even when we do not understand where He is leading us, we will be at peace and blessed. When we encounter obstacles and bumps along the way, we fully know that they are only temporary. God will prepare the way for us.

A friend shared a story with us. She owed an insurmountable amount of money. When her business experienced a hiccup, she could not see a way through or did not have a clue how to pay the money back to her lenders. But she was determined that she would trust God and continue to be His responsible and faithful steward. She paid a faithful tithe from her meager resources. Guess what? God came through for her and she paid all her debt in less than two years. Later she reestablished her business.

The statement that got to me was when she said that she knew she was in deep water, drowning in debt, but she had joy on her mind, and she said with confidence, "I was not being punished by God but was just experiencing problems of living, not God's chastisement." So, although she was going up the rough side of the mountain, she found that God's promises to and provisions for those who are faithful and who trust in Him are true and stand forever. She began to claim His assurances and gained the peace that passeth understanding. She could sleep at night with a clear conscience that she had done what she was supposed to do, and with assurance that God would do the rest. The closer to Jesus Christ we are, the more we desire to seek and obey God's ordained plan for our lives. The opposite is also true.

Last Word

Trusting and following God's ordained will is the way to go. Proverbs counsels us, "Trust in the Lord with all thine heart, and lean not unto thine own understanding. In all thy ways, acknowledge Him, and He shall direct your paths" (Proverbs 3:5–6 KJV). This reminds me of a quotation from one of my favorite preachers, Dr. William T. Cox: "If you do what

God has commissioned you to do, He will make Himself personally responsible for your success!" I subscribe to this sentiment because God has done a great deal for my husband and me, repeatedly, in many ways, through the years. The key is trusting Him and believing His plan is the best. Just follow His timetable, even when you do not understand. Trust Him with your resources, your marriage, your family, and all that you have. Be a faithful steward and God will bless you not based on your needs, but according to His riches in heaven, far beyond your earthly needs. Choose to seek, obey, and follow God's ordained will and your life will be secure under His wings of glory. Joy comes with obedience to the will of God for your life. Peace and success are a bonus!

Pillar #9
Friendship of a Lifetime

Foundation

If you want a friend, be a friend! If you want
love, give love! All starts with you!

—Anonymous

Under pillar #1, I addressed the concept of looking at your mate with a *four-dimensional perspective, as lover, family, friend, and roommate.* I discussed under My Story the idea of being your spouse's responsible roommate (the fourth segment). In this section, we will look at the value of perceiving your mate as a friend and kinsman to add value to the relationship.

Gift of a Spouse as a Friend

Friendship is one of the most rewarding social relationships. Couples should enjoy being best friends with each other more than they enjoy any other friend out there. It is crucial to establish friendship early in the marriage because the joy that emanates from this bond of friendship can be a standby in times of trouble. When love is tested in hard times, friendship kicks in and fills the void. Be friends even when you disagree. Amazingly, some people's friendship with their ex-mate shines through even after they are divorced, when the love affair is long extinct. This tells me that a couple may be friends without being lovers, but they cannot be lovers without being friends.

Given this fact, couples should seek to be close friends and enjoy each other's company as friends first and lovers second. In this way, your love will regenerate when tested. Friendship is to a love affair what a backup generator is to the main source of power. For instance, when the electricity cuts off, the generator kicks in and keeps on running, until the power comes back. In light of this metaphor, let's look at friendship with a fresh lens, as follows:

1. *Friendship is a gift from God.* The biblical story of David and Jonathan reveals the prototype of a friendship made in heaven. Jonathan, rightful heir to the throne and seat of power, saved the life of his friend David from the ruthless hand of King Saul, knowing very well that David was favored by the Lord and would take over the throne from Saul. "Jonathan' s soul was knit to David, and Jonathan loved him as his own soul" (1 Samuel 18:1 ESV). If the friendship between spouses could rise to this level, there would be less strife in homes. Even Jesus felt at home with his friend Lazarus and his two sisters, Martha and Mary, of Bethany. He valued their friendship, which was made particularly clear when He had declared, "Foxes have holes, and birds of the air have nests, but the Son of man hath nowhere to lay his head" (Matthew 8:20–22 NKJV). He found a home where He could come inside and rest with His friends Martha, Mary, and Lazarus.

2. *Friendship is value added to the union.* No doubt, a friend can be an added value to the couple, especially, if the person is a mutual friend to both spouses. Conversely, if friendship is not well handled, it can be destructive. I have heard horror stories where a friend is implicated as the cause of separation or a painful divorce because he or she was too close for comfort to one party.

3. *Friendship can escalate to family status.* A friend can sometimes do more for you than family members. Just before His death on the cross, Jesus entrusted and bequeathed His mother, Mary, to John, His dear friend and disciple. Interestingly, He did not leave the care of His mother to His brothers, James, Juda, Joseph, and Simion, who were Joseph's sons (Mark 6:3 NIV). Even with you and me, Jesus "sticketh to us closer than a brother" (Proverbs 18:24 KJV). Jesus felt at home among His friends in Bethany, as we should feel in His presence. I know of several friends in my own life who have risen to a family status at one time or another. I am sure you could name a few too.

My Spouse Is Family

It appears that some spouses forget the idea that their spouse is a gift from God and is a member of the family too. The benefit of embracing a mate as family is that family members usually stick together no matter what. However, there are several responsibilities that come with embracing your mate as a kinsman. With these in mind, I caution you as follows:

1. Be mindful of what you say about your mate to relatives on each side of the family. Believe me, any negative things you divulge to your mother or siblings about your spouse will be indelible and will remain in effect long after you and your mate have kissed and made up.

2. Be cautions of airing your dirty laundry in the street among strangers. The devil is like a roaring lion, seeking whom he may devour. Before spilling the beans and airing your grievances, think twice because some dogs in the street may take the opportunity to lick the wounds. Be careful! Dr. Brené Brown, author of *The Gifts of Imperfection*, reminds us that while we open ourselves and become vulnerable with our friends, we need to be cautious with whom we share information because, a person can easily become "one more piece of flying debris in an already dangerous storm!" Think about this statement before you spill the beans.

3. Be ready to fight to defend and protect the family name and things that are important to you and your spouse, instead of compromising your family values, integrity, and legacy. Thus, try to find meaning in all your challenging circumstances. Pray, forgive, and move on! If you must fight, then fight fairly behind closed doors and not in the street. Remember, your spouse is *family*!

4. Be aware that some members of the family are not pleasant. Embrace them anyway. Do not get into family squabbles. Instead, help your spouse to repair bridges. This is better than tearing down the towers. One friend of mine once commented, "Family is like a chocolate fudge. It is sweeter with some nuts in it."

Your Spouse Is Not Perfect, and Neither Are You

"For are all have sinned and fall short of the glory of God" (Romans 3:23). Each spouse is a sinner married to another sinner. So, we need to give up the notion of an innocent victim, the perfect mate, a superman or superwoman, and the like. We all have good qualities and shortcomings alike. The key is to accept and embrace the human condition of being gifted in some areas but being deficient in other areas. Educators refer to this phenomenon as *twice exceptionality*. Thus, by acknowledging your double-sided nature, for example observing that you have a spark of genius as well as a spot of imperfection, you remain humble and tolerant of others. This type of healthy introspection will help a mate to dissect his or her own mistakes and work to repair them, rather than concentrating on the other mate's shortcomings. This perspective also helps a spouse to embrace the other mate's personality, celebrating the differences and imperfections as strengths to complement the areas where he or she may be weakest.

Just Be There for Your Spouse as a Friend

Real friends are those who will stick with you when you are in a rut. But this does not always happen. So the question is, how do you deal with those who are not responsive to your needs? You do the following:

1. Acknowledge that others have a life too; you are not the center of attention.
2. Realize that your friends may be busy like you, or even busier. Have no expectations. Accept the help they can give you and expect nothing more.
3. Accept the reality that some who disengage from your friendship are not meant to be in your future. However, make sure that if a friendship ends, it is not because you failed to hold up your end of the bargain.
4. Understand that sometimes God will orchestrate things so that everyone around you, especially those you depend on, moves far away so you can discover or realize, without a doubt, who is in control of your existence.
5. Understand that God is the giver and your friends are a gift. Even your spouse is a gift from God. There is a tendency sometimes to glorify the gift and push God away, forgetting that He is the source and giver of all good things. This distinction is crucial because God can choose to use anything or anyone to solve your situation as He appoints and sees fit.

6. Embrace the fact that God wants us to belong and coexist in peace, not in pieces. We all come in different shapes and sizes and have different strokes and needs. It is not our duty to try to change the other person, but it is our duty to seek to understand that person and to embrace his or her differences as strengths that unite us, being complementary to our weaknesses.

7. Refrain from using your friends as a crutch or being critical when a friend cannot help you for whatever reason. Jesus is all that you need. He can show up and solve your problem in nontraditional ways rather than in a way that is familiar to you.

Types of Friends to Avoid Sharing Personal Matters With

Brené Brown has identified six types of friends you should avoid or with whom you should exercise care when deciding what to share with them. These friends tend to display one of the following behaviors:

1. Confirming how horrified you should be at your imperfections.
2. Responding with sympathy, rather than empathy.
3. Feeling disappointed by your imperfections.
4. Getting uncomfortable and chastising you with words for being vulnerable, saying things such as "How in the world could you do x, y, or z, or let that happen?"
5. Refusing to acknowledge that you might actually make terrible choices ("You're exaggerating. It wasn't that bad").
6. Using your situation as a peg on which to hang his or her own story by downplaying and trivializing your case and taking it as an opportunity to elevate his or her own case, such as saying, "Oh well, that's nothing. You won't believe what happened to me."

I have noticed another behavior of people who may fall into Dr. Brown's category of friends one should not share personal matters with, as follow:

7. Sharing a piece of gossip and then warning you not to tell anyone else about it (e.g., saying, "Please keep it to yourself" or "Please promise you will not share this with anyone"). I usually feel like responding, "But you could not keep it to yourself. Why tell me now?"

Opposites Attract

It is amazing that people in many cases are attracted to mates who are different from them, but then they spend their precious time trying to change the spouse into someone who looks more like them. This ultimate insanity is a waste of energy and is like chasing a mirage! So, please, do not try to change your mate. The ultimate fallacy is that you can change other people. Are you kidding me?! We are not even able to change ourselves without the help of the Almighty God, let alone able to change another person, especially our spouses. I have tried that—been there, done that—and failed. My husband and I are so different, it is not funny! Rather, I have chosen to expend my energy cultivating joy and building our marriage based on a perspective of strength. When you seek ways to deliberately embrace each other's differences, you will discover that your strengths complement each other's weaknesses.

Another concept to explore in this pillar is the phenomenon of androgyny. Androgyny is the innate existence of male and female characteristics within each gender, whereby a female or male may exhibit qualities that are normally ascribed to the opposite gender. In my experience, androgyny, if embraced, can be an added value to the human condition. It breaks the imaginary barriers and defies traditionally ascribed social roles. This trait can lead us to leverage our unique abilities and carry out responsibilities normally delegated to the opposite sex. For example, androgyny enables a woman to be tough or have an extraordinary ability to raise a male child in the absence of a father figure. Likewise, a man can exhibit tender nurturing and tender graces when raising a little girl in the absence of a mother. Therefore, one should be sensitive to criticizing a spouse for exhibiting opposite-gender tendencies. Instead, a couple should acknowledge and accept these anomalies as strengths, not weaknesses. God is able and faithful in spite of our shortcomings.

Song

Great is Thy faithfulness, O God my Father.
There is no shadow of turning with Thee;
Thou changest not, Thy compassions they fail not;
As Thou has been Thou forever will be.

<u>Chorus:</u>

Great is Thy Faithfulness! Great is Thy Faithfulness!
Morning by morning new mercies I see;
All I have needed Thy hand hath provided,
Great is Thy faithfulness! Lord unto me!

—Thomas O. Chisholm

My Story

The story I am going to share is a classic example of a couple who possessed androgynous qualities and how they reconciled these differences, creating a harmonious tapestry in the milieu of their marriage.

Pam and Joe were our neighbors. They grew a beautiful vegetable garden that was the envy of everyone around. Pam had a green thumb and was responsible for the upkeep of the garden, planting, weeding, watering, and tending to the plants. Guess what? Joe spent his time in the kitchen, cutting and cleaning the veggies and cooking finger-licking-good gourmet cuisine. You could tell that Joe was comfortable in the kitchen. The kids were always around him salivating for the next treat. Pam's domain was in the garden, where she sang songs and enjoyed herself.

I tell you, it was a sight to behold, especially in African society, where male and female roles are rigidly cut-and-dried, even among educated and supposedly enlightened professionals.

The purpose of this story is to encourage couples to celebrate differences and capitalize on the strengths of the other mate to enhance the quality of the marriage relationship, and to refrain from spending quality time bickering and trying to change the other spouse to conform to arbitrary social mores.

Last Word

Indeed, our Father God hates sin with a passion, but He loves sinners with ultimate compassion, to the extent that He sacrificed everything to come to earth and die for sinners such as I. This makes me sober-minded each time I am tempted to judge or criticize my husband. Being tolerant of each other and learning to embrace each other's differences is a conscious choice.

God did not make us as robots, but in His divine wisdom, He deliberately designed the human species (men and women) as intelligent moral beings with a choice to do and to will. He does not force us to change, even when our behavior is destroying us. We should exercise our God-given power of choice to change ourselves and embrace our mates, shortcomings and all, as dear friends, brothers and sisters in Christ. We are not commissioned to change our spouses, although it is flattering to think otherwise. We are commissioned to love them as Christ loves us. Oh, that is scary! But it is true! It is amazing that we seek and are attracted to people who are not like us, but then we expend our energy trying to change them into our clones. How silly is that! In my observation, there are times when we begin to think or sound alike, or when we emulate each other's strengths through interaction and observation without pressure. You cannot force this merging of personalities, but it will happen in time through kindness and embracing each other's uniqueness. Be friends and lovers for a lifetime!

Pillar # 10

Jesus-Centered Marriage

Foundation

> Jesus you're the center of my joy! All good and perfect
> comes from you; You're the heart of contentment, hope
> for all I do. Jesus you're the center of my joy.

> —Richard Smallwood

This section examines scenarios that generate *joy* from being connected and grafted to Christ Jesus through anchoring your marriage on Christ the Solid Rock, as commanded in God's Word.

Joy through Anchoring Your Marriage on the Solid Rock
A Jesus-centered marriage is the key to guaranteed joy, peace, and contentment, even in the face of the storms of life. That your marriage is anchored to Jesus Christ, the Solid Rock, is evidenced by the following factors or principles:

1. You both have developed a personal spiritual relationship with God.
2. You both have internalized God's Word and His promises.
3. You each spend time in prayer alone with God.
4. You and your spouse spend time together with God, praying for each other.
5. You embrace your differences and capitalize on each other's strengths, rather than being preoccupied with each other's weaknesses.
6. You have built a culture of fun and mutual friendship in your home.
7. You have adopted a posture of unconditional love, giving to and forgiving each other.

Joy through the Triangle of Submission and Love

The wife's submission to the husband does not sit well in some societies. To some, *submit* is like a curse word, particularly to well-educated, liberated postmodern women. Historically, a wife's submission to her husband was perceived, perhaps, as a sign of weakness, domination, or enslavement. However, if we examine God's plan of submission with an open mind—(1) Christ submitting to God His Father, (2) husbands and wives submitting to God through Christ (*vertical relationship*), (3) men and women submitting to each other (*horizontal relationship*)—couples will not be confused about what God intends submission to look like. The triune God—the Father, Jesus Christ the Son, and the Holy Spirit—works in harmony. The Lord confirms that He and His Father are one (John 10:30). In Ephesians 5:21–32, God's call for submission as directed to the man is that he is to *love* his wife as Christ loves the church, to *cleave* to his wife, forsaking all others, and to love her as he loves his own flesh. The call for a woman is to *submit* to her husband as unto Christ. Furthermore, God calls for both the man and the woman to submit to one another as well (Ephesians 5:23). Thus, the relationship and definitive order of submission, from the biblical perspective, is clear. Figure 10.1 shows that trifactor submission is a function of a husband and wife's love relationship to Christ; the love of a husband for his wife and the submission of a wife to her husband as unto Christ; and the couple's submission to each other.

FIGURE 10.1. Trifactor vertical and horizontal submission

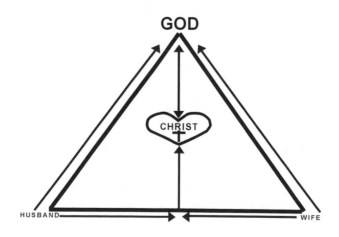

There are practical applications to be drawn from the triangle of submission illustrated in figure 10.1.

- *Centerline*—Christ should be at the core of our marriage, the center and heart of a love relationship, for the husband and wife to achieve mutually fulfilling spiritual intimacy.
- *Baseline (left)*—Love of a husband for his wife should be as Christ loves the church with all its imperfections.
- *Baseline (right)*—Submission of a wife to her husband as unto Christ should be unconditional, regardless of her husband's imperfections.
- *Baseline arrows*—Submission of a husband and wife to each other should connect at all levels of intimacy, that is, the physical, spiritual, intellectual, and emotional domains.
- *Vertical arrows*—Relationship of each spouse with his or her Father God is an individual responsibility and choice. Connection is direct and personal.

The triune God's hierarchy of submission is three-dimensional: (1) Jesus Christ as submitting to Father God, (2) the man submitting to Jesus Christ, his Lord, and (3) the woman submitting to her husband as unto Christ. So where is the problem? This is fair, and it is easy for a woman to submit to a man who submits to Christ, and who genuinely loves her as he loves his own body, cleaving to and not cheating on her! Husbands and wives are the church, and the Holy Spirit guides, teaches, and enables us to follow God's order of submission. This is the model of submission in heaven's eyes.

I have heard men argue that women should submit to their men, without considering the last segment of the Ephesians 5:23, namely, the vertical model of submission to Christ first. In some cases, men say, "It is a woman's duty to submit to her man, period!" Wow, hold on! Unfortunately, such an attitude reflects a distorted view of submission. The problem lies with our earthly imposed modality of submission, outside the hierarchy of submission of the man (the vertical relationship) as prescribed by the Bible. Biblically, wives should submit to their husbands as husbands submit to Christ. Without the biblically ordained practice of submitting to Christ first, husbands end up not wanting to take responsibility or be accountable for the decisions they make as head of the family. This is called wanting the glory of the crown without the cross. P. B. Wilson, author of *Liberated through Submission: The Ultimate Paradox*, makes the sobering statement that a submissive wife is a "woman of faith" and is liberated by the very principle the devil worked so hard to distort (p. 101).

Likewise, if wives would understand the virtue in submitting to their husbands, in the context of the vertical mandate to submit to a man who himself submits to the Lord as Christ submits to God the Father, they would derive joy in submitting to such a husband and assume the following posture.

1. Instead of arguing or freaking out, wives would commit their men to the hands of the Lord, constantly asking God to help them to submit to Christ, as He submits to Father God.

2. As the helpmate, a wife, once she has given her honest view of the decision at hand, but still the husband is adamant about taking a certain course of action, even if it does not make sense or if it is apparent that it is a wrong or unwise decision, should let go and let God do the rest.

3. A wife should remind her husband that he is responsible and accountable to God for such a decision, but she must also indicate that her support is unconditional. The wife, then, must continue to support her husband moving forward the best she knows how. In my experience, my husband appreciates it when I assume this position. He has not been shy in affirming that I was right. Likewise, I have not been ashamed to affirm to him that, although I did not see the forest for the trees, I was glad I let him move forward as the Lord led him as the head of the household, regardless of how I felt at the time he made the decision. I derive joy from supporting him no matter what the outcome is. The peace and joy come from knowing that if things blow up, it is between him and the Lord.

Joy of Being in Partnership with Christ

There are two special songs that come to my mind when I think of joy as generated through partnering with Christ: my aunt's favorite, "Joy Unspeakable," and "The Center of My Joy." Jesus gives us *full joy* and a better perspective on our life with Him when we embrace His Word and fellowship (1 John 1:3–4). When Christ occupies space in our hearts, our perspective changes and we experience unspeakable joy. Happiness is fuzzy, instantaneous, circumstantial, and short-lived, whereas *joy* is a state of mind and is lasting (Frank W. Hale). Someone once remarked, "The opposite of happiness is not unhappiness but apathy." Joy counters apathy. The two are mutually opposing constructs. Like light and darkness, they do not coexist. Joy is a choice; you must choose joy in the presence of unhappiness and amid a situation that could induce apathy. Thus, when we choose Jesus as the center of our joy, the devil has no chance of stealing our joy, unless we allow him.

Joy of Knowing Whose You Are

I remember as if it were yesterday how my dad would pat my shoulder and offer his last-minute words of counsel just before I left home for boarding school "Baby, remember your family name, whose you are, and what you represent. I will always be with you in my prayers!" This used to make me cry and make me realize that my dad believed in me. He trusted that I had the guts to stand up to my peers and say no to sleazy suggestions that would make a mockery of me or dishonor my moral values and upbringing. Likewise, I remember my Jesus now. When I am facing situations that threaten to dishonor His name and all that He is about, I imagine His loving hand touching my shoulder and His voice saying, *Nozipho, My child, you are Mine. I bought you with the price of My blood. Honor Me and remember whose you are. Call on My name in times of trouble and I will deliver you and show you great and mighty things you did not even know about. Ask for anything you need, for My possibilities are unlimited and I will bless you, not per your needs, but based on the bountiful supply of My riches in glory* (Psalm 50:15; Jeremiah 33:3; Luke 1:37; Philippians 4:19).

Even in the corporate world, before one is hired for an important job, one must produce a resume. A diplomat must represent his or her country's credentials before the ruler, the president, or the powers that be in the foreign land will agree to his or her company. A pilot or captain before operating an airplane or ship, respectively, must show his or her worthiness to operate the craft. A driver is required by law to have a license to operate a vehicle. The list goes on. None of us can even dream of asking a lawyer to represent us in a court of law without necessary credentials, graduation from a reputable law school, having passed the bar examination, and having shown a successful record of winning similar cases in the past. It is the same way with a physician. None of us would want an unqualified doctor to amputate a limb or operate on our heart or kidney, or any other limb or organ. No, we would want to research that doctor's track record and see certificates hanging on the wall attesting to his or her expertise and worthiness to operate the clinic or office. We would not even try to take our cars to a novice mechanic, but rather to the dealer, to ensure that we get the best service. It is sad to say that with all those qualifications and all that scrutiny, things still happen, mistakes, misdeals, greed, and fraudulent outcomes can arise, but we still go to these professionals anyway. In short, no institution of higher learning will award a diploma to a person before he or she qualifies for the degree.

Listen very carefully. What I am trying to emphasize here is that qualifications and the practicum precede the license. Yet when it comes to marriage, check this out, couples are given a license prior to receiving any training and earning any qualifications. It is left to chance whether a couple will sink or swim, under the guise of "We are *in love*!" We then wonder why marriages are in trouble. Seriously, society is obligated to hand out licenses to individuals who have not been prepared in any way for marriage. On the other hand, God qualifies you, hoping you will depend on Him for practical training and apprenticeship in marriage as you take the tests of life. That is why some refer to marriage as a university from which one never graduates.

See, marriage can break or make a couple, and jeopardize their chances of making it to glory and enjoying life eternal. Why and how in the world do couples run with marriage as if they own it without Christ? How do they hope to succeed in the marital journey without the author and creator of the marriage union? Without Christ as the chaperone, shepherd, author of the institution of marriage, expert, consultant, and mighty counselor, marriages are doomed to fail dismally. Some may say, "Well, we had weeks of counseling with a pastor or priest prior to our wedding." Now when you look back at your marriage journey, do you think that was enough provision? Did that prepare you for a lifetime journey? If not, I encourage you to embrace Jesus Christ as the personal center of your marriage. Genuinely invite Him to be your personal confidant and guide you through mountains, rough terrain, dark alleys, twists and turns, and the dangerous curvy roads of the matrimonial journey. If you think I am painting a gloomy picture, keep on living, honey. You will understand by and by.

Thank God for my Christian parents who drilled into me the importance of having Christ as the center of my joy in marriage. Neither are no longer here, but they left me a treasure and the pearl of great price, Jesus! Through the fifty years of my marriage, the Lord Jesus Christ has been everything I needed and wanted. He has been the A to Z of my existence and the center of my marriage, as outlined below:

A—author of my marriage and my salvation, the Alpha and Omega

B—my brother, divine friend, confidant, and soul mate

C—the cornerstone upon which I built my existence, hope, and joy

D—deliverer of my sins and restorer of my peace and understanding

E—Emmanuel, God among my family, and my ever-present consultant

F—fear blocker and my divine assurance who fought and won battles

G—He who is gracious to me despite my pathetic foolishness

H—my High Priest and my advocate to those who judge me ruthlessly

I—the Intercessor who pleads my case before my heavenly Father daily

J—Jehovah-Jireh, my provider and the sustenance of my family

K—my King and Savior, my joy, and my hope of eternal life

L—He who looks beyond my faults and sees my desperate needs

M—my miracle worker, who gives a fresh supply of new mercies daily

P—my perfect peace in storms and my protector against the Goliaths of this world

Q—the qualifying legend who gained victory over sin and won the war

R—Redeemer and restorer of my soul and my marriage

S—the secret code and password to accessing His timeless blessing

T—He who transformed me from hopeless sinner to heir of the kingdom

U—universal affordable care provider and restorer of my spiritual health

V—He who delivers victory in my setbacks and adds value in the face of my enemies

X—the x-ray that gives me introspection/perspective in times of doubt

Y—the yoke that is easy to carry when life's burdens are too hard to bear

Z—the zealous shepherd seeking to anoint me and guide me to eternal life

The question is, what is He to you?

Song

Jesus, you're the center of my joy
All that's good and perfect comes from you
You're are the heart of my contentment, hope for all I do
Jesus, you're the center of my joy

When I've lost my direction, you're the compass for my way
You're the fire and light when nights are long and cold
In sadness, you are the laughter, that shatters all my fears
When I'm all alone, your hand is there to hold.

—Richard Smallwood

My Story

The best thing that ever happened to me during my marriage journey was that I learned in my earlier years to depend on the wisdom of God and be submissive to His will to pilot my existence. When I look back at the inception of my matrimonial union and the litany of hurdles I had to jump over to get to where I am now in my life, I have no doubt that being spiritually grounded and grafted in the Lord, the True Vine, is the main ingredient for attaining a joyful and mutually satisfying marriage.

I can just hear the reader arguing, "Well, I hear you, but if that be the case, why do Christian folks tend to be subjected to and assailed by the same challenges and experiences as nonbelievers?" I am glad you asked. See, God has not promised that saints will be free from trials. Rather, He promises an assurance of perfect peace that passeth all understanding amid the storm and an unspeakable joy amid tribulation. The Bible is silent about happiness and is explicit about joy, especially joy in tribulation. The difference is that without Christ, one experiences nothing but troubles and tribulation, undiluted, and has no one to turn to. In Christ, you have the backing of the God of peace and His unlimited resources!

In my life's journey, I have come to realize that without Christ I am nothing, but with Him in my life I have everything. He has been the undergirding pillar and the tower of strength lifting me up, guiding my marriage, and tending my garden of love. He has been instrumental in plucking out the weeds of pride that threatened to suffocate mutually fulfilling intimacy or spiritual growth in our marriage vineyard. He has been a prescription and potent antidote for "marriage killers" in my life, making it so that our love garden can thrive and blossom. I am confident that embracing Him in a multidimensional way, as articulated under pillar #1, has been the active ingredient for our love garden to grow. He can do the same for your marriage. His diverse and unique multifaceted approach to addressing marital dilemmas and enriching the marriage has fulfilled my spectrum of needs. I appeal to you to offer Him a genuine invitation into your own love garden. Whether your situation requires major landscaping, weed control, or just simple maintenance, you can surely depend on Him. He is the *one* and *only* Master of weed control, termite extermination, and aphid eradication in your marriage vineyard. He is it. Try Him!

Last Word

Can we pause a moment and reflect on the cost of a wedding ceremony? Think of the money and energy spent on the elaborate preparations, from the bride's dress and bridesmaids' gowns; to tuxedos for the groom and his ushers; to the venue, including decorative flowers, place settings, the wedding cake, food, and other refreshments; to limousines; to photographers and videographers. Can you picture it? And yet, this is just one day's event. And it is all for a glamorous ceremony, not the marriage itself. Do not get me wrong, these things make for important memories, if a couple can afford them. However beautiful and glamorous the ceremony may be, the amount of energy expended does not prepare a couple for the marriage journey. Instead, when reality sets in, the humongous price tag of the wedding preparations can cause stress to the new union. The real marriage starts after the honeymoon. Having said this, and knowing what I know now, after decades in this marriage marathon, I, if I had a choice, would counsel couples who are courting or engaged to be married to do the following things:

1. *Seek to know more about the God* who created your mate and the marriage institution before seeking to know more about your potential mate or spouse. If Jesus relies on His Father, how much more must we sinners rely on Him? Yet we often have the audacity to run our lives without Christ and hope that we will be successful!

2. *Spend a year in counseling, exorcizing the demons of the past* and breaking generational curses. Also, save the money for a home. Empty yourselves of selfishness. Learn how to share resources and how to focus on the love needs of a spouse. Until you are ready to share, negotiate, and compromise, you are *not ready to be married.*

3. *Vow to put Jesus at the center of your marriage and to build an altar of the sacred vow* to offer up the marriage to God's care. There is no better place to learn all wisdom and proper behavior than at the *feet of Jesus Christ.* "If I am lifted from the earth, I will draw all men unto me" (John 12:32 NIV). Jesus paid the debt at Calvary. All He requires is your heart, and He will do the rest.

Pillar # 11
Objective Ordinal Selection

Foundation

> The core of spiritual maturity is the ability to marshal
> the interaction among knowledge, choices, and faith
> in Jesus Christ, the vertical locus of control.

—Nozipho N. Nxumalo

The joy of living as a child of God is predicated on knowing that in whatever state you find yourself, you have learned to be content. Once you make your desires known to Him and put your requests on the altar in prayer, trusting in God's ordained will and His wisdom, power, matchless love, and plan and direction for your life, whatever the outcome, you will be okay with it. You will sing, "It is well with my soul!"

Objective Ordinal Selection Protocol

Life sometimes presents us with difficult or complex options to choose from. Objective ordinal selection protocol defines what is important in the order and scheme of things. In my experience, it is an intentional prioritization that helps us make informed choices and decisions based on the knowledge we have, our innate freedom of choice, and our dependency on God to direct us through faith. There are so many situations that couples need to address before the altar of prayer. If we do not make our requests known to God through prayer and guidance of the Holy Spirit, who "guides us into all truth" (John 16:13 NKJV), we run the risk of making haphazard decisions and choices under duress and, thus, taking a course of action only to realize that the results are disastrous. Meanwhile, we have entangled ourselves in situations we can't undo, or signed off on something we may regret later. This may compromise our integrity and our family image. This is where faith in the guidance of the Holy Spirit comes in, as an intervening shield between us and our impulsive choices, which sound good at the time but are bitter in our bellies later. This is especially true when the outcome proves to be sealed and irrevocable. Because the Holy Spirit does not coerce us into obedience or force Himself upon us, we should solicit the direction of a divine guide.

In ordering and prioritizing choices, it is crucial to ensure that the most important value is realized. That is where prayer comes in, praying for the power of the Holy Spirit to give us *discernment, clarity of purpose,* and *wisdom* to make right decisions. The understanding of the interaction of the three virtues at the threshold of uncertainty has proved to be priceless and has guided me when making critical decisions. I discussed at great length in pillar #5 the importance of prayer and praying. This section picks up on the practicality of prayer and operationalizes the strategies in the order of events, sequencing the channel for our requests in a way that is concrete and easy to comprehend. When we have followed this protocol, there is no doubt who really deserves the glory!

It is not being rude to ask God for a sign to ensure that we are in sync or harmony with His ordained will. In the Bible, Gideon asked for a sign and God honored his request (Judges 33:6–40 NLT). This section explores the art of ordering your requests before God using the following protocol, discussed as postures.

- *Posture 1: genuinely seeking what God wills for you as a couple.* This is based on understanding the virtue of choices guided by God (i.e., *the vertical supreme order*).
- *Posture 2, avoiding self-pleasing.* This posture is predicated on valuing the collective decision of both parties, "the us as a couple" (i.e., *mutual horizontal order*), *sequencing your needs as a couple before the Lord.*
- *Posture 3, depending and holding on to God's unchanging hand.* This posture allows total dependence on and vulnerability before the Lord. (i.e., the source of power and direction).
- *Posture 4, channeling your desires and requests through Christ.* This posture is predicated on acknowledging Christ as your mutual

connecting link and the overseer of your plans (i.e., *horizontal and vertical locus of control*).

- *Posture 5, asking God for a sign and wisdom to discern His ordained will.* This disposition is based on *believing* in His promises, *trusting* His Word, and *claiming* His assurances. "For I know the thoughts I think towards you, says the Lord, thoughts of peace and not evil, to give you future and a hope" (Jeremiah 29:11 NKJV).

- *Posture 6, requesting enduring power.* This is based on yielding to the timeline of God and to His guidance regarding when to move forward and attack, while relying on His wisdom to know when to withdraw from the battle if necessary (i.e., *formidable strategy guided by the spirit of discernment*).

- *Posture 7, accepting God's ordained will for your life.* This demonstrates total submission to the will of God and the understanding that whatever the outcome is, you will be okay with it. (*It will be well with your soul*).

When we have followed the protocol outlined above, we derive unspeakable joy and peace, knowing that we have left everything in the hands of the all-knowing God. If things do not turn out the way we anticipated, we do not fall into the trap of ascribing power to the devil or believe that he meddled or derailed our progress. Rather, we go back to the altar to find answers from God. In most cases, He has a better plan for us in His time. Dr. William Cox once said, "Prayers outlive the praying!" Some answers to our petitions may come through after we have departed from this world. Especially as it relates to praying for our children or another family member, our job is to stay the course and trust His divine wisdom and will for us.

Don't get me wrong, the devil does try to derail us from the course the Lord has ordained for us. But he is a defeated enemy and has been since the foundation of the world. When we put all our focus on and trust in God, we can discern and discriminate between the plan of God and the works of Satan. The Holy Spirit will tell us, "The enemy has done this." Sometimes it is neither God nor Satan who has a part in our failures, but our own impulses. We tend to act too quickly, pull out too soon, or give up prematurely when we hit a bump or turbulence. That is why it is crucial to rely on implementing strategies that are bathed in prayer.

When we have truly presented our petitions before our Lord and the outcome tends to be contrary to what we envisaged, we can attain peace of mind, the peace that passeth understanding, from knowing that God may solve our situation in a different way than what we expected. Sometimes God's strategies employ nontraditional means rather than familiar methods. Our job is to believe and trust Him even when we cannot trace Him. We must trust His heart, especially when we do not even understand where He is leading us. Give glory to Him and meaningfully praise Him always for His unfailing hand! Such is my story that I will be sharing under this pillar. Keep reading!

Song

Lord, in the morning Thou shalt hear
My voice ascending high;
To Thee will I direct my prayer,
To Thee lift up my eye—

The men that love and fear Thy name
Shall see their hopes fulfilled
The mighty God will compass them
With favor as a shield.

—Isaac Watts

My Story

I remember one winter while living in the USA, I felt so sick and was very weak. I could not figure out what was going on with me. At first, I figured that if I could sleep it off, I would feel better. Instead I was sicker. I'd never felt that way before. I felt as if something was sucking the life out of me. My good husband urged me to see my doctor. I said, "I will be fine," insisting that it must be jet lag or something. We had just returned from an overseas trip, having spent six weeks visiting family in Johannesburg and Cape Town. Because of my husband's persuasion, I called my family physician and was told that he was overbooked and could not see me and that I should go to an emergency care facility. I was not a happy camper. I wanted my family doctor for selfish reasons. However, I prayed for the Lord to guide me to a good substitute.

To my surprise, the alternate doctor proved to be the best thing that ever happened to me. She diagnosed me with vitamin D deficiency, prescribed a very high dose for six weeks, and instructed me to follow up with my regular physician for maintenance. My blood work showed negligible low levels of vitamin D even after the high dose of therapy. I remember asking the attending physician, "How is my vitamin D so low after spending almost two months basking in the African sun?" She smiled and responded that it was a blessing I had, saying that I should consider the alternative if I had not vacationed in South Africa and soaked up all that summer sun. Apparently, some doctors do not check for vitamin D levels as the norm. She also told me that brown-skinned people use more vitamin D to maintain their skin color. During the winter season, that causes a problem because there is not much vitamin D present in the Northern Hemisphere. I also learned that a vitamin D deficiency is associated with several other serious conditions, including fibromyalgia and skin cancer among African Americans. I share this story because it has several implications, as follows:

1. I wanted my family physician, but God gave me a substitute I did not want. God's provision is always the best.
2. God answers prayers even when we are selfish and think we are in control of our situation, or when we are expecting a shorthanded blessing as I was.
3. My regular doctor, perhaps, would not have checked my blood for vitamin D.
4. God in His goodness allowed me to visit home in South Africa to bask in the summer sunlight so as to fortify me with the vitamin D I did not know I needed in order to prevent a more serious ailment that may have cost my life.
5. I tried to solve the situation using my own wisdom through the familiar means of sleeping the illness off and seeking my family physician, instead of seeking the Lord for guidance in the first place.

6. My teammate (husband) saved my life by insisting that my condition needed medical attention, even though I downplayed it. If he had not forced me to seek medical help, I may have died still thinking I had jet lag.

7. Sometimes God solves our situations using nontraditional means just to make the statement that He is in control of our existence. For example:

    a. He used a *raven* to feed Elijah.

    b. He used a *fish* to provide money to pay taxes for Him and Peter.

    c. He used a *donkey's jawbone* in the hand of Samson to kill the Philistines.

    d. He used a *smooth stone* in the hand of David to bring down Goliath.

    e. He used a little boy's lunch of *two sardines and five barley loaves* to feed a multitude of people.

Last Word

God loves us all. "In truth, I perceive that God shows no partiality" (Acts 10:34 NKJV). Differences do not make us inferior; they just make us different! So, we should "come boldly to the throne of grace that we may obtain mercy and find grace to help in time of need" (Hebrews 4:16 NKJV). That is the case even within our marriage. If we believe these promises, we will not be shy to ask our heavenly Father to lead and guide us through the maze and intricacies of life and when we are at a crossroads facing decisions. We cannot achieve our plans, hopes, and dreams without consulting His wisdom. "I am the vine, you are the branches. He who abides in me, and I in him, bears much fruit; for without Me you can do nothing" (John 15:5 NKJV). "With man this is impossible, but with God all things are possible" (Matthew 19:26 NIV). "For with God nothing will be impossible" (Luke 1:37 NKJV).

After Nehemiah's moving prayer, "Lord, let your ear be attentive to the prayer of this your servant and to the prayer of your servants who delight in revering your name. Give your servant success today by granting him favor in the presence of this man" (Nehemiah 1:11 NIV), God opened doors

Nehemiah never imagined and touched King Artaxerxes to work things out in Nehemiah's favor. God has promised to make even our *"enemies to be at peace* with us" (Proverbs 16:7 KJV, emphasis added). So, even after we have prayed and do not get the answers we were expecting, or even when we face contrary evidence, we should have courage enough to go back to the drawing board of prayer, believing and trusting that God has something better for us than what we had in mind. Our job is to sincerely desire to walk with Him, to understand and appreciate His agenda and timeline for us.

> I want Jesus to walk with me.
> I want Jesus to walk with me.
> All along my pilgrim journey,
> I want Jesus to walk with me.
>
> In my trials, Lord, walk with me.
> In my trials, Lord, walk with me.
> When the shades of life are falling,
> I want Jesus to walk with me.
>
> —Eurydice Osterman, 1984

Pillar #12
Yielding to and Yearning for the Way of the Lord

Foundation

> If you do not bump heads with the devil, you may be
> traveling in the same direction, side-by-side!

—E. S. Moya

What Is Yielding?

Joy is derived from yielding to the way of the Lord. Yielding is arrogance dipped and sanctified in the blood of the Lamb. Naturally we are stubborn, haughty, opinionated, self-righteous, and self-pleasing. Watch the newborn upon arrival in this world. It does not come smiling and giggling but comes screaming and agitated. Watch it again when it is hungry. It wants food now! Its concern is the food; nothing else matters. If Mommy is sick or sleepy, too bad! If truth be told, some of us have not outgrown the tantrum stage or the tendency to be demanding, selfish, and haughty. Dr. Calvin Rock labels the condition of humankind mutated by sin as "born dead on arrival (DOA)." Thus, the key to extending our existence is in being connected to the heavenly life support of the will of God. The idea of yielding to the will of the Lord's leading is foreign and does not come naturally to humans. It can be accomplished only through (a) deliberate prayer, (b) intentional desire to surrender the reins to the Lord, (c) being grounded in and grafted to the True Vine, and (d) being willing to succumb to the will of God and the direction of His hand.

Elements Resulting in Failure to Yield

The genesis of sin was discussed in the introduction of *Pillars of Joy in Marriage* under the subhead "Pre-Sin Condition." There are three underlying elements of sin that can be established. They are as follows:

1. *Appetite*

Appetite refers to human beings' quest to be gods, which, on its own, distorts our allegiance, defies the lordship of Christ, and leads to disobedience of God's ordained order for humanity. In the context of the Bible, appetite is the desire, urge, and craving to experience a state of being like gods, so promised by the serpent. Hence, yielding to the way of the Lord and focusing on His will for us curbs the appetite for sin and sinning.

2. *Selfishness*

This emanates from an urge to do what pleases us rather than what pleases God. A self-serving focus distorts the view of God's sovereign power, and undermines and disregards God's absolute authority.

3. *Pride*

This entails elevating one's view of self above all that is required and good in the eyes of the Lord. Pride refuses to change or give up destructive practices to relearn new constructive pathways. Pride prevents us from forgiving others and embarking on a fresh start. Likewise, pride gets in the way of seeing one's own mistakes and the ability to say, "Thank you," "I am sorry," and "Please forgive me!"

In the context of the marital relationship, the interaction between *appetite* for sinning and *self-serving* notions compounded by *pride* predisposes the continuation of sin and sinning, and ultimately contributes to lack of joy in the marriage and the family at large, as delineated below.

Uncontrolled Sexual Appetite

In the context of a marriage, the sour relationship and devastating divorce that has torn some marriages apart have sometimes been caused by extramarital affairs, instigated by an uncontrolled sexual appetite. When we engage in sin or destructive behavior, this is not a reflection of God's lack of power to help us overcome sin but our hardness of heart and absence of trust in God. Paul fortifies us with the power to control our appetite for engaging in any form of sin: "I can do all things through Christ, who strengthens me" (Philippians 4:13 KJV). Hence, an uncontrolled sexual appetite destroys the pillars of joy in marriage, physically, spiritually, emotionally, and otherwise.

Yielding to Temptation

Another aspect of yielding relates to the ability to detect temptation. Temptation by itself is not a sin; yielding to temptation is. God does not tempt us; He tests us. It is the devil's job to tempt us. The joy comes from knowing the difference between tests and temptation episodes. God will not test you more than you can bear, and He supplies you with resolve and strength to stay true amid the test and overcome. But appetite, pride, selfishness, and a self-serving lifestyle disregard marital vows, fuel the appetite to violate the integrity of the sacred circle of marriage, and propel the desire to continue unbridled along the pathway of destruction without regard for what God wants and has ordained for the marriage.

Failure to Yield to God's Will

Yielding to God's will means applying the brake and exercising caution while traveling this marriage journey. Most spiritual casualties are usually caused by failure to yield to the way of the Lord.

The following is a summary of terms used herein to describe symbolically the conditions a couple may encounter on the marital journey when traveling without Christ.

> a. *DUI*—Driving under the influence of something or someone other than God, which results in an impaired vision and distorted allegiance to God.
>
> b. *Speeding*—Running your life and being suffocated by the problems of life with no space for the Lord and no time to worship Him. Thus, you get caught off guard and become potential prey for the wiles of the devil, who is a roaring lion looking for someone he can devour (1 Peter 5:8).

c. *Failure to yield*—Trusting in your own wisdom and understanding independent of God's ordained will and plan for your life.

d. *Running red lights of the Holy Spirit*—Ignoring warning signs or danger signals in your relationship or not listening to that small, soft voice saying, "You'd better stop doing what is breaking your mate's heart!"

e. *Facing a hijacker*—Trying to face the devil (hijacker) on your own instead of calling for a heavenly "all-powerful" backup to fight the enemy on your behalf. Jesus is able, and He is the number one weapon in a Christian's arsenal.

f. *Missing the turn and following a wrong road*—Deviating from principles or strict integrity. Following the crowd and not upholding the moral compass or standard to guide you in the marriage marathon.

g. *Driving in the wrong lane*—Engaging in practices that are offensive to your spouse, that may cause your mate to stumble, and that may block his or her spiritual growth and development.

h. *Falling asleep at the wheel of prayer*—Living a life without prayer is tantamount to falling asleep while driving and failing to be vigilant as a watchman or steward of the kingdom.

i. *Failing to realize that one is lost*—Being oblivious to what is going on in your house and relinquishing your role as a faithful steward, spouse, and parent whose job it is to guide the family to eternal glory.

These conditions outlined above are the devil's tools used to instill distorted allegiance to God, fear, worry, and hopelessness.

Trusting in Human Intelligence

A friend once cautioned me that before you do something, it helps to ask yourself the vital question "Then what?" I have used this in the process of making the decision to yield or not to yield. Another important factor to consider is whether it is wise to do something, or follow a certain course of action. Yielding to wisdom has saved me from taking a destructive path. Yielding to wisdom is always right! But doing what is right may not always be the wise thing to do. At the same time, doing what is wise may not always be a better thing to do if we trust in our own wisdom alone.

Losing It All After All

"What shall it profit man, if he shall gain the whole world, and lose his soul? or what shall a man give in exchange for his soul" (Mark 8:36–37 KJV)? Serving other "gods" such as extramarital sex, power, fame, and fortune over our Father God in search of a better life or a thrill has led many couples onto a path of destruction, a dead-end street, where they lose all instead of gaining a better life. God is our existence and wants the best for us. Yielding to his prescription for marriage is the best antidote for the sin virus and is the cure for sin. The devil himself knows his time is short, and his imps are afraid of Jesus. They have a panic attack in the presence of Jesus, who, to them, is like chemotherapy to cancer cells. Listen to what the demons said to Jesus: "Thou son of God, art thou *come to torment us before time* (Matthew 8:29 KJV, emphasis added); "Art Thou come to *destroy us* (Mark 1:24 KJV, emphasis added)? So why are we so stubborn and lax about sin? How in the world do we allow ourselves to be hijacked by the devil? If we know and believe in God's supreme love for us and His absolute power to conquer Satan, why do we toy with the devil and not invite Jesus to be Lord of our household? Submitting to God's guidance is not a weakness but a superstrength. Yielding to His purpose for our lives, especially when we do not understand where He is leading us, is a sign of wisdom, maturity, and sure, safe road-worthiness. Brenda Walsh, author of *Moments with God: One-Minute Devotions to Encourage, Inspire, and Spiritually Change Your Life*, summed it up well when she wrote, "When we allow God to push us away out of our comfort zone, it is then we are really leaning on Jesus. There is no better place to be on this journey of life than holding his hand" (p. 62).

Song

Have Thine own way, Lord! Have Thine own way!
Thou are the Potter; I am the clay.
Mold me and make me after Thy will,

While I am waiting, Yielded and still.

Have Thine own way, Lord! Have Thine own way!
Search me and try me, Master today!
Whiter than snow, Lord, wash me just now,
As in Thy presence Humbly I bow.

—George C. Stebbins

My Story

It was in 1976 that I was expecting our long-awaited for child, after seven years of waiting and trial and error. We had just built our new home, which sat on 2.5 acres in Swaziland, Southern Africa. Life was good. I felt sick, and my doctor told me the sweet news and the bitter news. The sweet news was that I was about two months pregnant. The bitter news was that he was concerned that I might miscarry. He counseled my husband and me that I should put a pause on my career and stop working for a period. I needed to have immediate bed rest and elevate my feet. My poor husband! He had to endure sleeping like that for seven more months to come. That is what love is all about, and what "we are all in this together" means. Since both of us wanted the baby, we complied. I was concerned that my husband would now singlehandedly be paying all the bills, paying for two cars, an Audi and a Volvo, paying the mortgage for the new house, and preparing for the newborn to come. Well, I can attest that God honors those who comply with His ordained will, even if they do not understand. These are the events that transpired:

1. I stopped working and followed the doctor's orders and instructions.
2. My boss told me that since the notice was from a private doctor, I needed clearance from the superintendent at the government hospital (who was on special assignment overseas), and sign-off by the secretary of health. But the wheels of government move slower than a tortoise. By the time the clearance letter came, I was nearly seven months pregnant and receiving my full pay while sitting at home. I was anxious about this delay and worried that I would end up having to repay all the money. Not so fast. God was in control of the situation.

3. When I went to see my boss, he told me that it was not my fault that I had been paid in full. No adjustments to my paychecks were made. "Just take it as if you've been working for the past seven months. We will apply your accumulated vacation to cover the eighth and ninth months. The Government General Order allows you three months' maternity leave, that is, six weeks before and six weeks after delivery." Thus, I received full payment throughout the full term of my pregnancy, and a month's bonus pay after the baby was born. Halleluiah! "For with God, *nothing shall be impossible*" (Luke 1:37 KJV, emphasis added).

Last Word

True joy comes with yielding to the way of the Lord and allowing Him to take us on paths we do not understand and do not know where they will end up. Our job is to relax and let Him drive, enjoying the ride and scenery. We must not worry about the destination. In real life, many casualties are caused by taking matters into our hands, speeding, driving recklessly, running stoplights, falling asleep at the wheel, and driving under the influence of the enemy. In *Pillars of Joy in Marriage*, the concept of yielding applies to succumbing and allowing *wisdom the right-of-way*. Wisdom is viewed as the ultimate *red light* or yardstick measuring whether we are traveling in the right direction and making sound decisions. Wisdom guides us to stop, or move forward, or follow the direction of God, our GPS, without regret.

In relation to married couples, the concept of yielding manifests itself in surrendering and taking responsibility for a course of action. It means loving your mate unconditionally, even when there are plenty of reasons not to give your love; committing to fulfilling your mate's needs despite his or her shortcomings; exercising a forgiving spirit, even in the face of neglect or betrayal or when there is no reason to forgive; yielding to and allowing your spouse the right-of-way; and acknowledging that he or she is right and accepting the blame for the sake of peace, even when a certain outcome is not your fault. Simply put, yielding your stubbornness will be beneficial to you in many ways. Also, it allows the Spirit of God to work with your mate's heart.

Pillar # 13
Investing in the Marriage Partnership

Foundation

> When you do what the Lord has asked you to do He will
> make Himself personally responsible for your success!

—Dr. William T. Cox

What Is Investment in Marriage?

Ordinarily, investment refers to monetary funds held in deposit accounts, as well as tangible assets of financial value, such as machinery and production equipment in factories and other manufacturing facilities. So, when people think of the word *investment*, they think of money, that is, in terms of dollars, euros, pounds, and so forth. They imagine portfolios, financial stability, and the amassing of wealth and the accumulation of land and property (real estate). However, in the context of marriage, investment looks beyond the cash value to assets that contribute to the optimum health, enrichment, and quality of the union. Granted, investing in your marriage is hard and is not an instantaneous effort. It takes time, but it brings joy and great dividends in the long run through seeking innovative ways to keep the love fire glowing, especially through challenging times. Thus, in this pillar, when we speak of investment, we look beyond the financial gains to the overall health quotient of the relationship.

Elder Sam Davis and his wife Rowena from England, visited our church, Metro Mission SDA, Johannesburg, in May 2017 to conduct a weeklong seminar about making deliberate and intentional choices and lifestyle changes to live a healthy life. One of the gems that sank deep in my mind was the statement "Just like with depositing money into one's bank account for a rainy day, one needs to do the same to maintain a healthy physical investment portfolio to cash in on later years. If one makes reckless health and lifestyle choices in younger years, one's cash investment portfolio can be swallowed all up by ill health and just trying to stay afloat in later years." This inspired me to look at marriage from a different perspective. Similarly, it can be argued about marriage that burning your marriage investment capital by doing things such as making uncalculated decisions, committing indiscretions, neglecting and overdrawing the account by engaging in foolish behaviors, making bad choices, committing infidelity, and engaging in other related destructive behaviors will not yield a good investment portfolio or contribute to the overall health of the marriage. It is important to note that the marriage capital investment, like any other investment portfolio, should be diversified to yield better dividends. Some of the investment assets that will be discussed in this pillar, as they relate to building a diversified marriage portfolio, are as follows:

1. Spiritual asset building
2. Physical health asset building
3. Emotional asset building
4. Marriage investment capital gains

Spiritual Asset Building

A joyful marriage does not come easily or just happen. The two people in the union must be deliberate about investing in the marriage and intentional about building a spiritually sound marriage portfolio. A major spiritual asset to achieving a joyous marriage is the commitment to building a relationship with the Lord Jesus Christ and having the triune God—the Father, the Son, and the Holy Ghost—as the foundation of your life, including your marriage. Hence, the pillars discussed in *Pillars of Joy in Marriage* seek to build a strong biblical foundation of joy in a marriage in terms of understanding the source of joy and the fundamental principles to uphold, as follows:

1. Joy is attainable only when the marital relationship is founded and grafted on Jesus Christ, the *True Vine* and the *guide* of our marriage.
2. Couples should be intentional about building strength-based relationships, embracing and celebrating differences as strengths rather than weaknesses.

3. Couples should understand the virtue of embracing differences as strengths, not as weaknesses, and of seeing them as complementary to each other's personality.

4. Couples should build a culture of humor wherein positive communication can thrive and should utilize humor to deflate potentially volatile situations that may cause distress in the marriage.

5. Couples should endeavor to meet each other's needs and look beyond each other's faults to see the need.

6. Couples should seek to resolve conflicts early, before they escalate to an irreconcilable or irreversible outcome.

7. Couples should learn to love and cherish the spouse they have and avoid getting into a love triangle with a third party other than Christ.

8. Couples should make every effort to build a spiritually healthy marriage that entails a moral climate conducive to reinforcing the hope of the *coming King and real Prince Charming*, Jesus Christ our Lord and Savior.

9. Couples should strive to develop the moral fiber and character conducive to a spiritually healthy marriage and mutually satisfying spiritual intimacy.

10. Couples should develop a posture of readiness to meet Jesus Christ in the *altar of the sky*, adorned as His bride, for an everlasting honeymoon where perfect happiness and holiness will culminate in a post-sin condition for eternity.

Physical Health Asset Building

Health is the best form of wealth and is a viable asset in developing a sound marriage investment portfolio. There is a relationship between marriage joy and health. A healthful lifestyle yields great dividends in a marriage. The favorite slogan of one of my surrogate daughters, Grace Brown, speaks volumes in this regard: "He who has health has hope; and he who has hope has everything!" In other words, plain and simple, the genesis of a hopeful future for the marriage is health wealth more than it is cash wealth. Health promises bright hope for the future, and without health, the future is uncertain. Health impacts every aspect of a marriage and one's quality of life, including energy, disposition, daily activity, mood, intimacy, patience, and outlook on life in general. Good nutrition has benefits spiritually, emotionally, intellectually, physically, sexually, and otherwise. The question is, how does your health lifestyle measure up? With the permission of Pastor Sam Davis, presenter of "Healthful Living," on behalf of Dr. Jim Sharps, author of *Basic Principles of Total Health*, which includes the Hierarchy of Nutrients, I have included for your convenience a Health Quotient in appendix D to help you determine a baseline for where you are in matters of healthful living. Knowing how you measure up in relation to healthful living and the trajectory of where you need to be in terms of an optimum healthy lifestyle will give you the impetus to change, unlearn old pathways, and make new healthy lifestyle choices, starting by adopting basic principles of healthful living outlined in appendix E. Thus, by redirecting your life, adopting changes, and making a *new start*, including positive incremental gains toward achieving an optimum healthful lifestyle, you deposit an invaluable asset into your marriage investment portfolio to cash in, in the later years.

Emotional Asset Building

Dr. Wayde Goodall identifies *commitment* as one of the most active ingredients in building an emotionally healthy marriage. Hence, this pillar includes commitment as one of the prime assets for building an emotionally sound marriage capital investment portfolio. Types of commitment are as follows:

A. *Long-term commitment*—True marriage investment is manifested in the determination to make each other's life better for the rest of your lives. Being married to your spouse means remaining committed even if things are not working well. Commitment is not predicated on how you feel each day. Like joy, it is a choice and an attitude you uphold no matter how you feel. Therefore, commitment is not an instantaneous fix based on whims but is a deliberate and intentional choice to commit to one person for the rest of your life. Such a promise is serious, and if kept and nurtured, it is a true investment in your marriage. This type of commitment is observable and measurable by positive actions and the long-term quality of the marital relationship.

B. *Commitment to building healthy communication*—The marriage investment for couples includes the commitment to develop mutually engaging positive verbal and nonverbal communication. This is a critical component for sustaining a healthy marriage portfolio. Researchers have identified a distinct difference among men and women when it comes to the value of communication. For women, the quality of the communication is a major indicator of a healthy marriage investment in intimacy. Dr. John Gray, in his book *Men Are from Mars and Women Are from Venus*, estimates that women speak about fifty thousand words a day, whereas men use only five thousand words per day. Dr. Gary and Barbara Rosenberg have confirmed the value of communication as an investment asset, especially in the eyes of women. For example, in their research on the love needs of men and women, they discovered a huge difference between how these two groups viewed intimacy. For women, intimacy equals talk, whereas for men, it means sex. This difference in needs or value can cause deficits and stress in the marriage relationship. So, learning and practicing strategies for building a culture of healthy communication and mutually fulfilling intimacy is a duty that couples should not take lightly. Men should not use silence to punish a woman. Women, likewise, should avoid using sex to punish a man. "Let the husband render to his wife the affection due to her, and likewise also the wife to her husband. The wife does not have authority over her body, but her husband does. And likewise, the husband does not have authority over his body, but his wife does. Do not deprive one another except with consent for a time that you may give yourself to fasting and prayer; and come together again so that Satan does not tempt you" (1 Corinthians 7:2–5 NKJV). Thus, investing in meeting the needs of both marriage partners can yield great dividends in the marriage investment portfolio.

Furthermore, couples should refrain from engaging in negative communication, which includes name-calling, insults, and put-downs. Such behavior drains the emotional investment account. Brenda Walsh has suggested sending a distress signal to heaven: "When tempted to speak a harsh word, react in an unkind way, or explode in a fit of rage, send an SOS to heaven and pray, *Jesus help me be like You*" (p. 63)! Having the triune God and heavenly lifeline to keep you from overdrawing your emotional investment account is added value for Christian couples and should not be neglected.

C. *Commitment to conflict management*—Invest time in conflict resolution. Conflict is part and parcel of life. In a marriage, there are several areas that can spark conflict. These areas include different assumptions, needs, interests, and overall perspective. The fact that we marry people who are not like us, with differences in cultural background, ethnicity, religion, tastes, and interests, may be a source of conflict. The question is not whether conflict can exist, but whether a couple has the technical know-how to address conflict when it arises. So, the commitment to address conflict, and developing skills for resolving conflict, can prove to be viable assets in building a healthy marriage portfolio. It is important to understand that unresolved conflict is detrimental to the health of the marriage and, if left unaddressed, may fester into animosity, hostility, grudges, and residual anger. All these are cousins of an unforgiving spirit and indifference. Thus, a deliberate and intentional commitment to resolving conflict is a part of a good investment portfolio. Couples who lack conflict management skills should seek professional help early on, when the situation is benign, before it escalates or progresses into an ugly cancerous growth that is beyond recourse or remedy.

D. *Commitment to studying what is real*—Study the real deal, the genuine article (God's Word), and do not spin your wheels examining the counterfeit (bogus or fake) assets, imitations, shades of tradition, or false doctrine. This last comes in a variety of colors, shapes, and sizes. Once you know the *truth* from the mouth of God, the rest will take care of itself. The Bible makes convincing assertions.

1. Jesus proclaims to investors that He is the real *"pearl* of the *great price"* (Matthew 13:46 KJV, emphasis added).

2. He confirms to the sojourners that "I am the *way*, the *truth* and the *life*, and no one comes to the Father except through Me" (John 14:6 NKJV, emphasis added).
3. God assures the investors that He is the prime asset and the source of wealth: "*Gold* and *silver* is Mine" (Haggai 2:8 KJV, emphasis added).
4. God declares to the clergy and ecclesiastic enthusiasts, "All *souls* are Mine" (Ezekiel 18:20 KJV, emphasis added).
5. God captures the traditionalists who invest in livestock: "All *cattle upon a thousand hills* are His" (Psalm 50:10 KJV, emphasis added).
6. He clarifies to the property developers, "The *earth* and the *fullness thereof* is Mine" (Psalm 24:1 KJV, emphasis added).
7. He assures the tentative investors and skeptics that He is the *great I AM* and that, simply put, before the trusted financial institutions and CEOs were established, He *was* there.
8. To the politicians and lawmakers, He declares that "He puts kings in power and removes them" (Daniel 2:21; 1 Kings 20:24) and "the *government* is in *His shoulders*" (Isaiah 9:6 KJV, emphasis added).

E. *Commitment to jettisoning the dead weight*—Forgive and get rid of anger and a spirit of resentment. A forgiving spirit is one of the central sources of joy and of exponential growth in the investment portfolio of a married couple.

F. *Commitment to renew the mind*—The apostle Paul in Romans 12:2 (KJV, emphasis added) counsels us not to be conformed to the ways of this world but to be transformed by the *renewing of the mind* consistent with what is the *"good, acceptable and perfect* will of God." The need may be there to change oneself or please the Lord, but the test of character is in one's willingness to follow through in doing the will of God. We need to fortify our minds by showing the following:

1. Willingness to unlearn old ways, unacceptable habits, and practices.
2. Willingness to learn new pathways and incorporate the new requirements.

3. Willingness to comply with demands, challenges, and even setbacks.
4. Willingness to be patient and wait for the expected results.
5. Willingness to celebrate small incremental successes.
6. Willingness to stay the course, getting up to start again and continue fighting when we have fallen. Change does not often occur instantaneously. Success is better measured by progress, not speed.
7. Willingness to depend on God for your success and giving Him the glory and praise for accomplishing your goal(s).

Marriage Investment Capital Gains

Earning the respect and trust of your mate is a priceless gain on all the hard work, commitment, and time you invested in your marriage portfolio. The prevailing popular sentiment that marriage demands each spouse to bring 50 percent to the investment is a fallacy. You are not ready to get married and experience the fullness of joy and benefits of the union unless each one of you is committed to invest 100 percent of *yourself* as an asset. Anything less than that—forget it! You may ask, what do you mean? I'm glad you asked. Well, among other things, these assets are manifested through being (1) faithful to your spouse, (2) loving, (3) selfless, (4) committed to meet each other's needs, and (5) responsible and accountable for the resources God has given you. This is demonstrated by how and with whom you spend your time, how you use your talents, and what you do with your treasure. Thus, with serious introspection, please respond to the following questions:

1. With whom do I spend my quality time? Who is the beneficiary: my spouse, others, or something else?
2. To whom do I give the best of myself? Who is the beneficiary: my spouse, others, or something else?
3. On whom do I spend the lion's share of my resources? Who is the beneficiary: my spouse, others, or something else?

Dr. Chapman, in his book *Marriage for All Seasons*, defines a successful marriage investment not as the amassing of wealth or fame, but as being a responsible steward in utilizing the resources God has bestowed upon you, which, I might add, include the three items mentioned above.

Please Don't Let Me Cry Twice

Crying twice here refers to (1) crying the first time because your mate has died and (2) crying the second time because he or she failed you by living you in debt or making bad investments. It is one thing to die a natural death, but another thing if the death is untimely due to reckless lifestyle, bad choices, or neglecting to make a wise investment in healthy lifestyle. I have observed that in modern society, the tendency for couples is to overwork and stress themselves to the point of ill health trying to provide material things for their children, often because they themselves did not have these things as children. In some cases, these parents neglect to pass on the moral and spiritual virtues and values of common decency their parents held dear and passed on to them. Like with any investment, we want to leave a legacy for our family and children, so they can remember us after we have passed on. I wish I could say it is material worth that matters most, but it is not. Yes, money helps, but it is not all there is to life. When we neglect to develop a sound vertical relationship with God, or recklessly squander every virtue we possess, then what will we be remembered for? If we fail to share meaningful and lasting virtues such as wisdom, morality, fundamental values, decency, and common sense with our children, we leave them with an empty existence, like a dried-up well, and no real meaning in life.

Building and *destroying* are equally important terms to understand when it comes to making sound marriage capital investments. Asset building and eliminating dead-weight debts are part of good investment. Unnecessary debts can drain cash flow that otherwise could be infused into meaningful investment. Similarly, in marriage, a deadbeat lifestyle, extramarital relationships, and sleazy affairs can bankrupt spiritual intimacy, drain spousal love, and paralyze the desire to continue investing in the marriage. Listen, it is enough for your loving spouse and family to cry because you are gone, but to have them *cry twice* just because (a) you made poor marriage investments and (b) you were not a vigilant, responsible, or faithful steward who taught and nurtured your family and left them a legacy of meaningful values and dependence on God to navigate this treacherous world would be a shame. Heaven will mark your tombstone, "Here lies a spouse who failed his [or her] family dismally!" Please do not get me wrong, money and material things are good, but they do not last and should not possess you. Character lasts forever and is the only possession we will take with us to heaven. E. G. White, in *Christ Object Lessons*, p. 332, states: "A character formed according to divine likeness is the only treasure that we can take from this world to the next." So, as you invest in your marriage portfolio, remember that character building is a lasting asset. Please do not make your spouse cry twice because you were not a faithful steward of values, morality, talent, time, or treasure, or because you did not live a healthy lifestyle. Let me be clear: your duty as a parent is to do your part, with God's grace. Your children may still choose a path of rebellion and destruction, but that will be their own problem. As for you, your *investment duty* before God is accomplished. Thus, in terms of the marriage investment, it is not money alone that defines wealth but character, integrity, and a mutually fulfilling marital relationship; such virtues money cannot buy. According to Solomon, the wisest person who ever lived on earth, it is "better to have little with godliness than to be rich and dishonest" (Proverbs 16:8 NLT). In the light of all that I have discussed, what do you say? Is your marriage investment portfolio sound in heaven's eyes?

Song

Lord, I care not for riches, neither silver nor Gold;
I would make sure of Heaven, I would enter the fold.
In the book of Thy kingdom, with its pages so fair,
Tell me, Jesus, my Savor, is my name written there?

Chorus:

Is my name written there, On the page, white and fair?
In the book of Thy kingdom, is my name written there?

—Frank M. Davis

My Story

It's not easy to choose love, or to invest in others, but it pays great dividends in the long run. I remember about seven years into our marriage, my husband and I were looking for a nanny to take care of our son. A trusted relative referred us to a seventeen-year-old named Bulla. She had dropped out of school solely because she lacked the funds to realize her dream of being a nurse one day. See, in African societies, education at the high school level is not cheap. There are no free rides either.

Bulla was bright, well-behaved, kind-spirited, and very respectful, unlike many teenagers her age. Godwin and I fell in love with her and took her under our wing as part of the family in many respects, not just as a nanny. When our son was one year old, we encouraged Bulla to pursue and complete her O levels, equivalent to a high school diploma, at a distant school while she lived with us as our daughter. My husband would drop her at the school facility in the morning on his way to work at Salora, a TV manufacturing company, where he was a personnel manager. He would pick her up in the evening after work, on his way home. To cut a long story short, Bulla completed her studies and passed her O levels. She then qualified to apply to Maluti Hospital in Lesotho to train as a nurse. I wrote a letter of recommendation and expressed her personal goals to the admissions committee. The committee readily took her, based on the strength of my letter. Bulla finished her nursing program and earned the highest recognition as a phenomenal caring nurse (the King Bereng Moshoeshoe II Award). She also completed her BSc in clinical nursing. Now she holds a high position at a reputable clinic in Johannesburg.

Well, guess what, little did we know that more than thirty-five years later Bulla would be there for us in many ways. She singlehandedly helped us navigate the complicated medical system when we relocated back to South Africa following our retirement from the United States. I wish I had time and space to describe the nuances of resettling overseas. All I will say is that some other couples who went back home with excitement ended up returning to the United States because of complications of the laws and regulations covering the health-care system. Bulla found us the best doctor, and all is well. We are now settled thanks to her direction and support. Her husband, as well as her children, who are now around the age Bulla was when she came to live with us, were also helpful in so many ways. Bulla's children cannot stop thanking us for the investment we made in their mama when she was young, destitute, and powerless. They share sentimental stories of how she used to enjoy being dropped off at school and picked up in a brand-new Volvo, and many more things we could not even recall. Wow, we feel that we are the ones blessed because we gained a daughter and grandchildren for life.

Bulla told us that she lost everyone in her family, her mother, grandmother, and uncle, and felt very alone. I quickly interjected "No, you are not alone, and you are not an orphan. You have Jesus and us, the family God chose for you forty years ago." She smiled, and said, "Thank you for that assurance. That means the world to me. I did not know you felt the same as I do." I assured her, "Yes we do, and we will always be here for you as long as you need us. We feel that we are the ones who gained a daughter." We hugged! Wow! I now believe in the old African adage, "Throw your bread on the other side of the river; you will find it a sandwich one day."

Last Word

I was impressed to close this chapter by sharing a bit about the assurance of restoration considering the setbacks we undergo and the losses we incur from time to time in our lives. Loss is the opposite of investment gain. Sometimes we suffer losses despite carefully planning our investments. The question is, what do we do when we suffer an investment loss, or when the devil messes with our blessing and steals our joy? The answer is found in Joel 2:25, where God promises to restore what the enemy has taken from us, directly or indirectly. God has a prescribed restoration logistics as delineated below.

Restoration Logistics

Loss of Investment

Loss is part of life. We will sustain losses in this life to some degree, even when we have been faithful stewards. But the difference here is knowing that you have done everything you were able to do to hold up your end of the bargain. But without the Lord, we sustain a massive loss of assets and even the loss of our lives.

Prayer and Restoration

In Joel 2:25, God promises to restore what we have lost. But in my experience, when He restores, He does not give you the same thing or the same value you lost. See, God does not have anything to do with what the devil has touched with his filthy hands and teeth (*Umtamo-ka-Satan*, in Zulu and Xhosa languages). Instead, God will restore not according to your pain, but according to His bountiful resources or riches and His bank account of glory. So, if you sustain any kind of loss in your marriage investment, including loss of a spouse, health, children, or wealth, trust in the God of peace, stay the course, and be a faithful steward. God in His time will restore what you lost, as He did for Job. He will give you something *new and of better value* than what you originally lost, be it money, material possessions, a job, or even friends and associates. Just hang in there and anticipate a better tomorrow!

Pillar # 14
A Nice Disposition Is a Plus

Foundation

Good head and good heart, are always a Formidable combination!

—Nelson Mandela

Just Be Nice

There is an adage that says you can catch more flies with honey than with vinegar. It is our individual responsibility to develop and maintain a sweet disposition. Just be nice! It is good for you and your mate. Creating a culture of being a pleasant person, regardless of the situation and circumstances, is Christlike and is the right thing to do. It takes more energy to be grouchy, mean, and vindictive than it does to smile and be nice. Someone once said to me, "If you smile, people will smile back to you; and if you frown, the whole world frowns back at you." Get the point? I understand it takes more muscles to frown than to smile. "A merry heart does good, like medicine, but a broken spirit dries the bones" (Proverbs 17:22 NKJV). So, if you cannot do it for your spouse's sake, then be nice for your own good, for the sake of your own health and longevity. You have absolutely nothing to lose.

There are prevailing arguments out there that associate being nice with weakness, such as if you are nice, people will walk over you and take you for a fool. That could be a correct assessment, but at the end of the day, we are not responsible for how people treat us or interpret our motives. In my view, being nice or gracious is a virtue. Not a sign of weakness, it is a manifestation of strength of character. It takes strength to exude grace in challenging situations, especially when you don't feel people deserve it. Our job is to do what is acceptable and pleasing to our Master and Lord Jesus Christ. That's it! Be nice! Just do it.

The following section highlights some of the ways one can establish a culture of being nice.

Tell Your Story, but Check Your Story

Have fun together, but *do not make fun of each other*. What has helped me in my marriage and friendships, generally, is to check what I say using a three-dimensional ruler, as my mom, Mildred Tenyane, taught me:

a. Is it *true*?
b. Is it *kind*?
c. Is it *necessary*? Even if the narrative is true or is a kind thing to say, it may not be necessary for you to share it.

If the story does not meet one of these requirements, stop right there and then; it is not worth telling. A story or remark may be true or kind or even benign, but it may not be necessary to share. So, if the story does not meet these three criteria, it is not appropriate to tell. Jettison it or throw it in the garbage can and close the lid. Be sensitive of one another's feelings and guard against making the other person a laughingstock.

Beware of the Four T's

The four T's are as follows:

1. Trivializing Each Other's Concern or Pain

It is very easy to downplay your spouse's pain or concern if the matter does not impact you personally. This disposition is nothing but selfishness at its best. Adopt a posture of respect when listening to your spouse's story or concern. Be empathetic, showing that you care. Granted, you may not be able to resolve the situation or provide resources to mitigate the pain, but you can listen, be nice, and show you *care*! Sometimes that is all that is needed, just an ear to listen or a shoulder to lean on. You can provide that, can't you? In my fifty years of marriage, I have come to realize that we engage in trivializing when we are faced with layers of information or with scanty substantive matter. In such a situation, because nature abhors a vacuum, we tend to form opinions and paint imaginary pictures to fill the empty shelves with unsubstantiated facts or hearsay. Let it be clear that when we are trying to fill in the gaps in the presence of scanty or inadequate information, we find ourselves in an unfamiliar territory. At this juncture, we face the danger of negatively engaging by choosing to respond in one of three ways, as follows:

a. *Downplaying a situation* that may need serious attention.
b. *Getting excited* by magnifying or reading too much into a situation than is warranted, thereby jumping to conclusions, going overboard, and exaggerating the situation, making a mountain out of a molehill.
c. *Making hurtful remarks*, including statements that we can't take back. We then find ourselves in a bind, trying to clean up the mess or administering punishment that does not fit the crime. The results are devastating, to say the least. I have been there many times, and it's not funny!

In my observation of friends and associates through the years, I can attest that all three scenarios can bring negative consequences, such as loss of friendship, a sour or tasteless relationship, animosity, indifference, an unforgiving spirit, and a family feud. They can even lead to an estranged spouse. So, why experience these repercussions when all that you as a spouse need to do is to (a) pay more attention, (b) listen, (c) be nice, (d) reflect, and (e) evaluate the information at hand with an open mind. If you do not do these things, when the relationship is over you may hear yourself saying, "I wonder what happened?" or "I did not see it coming?" Really? Duh!

2. *Taking Each Other for Granted*

I asked several couples who have been married for at least fifteen years to name just one thing that has been helpful in building their relationship. All pointed to being nice and gracious toward one another, and not being shy about giving compliments or expressing appreciation toward their spouse for little and not so little things. Lack of appreciation discourages a mate from continuing to apply himself or herself and doing good things for the other spouse. Let's start by using the three magic words and phrases— "thank you," "please," and "I am sorry"— copiously. We should kindle the flame and keep the fire burning. We all like recognition and appreciation. Even God wants His children to praise Him!

3. *Teasing Each Other Mercilessly*

Humor is fun, but it should not be confused with teasing and making fun of another person, especially a spouse. Teasing and making fun can lead to irreparable damage and permanent scars. One young man said to me, "I really do not enjoy going out with friends with my spouse because she seems to enjoy making fun of me as if I am the dessert for the day." Well, familiarity breeds contempt! It is very easy to find yourself in this territory. Seek to get along! Study your spouse's likes and dislikes and know when to disengage your fun gear. None of us likes to feel uncomfortable. The Lord spent time admonishing His disciples and teaching them how to get along. Have fun together and laugh together, but not at each other. Be attentive and quickly pick up your partner's nonverbal cues of discomfort. Laugh at yourself, but don't confuse sarcasm with humor. Sarcasm isn't funny.

4. *Threatening Each Other with Ultimatums*

Refrain from using threats, period. Threatening a spouse with ultimatums is an intimidation tactic and the worst form of bullying. Ultimatums have no place in promoting intimacy in a marriage. Instead, ultimatums are destructive negative strategies used to bring the other mate into submission or compliance under duress. Ultimatums should be avoided at all costs. They play on the "zone of the unknown," just like the phenomenon that propels an individual from social drinking to bingeing on alcohol, a dangerous zone, such as playing with fire or playing Russian roulette. The latter is a lethal game of chance, whereby the participant spins the cylinder of a revolver loaded with one bullet, aims the muzzle at his head, and pulls the trigger, hoping not to blow his brains out. Well, the odds are fifty-fifty!

Assert Yourself without Compromising Your Moral Virtue

When your mate is upset or not agreeable about something, you should at least try to understand why your mate has a problem. Be calm, be vulnerable, be upfront, and have no hidden agenda. State the facts of your case, your views, or your opinion with honesty and integrity. You do not need to be ugly or dirty to get your point across. It is not what you say but *how* you say it that can be damaging to the relationship. Trust me, just one uncalculated threat or ultimatum may just push your spouse over the edge or cause his or her already thin rope to snap. Indeed, marriage is sweet, but it is not easy. It can be delicate and fragile. Given all the points above, it takes a great deal of effort to sustain a mutually fulfilling marital relationship. What is clear is that without Christ at the center of your marriage and without a viable culture of prayer to sustain the union, there is no hope of making it together.

No Room for "Me, Myself, and I"

In the context of the marital relationship, the opposite of nice is not only sour or ugly but also includes selfishness. When I do premarital counseling, I tell young people, "Please do not bother to get married until you are willing to die to self and put your mate before yourself." A major indicator of *selflessness* is demonstrated in the collective whole, "the us and ours" and "for both of us." Conversely, the narcissistic selfish posture is directed at looking out for "me, myself, and I." To put it succinctly, the focus is on "what is in it for me," the WIIFM radio station for airing one's self-interests and forgetting about the "we," "us," and "our" part of the story. That is sad! It takes a profound self-search and introspection to identify the bent or posture ruling the marriage relationship.

I have met several married friends who shared that they felt like strangers, or somewhat displaced and marginalized, in their own homes because of a selfish and controlling spouse. In some cases, this climate has opened the door for the afflicted mate to look for tender care outside the confines of marriage. I have heard others voice, "My mate treats the kids better than me." Being nice to your mate gives him or her a sense of belonging, a feeling that he or she is needed and wanted. The sense of belonging should not be trivialized. It is crucial in a marital relationship. A friend once said that before people fall in love with your rules and doctrine, they will be attracted by your warmth and friendliness (i.e., sociology should come before theology).

At the same time, not everyone who smiles means well. Many men and women have fallen prey to Ms. Phony or Mr. Nice Guy, who are nothing but wolves in sheep's clothing. They are smooth and sleek, but they are venomous snakes. They entice innocent and naïve souls with the guise of a smile and sweet talk. They have nothing substantive to offer and use only their charm as collateral. I wish I could say the phenomenon applies to naïve girls or single women only, but it also happens even to couples, married women and men, who leave their spouses and fall prey to these scoundrels who are up to no good. If being *nice for the wrong reasons* works out there, why not employ the strategy of being *nice and sweet for the right reasons* at home with your spouse and family? *Just be nice* to your spouse.

Song

'Tis so sweet to trust in Jesus,
Just to take Him at His word;
Just to rest upon His promise,
Just to know, "Thus saith the Lord."
I'm so glad I learned to trust Thee,
Precious Jesus, Savior, Friend;
And I know that Thou art with me;
Will be with me till the end.

—Louisa Stead

My Story

I had a friend who did not want to face up to any challenge. She would shy away from addressing conflict. When her mate mentioned his concerns to her, her sure response was "I am leaving you" or "I'm getting out of this marriage!" Lo and behold, one day her caring and patient husband got tired of her threats and granted her wish. He said, "Please pack all your belongings and *hit the road, Jackie*, once and for all. She went to the dark and unknown world she had been romanticizing and dreaming about. Meanwhile, he moved on, improving himself academically and professionally. He ultimately found the love of his life and never looked back. Unfortunately for his former wife, it was the opposite experience. She now regrets every adverse word she's ever uttered. She confessed to me, later, that she indeed said some ugly, demeaning things and exhibited a condescending spirit that was downright nasty. She said she really regrets all the threatening stunts she pulled on her spouse and that she is very sorry. Unfortunately, by the time she had this epiphany, it was too late to mend the relationship or reverse her decision.

A male friend, Greg, shared a similar situation involving him and his wife Kay. His wife had had a secret love affair with a tycoon, and all seemed well for her. Once Greg moved out, Kay's lover neither left his wife nor marry Kay as promised. The reality set in, but it was too late for Kay to make amends with her husband. Greg had moved on and was enjoying his peaceful and quiet life. Kay realized that life was not a bed of roses, as she anticipated it would be, and found that she could not even keep up with mortgage payments now that Greg had moved out. Mr. Nice Guy was cleaving to his wife and was not willing to rescue Kay. Unfortunately, spouses fall for this trap, kidding themselves that "It cannot happen to me!" Sad to say, there are countless similar stories out there. This phenomenon is not a male or female thing but a sin thing!

Last Word

It is crucial for couples to consciously create a sustainably kind culture devoid of selfishness. They must be nice to each other, care for each other, and stand ready and willing to help each other, instead of looking for what they will gain in return. We are admonished in Galatians 6:9–10 (NKJV), to "not grow weary while doing good. … As we have opportunity, let us do good to all, especially to those who are of the household of faith." Your noble gesture may not be reciprocated by your mate. In that case, you may get no encouragement but instead be faced with criticism, whining, and ungratefulness from the very person you are trying to help. You may hear innuendoes and want to retaliate. Be nice regardless of your spouse's response. What I am trying to emphasize here is, do not look for a thank-you or accolades all the time. Just be nice! Do it because it's the right thing to do. Emulate Jesus's love and His love for sinners, even His enemies. When you surrender your life and give your heart to the Lord, His love will flow through you and affect everything you do, as well as your attitude, perspective, and response toward life and people. "Let this mind be in you which was also in Christ Jesus" (Philippians 2:5 NKJV).

Pillar #15
Ministry of Marriage

Foundation

Rejoicing in hope, patient in tribulation, consistent in prayer.

—Romans 12:12. KJV

What Is a Marriage Contract vs. a Marriage Covenant?

Before I explicate the comparison of marriage to ministry, let me first address what marriage is all about, in terms of the notion of a marriage *covenant* vs. a marriage *contract*. I was impressed to share the distinction Pastor Marvin Brown made in his address at a ceremony for the renewal of wedding vows in Cape Town, South Africa, in 2013.

1. *Marriage Covenant*

    According to Pastor Brown, marriage is a covenant and not a contract. A covenant is made between God and His people. A marriage covenant is permanent, a *blood bond of life and death!* This is where the phrase "till death do us part" comes from. Thus, a covenant is permanent and unchangeable, and God Himself is the underwriter or guarantor of the marriage covenant.

2. *Marriage Contract*

    A contract is made between two parties and is temporal and changeable, depending on the behavior of those who enter the deal. A contract basically says: "If you keep your end of the deal, I'll keep mine. But the moment I don't feel like you're keeping up your end of the bargain, the deal is off! I'm out of it! The contract is canceled or annulled by the state—the guarantor of the contract.

How Is Marriage Like Ministry?

Marriage is like ministry in that it requires a bond and fellowship, an intimate covenant, between the couple and Jesus Christ. Furthermore, marriage requires a new set of ethical codes to govern its existence, just as joining the church fellowship requires a higher moral standard of the set rules to abide by. For instance, married couples may have never seen a Bible school or even walked the corridors or matriculated in a seminary, but when entering matrimony, couples instantly become ministerial students, enrolled in a seminary, Bible college, or Bible university from which they will not graduate until death do them part or Jesus Christ appears in the skies to take His bride, the church, home to glory. Three phases of human existence attest to this fact.

1. *What happens when lovers decide to get married?* Those who want their union to be blessed in a church setting, even though they never stepped inside the doors of a sanctuary, run around looking for a church and a man of God—a member of the clergy or a priest—to bless their marriage at the altar.

2. *What happens when the baby is born?* Couples take the child to church to be blessed, and the entire village, along with family and friends, aunts and uncles, cousins, and grandparents, comes to witness the child's blessing. The idea is to dedicate the child before a cloud of witnesses. Based on an African proverb, it takes a whole village to raise a child. So, the villagers, friends, and family are the cloud of witnesses, proclaiming and embracing the mandate to be their brother's keeper.

3. *What happens when a person dies?* Similarly, at death, some families take the body to a church for a celebration of the deceased's life and for burial rites. Even if a person never connected with Jesus before, the family respectfully takes the departed to church, where he or she belonged in the first place.

Thus, it is crucial to view the members of a marriage as coexisting and interacting in a form of a ministry. Just like any ministry on the face of this earth, marriage, among other things, demands a set of specific characteristics and foci, as follows:

a. for its existence in all phases of life, as explicated above;
b. for relevance in the community; and
c. for cultivating an intimate relationship with Jesus Christ.

This pillar will focus on the crucial traits that are part of any functional ministry—faith, giving, fellowship, worship and praise, service, forgiveness, and prayer—and how these traits relate to the ministry of marriage.

Faith Ministry in Marriage

Faith is at the core of God's ministry because "without faith it is impossible to please Him" (Hebrews 11:6 KJV). Likewise, marriage is a walk of faith. Every step of the marital journey thrives on faith.

1. *Faith in God* is based on mutually trusting your heavenly Father and relying on His wisdom to guide your marriage day by day, to eternal glory.

2. *Faith in yourself*—Have confidence as a wife or a husband to execute the commission and wait until He comes again. God gave each one of you, as members of the body of Christ, His enabling power to stand and remain faithful through difficult times and through the trials and tribulations of life.

3. *Faith in your spouse*—Embrace and believe in your spouse's role, that is, the wife as a helpmate, best friend, and confidant, encouraging the husband as head of the household, trusting in his strength and leadership abilities. Have faith when solving problems that arise together as a team, and cleave to your spouse, not allowing any third party to interfere.

4. *Faith in your family*—Invest all you have in your family, your support system, and do not lavish your resources on other gods. When things fall apart, all you have left is family. So, think twice before you sow your oats in the wilderness!

5. *Faith in each other's love*—Marriage is the only institution that is likened to the love Christ has for, and His relationship with, His church. Husbands are admonished to love and cherish their wives as Christ loves His church. Wives are commissioned to submit to their husbands as in Christ, and both the wife and husband are to

submit to each other. The key dynamic here is that couples need to be *loving*, need to *submit* to their mates, and need to be vigilant no matter what the devil throws at them. It does not matter how handsome "Mr. Six-Pack" or how gorgeous "Ms. Designer" is; he or she is not your spouse. Admire and care for the one God gave you and you will be rewarded by your Father in heaven.

6. *Faith in each other*—In the context of marriage, faith in each other is demonstrated by shunning acts of indiscretion. Believe in each other's love and show it by coming home to "drink from your own well," avoiding the stagnant, polluted, and poisonous waters out there that you do not know. Come home and quench your thirst by drinking from your own well. Why spill the water of your springs into the streets by having sex with just anyone? You should reserve it for yourselves. Never share it with strangers (Proverbs 5:15–17). Thus, be *faithful* to each other and keep the marriage bed undefiled. This is the true test of character and integrity, a virtue that God honors. Christ demands purity from His bride, the church.

Giving in the Ministry of Marriage

I had a discussion with several couples who have been married for over forty years to find out what one thing has kept their marriage alive, viable, and thriving through the years. I was amazed that all, in many ways, attributed their longevity and mutually fulfilling relationship to the giving of self, which was at the center of it all, and which entails all aspects of giving. Giving is defined as investing time, talents, and treasure for the betterment of the family and not chasing after other gods (i.e., sordid affairs outside the confines of holy matrimony).

1. *Time*—Invest quality time in each other and the family at large. This is the responsibility of each spouse, no exceptions. Couples must find the time and not use a job as an alibi for not spending time with each other.

2. *Talents*—The spiritual gifts of the members are intended to edify the church family. The focus for giving your talents is the advancement of the gospel. In the context of marriage permanence,

the spiritual gifts of spouses should be used to edify the family circle and maintain a mutually fulfilling and enjoyable marriage.

3. *Treasure*—Commitment to support and provide for the needs of the family is an honorable duty that God does not wink at. Give until it hurts, until you are "pressed down, shaken together, and running over" (Luke 6:38 NKJV). This includes making sacrifices, which characterizes the virtue of giving in marriage. That is, give unselfishly, without asking WIIFM, or seeking recognition or accolades, or having a pay-me-back attitude. Just give love unconditionally.

Ministry of Fellowship in Marriage

The essence of belonging and learning to get along with people of other cultures, creeds, and political beliefs must not be trivialized. No doubt, evangelism brings people to Christ, but love, belonging, and fellowship help people stay within the church family and feel part of the body of Christ. If fellowship and a sense of belonging are lacking, doctrine alone cannot make the church members feel at home and connected. Fellowship is the "Powerball" of faith in play.

Ministry of Worship and Praise in Marriage

Adopting an attitude of gratitude, praising the Lord in all things, and having an attitude of contentment at any stage in your marriage is reflective of one's character. It's easy to worship and offer praises to the Lord when things are warm, fuzzy, and glossy, but worshipping the Lord amid challenges or turbulence is the ultimate manifestation of real worship. The Bible gives account of several times when God's people suffered deadly consequences for their discontentment and for murmuring against other believers or the appointed leadership. For instance, Miriam was stricken with leprosy for her animosity and criticism of Zipporah. Moses had to pray for her healing and restoration (Numbers 12:1–13). God opened the ground so that it would swallow those who rebelled and murmured against God's servant Moses (Numbers 26:10–11). Likewise, in the church family, as in marriage, murmuring and discontentment can destroy peace.

Ministry of Service in Marriage

Compassion has *eyes, feet, hands, arms,* and *legs,* especially when it comes to those who have no capacity or potential to return a favor or give back. Compassion and hospitality are a conduit for attracting angels to your home. A friend once made a profound observation of what he called "Christian schizophrenia," saying it is ironic that certain Christians, while professing to be servants of God, do not want to be Christlike when it comes to service. He remarked, "Christians sometimes are slack in embracing the *servitude posture of Christ.* They want to identify only with the *lordship of Christ.*" If he is wrong, then there would be no proliferation of the gospel of prosperity, bickering about position, or self-serving attitudes among the body of believers and family of God. Couples, therefore, should focus on service and serving, in-reach and outreach evangelism. Instead of being jealous and faultfinding, couples should embrace each other's strengths and use their strengths and gifts of the spirit to minister to each other, edifying the body of Christ, the family, and the community. In-reach is crucial but is not sufficient to quicken the steps of Jesus Christ and hasten His resolve to come back soon to take us to glory. "This gospel of the kingdom will be preached in all the world as a witness to all nations, and then the end will come" (Matthew 24:14 NKJV). "Go ye therefore, and teach all the nations, baptizing them in the name of the Father, and the Son and the Holy Spirit, teaching them to observe all things whatsoever I have commanded you; and lo, I am with you, even to the end of the world" (Matthew 28:19–20 NKJV). "But he that shall endure unto the end, the same shall be saved" (Matthew 24:13 NKJV).

Ministry of Forgiveness in Marriage

The ministry of forgiveness includes, first, an understanding of God's justice, of the penalty for the transgression of His law, of His unfailing love for us sinners, and of His grace and mercy, all of which culminated at Calvary, where His only begotten Son, Jesus Christ, was crucified to pay the penalty for sin, so that we could live, thus redeeming and reconciling us unto His Father and our God (John 3:16). Second, it includes the understanding that we all have sinned and come short of the glory of God (Romans 3:23 KJV). Third, it entails the understanding that sin is offensive to God and the knowledge that there is no sin that is greater than the other. In heaven's eyes, sin is sin. The notion of categorizing sin as either small or big is a fallacy and the devil's pacifier at best. Fourth, it involves the understanding that God loves sinners like you and me, including your enemies or those you dislike for whatever reason. Fifth, it entails that knowledge that God can forgive us of our sins, but we must acknowledge them, confess them, humble ourselves before Him, ask for forgiveness, and repent of our wicked ways. He will hear us and even heal our land (2 Chronicles 7:14), and make our enemies be at peace with us, if we follow His will (Proverbs 16:7).

If God can forgive you, who do you think you are to withhold forgiveness when your spouse and others have wronged you? The next time you find yourself holding a grudge against those who offended you, either by spreading malicious rumors about you, openly or subtly discriminating against you, subjecting you to stifling criticism, hostility, or even venomous words, or being jealous of you, remember that those who offend you are all God's children and He loves them all as He loves you. So, what should you do? Let them go unpunished? Yes, do not avenge yourself, because vengeance is God's (Romans 12:19). The Lord commands you to do three things: *forgive* those who have offended you, *pray* for them, and *love* them (Matthew 5:43–44). In analyzing the Lord's Prayer, we find that Jesus tells us that God forgives us of our sins in direct proportion to how much *we forgive* those who trespass against us (Matthew 6:12). Remember, God loves all of us; He died for you and your enemies equally. I know, it is a sobering epiphany and a humbling thought. Try forgiveness. If you do, you will develop into a mature Christian. You will experience joy and the peace that passeth understanding, as well as immeasurable growth as a person and a spouse.

In the context of marriage, we should remember that the ability to forgive is a virtue and strength, not a weakness. We do not forgive from a position of weakness but from one of strength. This posture calls for dying to self, burying the hatchet, seeking deliverance from strongholds of grudges and animosity. This does not mean the offender does not have a part to play. In fact, the offender must surrender, confess, and seek forgiveness from the person he or she has wronged before asking forgiveness from God (Matthew 5:23–24). A dear friend once encouraged me when I was going through a rough time at work. She said, "Forgive them,

Nozipho, out of strength and not weakness. The essence of forgiveness is saying, 'I choose to give up the chance to revenge or harm an enemy, when the time, place, opportunity, and resources to retaliate are at my disposal.'" Forgiveness is a choice!

Ministry of Prayer in Marriage

Prayer to a couple is a formidable weapon to defeat our common enemy, the devil. If we neglect to pray for each other, we will miss out on connecting to, harnessing, and leveraging the heavenly arsenal to defeat the enemy. Our bodies are the temple of the Lord, and God considers the temple or church a house of prayer. Prayer to the church is the bread and butter of its existence, contributing to the direction and growth of the body of Christ. Likewise, the marriage relationship cannot flourish without the nutrients of prayer and the Holy Spirit. As discussed in pillar #5, prayer has several ingredients that bring joy and sustenance to the body of Christ and family:

1. Prayer is a powerful love letter to God.
2. Prayer does not change God; it changes us to align with His will.
3. Prayer does not bring God down to our level but lifts us up, so we can be close to God.
4. Prayer is intimate communication between us and God. It is like kissing God's face.
5. Prayer affords couples the privilege of interceding for family members.
6. Prayer is a two-way street, allowing us to speak to God and allowing God to speak to us in return. When we talk to God in prayer, we must listen to his voice responding to us.

"My Brother's Keeper" Model

To be one's brother's keeper is to participate in the ministry of evangelism inside (*for retention*) and outside (*for membership growth*) the church family, for several reasons. For instance, if the house next door is infested with rats or roaches (*inside problem*), this can become a problem for the neighbors. If not addressed, the problem will spread to adjacent homes in the neighborhood. Similarly, the church cannot be nonchalant and do nothing about things impacting families in the community because the church and the community cannot be separated. What impacts the families, good or bad, can taint or improve the behaviors of the church members. Viable in-reach and outreach programs are beneficial to the growth of the church family, and to *depopulating hell*. Like in a married couple's relationship, both in-reach and outreach programs are viable ministries and coexist in a symbiotic relationship for the nourishment and development of the church family. The aim of soul-winning should include both activities. Outreach adds to the relevance and existence of the church in the community, whereas in-reach addresses retention. There are many competing attractions out there that pose a great challenge and threat to retaining members, especially for the millennials. Couples are also battling with the same underlying challenges that face church families, namely, stability, rebellion, and the quest to serve other gods. Prayer seems to be the only powerful weapon in the arsenal of couples and the church that is effectively against the common enemy, the devil.

Song

Does Jesus care when my heart is pained
Too deeply for mirth or song;
As the burdens press, and cares distress,
And the way grows weary and long?

Chorus:

Oh yes, he cares—I know He cares!
His heart is touched with my grief;
When the days are weary, the long nights are dreary,
I know my Savior cares.

—Frank E. Graeff

My Story

For about ten consecutive years, I had the privilege of leading the family life ministry at my church. I found myself scraping for ideas to keep the department viable and dynamic given the confines of our meager resources and tight budget. It is puzzling that an institution as old as marriage is so misunderstood. Divorce trends show that the marriage institution is in trouble even among believers. Current trends in the divorce statistics in the USA reveal that first marriages have a 50 percent chance of ending in divorce. The odds are greater for second marriages, with a 67 percent likelihood of ending in divorce, and even higher for third marriages, at 73 percent (Banschick). Hence, "Marriage is a counter cultural act of throwaway society" (Doherty).

I knew that I had to think outside the box and dig deep in my own pocket to make something happen and to prepare for the awesome responsibility of heading up the ministry. First, I enrolled at Seventh-day Adventist Theological Seminary, an Andrews University summer program, as a self-sponsored student for three years to equip myself with the requisite biblical knowledge and necessary skills. It paid off. I graduated with a Marriage and Family Graduate Certificate. Second, I presented a comprehensive program to target married couples while serving the church family as well. It was crucial that the intervention plan meet the needs of families in the church.

Figure 15.1 illustrates (1) the extent of the commitment the church made in investing in intervention programs for families within the church and (2) how these programs were structured based on a needs assessment.

FIGURE 15.1 Family life enrichment programs framework (FEPF)

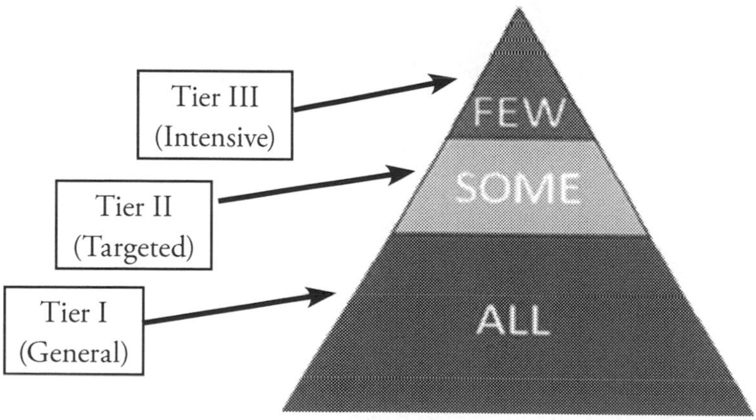

Three-tier framework adapted from the Ohio Integrative System Model (OISM).

Free diagram available at Businessball.com.

Note: The three-tiered model is a popular one that has been used in educational settings to target schoolwide student interventions, such as those created by the Ohio Department of Education. However, the framework has been adapted in *Pillars of Joy in Marriage* to explain intervention programs in the context of the church's family programs, which were established to provide assessment-based interventions to meet the needs of various groups, old people, young people, married couples, singles, men, women, and so forth.

The impetus was to provide relevant innovative activities to enrich the church family beyond the pulpit and strengthen the quality of social and spiritual relationships categorically. Among other things, I spearheaded church cruises for the church family and organized successful marriage retreats, read-a-thons, and symposia for couples on topics related to family dynamics, such as the differences between men and women, how to manage conflict, dealing with anger, pillow talk, boundaries, marriage vampires, the Christ-centered marriage, and coping with rebellious children.

Tier I—Church-Wide Enrichment Programs
These are inclusive church-wide enrichment programs designed to capture about 80–90 percent of the church family. At this level, programs are proactive for retention, teaching, and building a culture of belonging, and designed to address most members in the church. Hence, they *target all categories*, married, singles, and young people, based on assessments drawn from a collection and need analysis of data, generated from questionnaires or inventories of adults, men, women, young people, and senior citizens. Thus, type of programs planned and implemented included the following:

a.   church-wide picnics
b.   group Bible bowls
c.   mentoring programs
d.   family cruises
e.   symposia addressing topics such as healthy lifestyle, nutrition, and obesity.

Tier II—Targeted Group Enrichment Programs

These are core programs tailored to the unique or specific needs of some group members in the church, about 5–10 percent of the members. The programs are highly efficient and rapid-response, targeting a specific cadre of members with similar needs and interests, such as married couples, singles, senior citizens, widows, or young adults who often fall through the cracks in the scheme of traditional programming. Thus, type of programs planned and implemented included the following:

a. a *book read-a-thon*, with selected books to read as a group on specific topics
b. *guest speakers* to address selected topics to target a group need
c. symposia on selected topics, such as the differences between men and women, forgiveness, effective communication, conflict resolution, pillow talk, finances, dealing with difficult youth, and dating
d. couples' getaway retreats and singles' retreats
e. a family cruise, a singles' cruise, and couples' getaway dinners
f. programs and getaways for senior citizens.

Tier III—Intensive Individual or Small-Group Interventions

Intervention programs at this level are tailor-made for a significant group of people, 1–5 percent of the church family, who require more intense and durable counseling sessions addressing a specific need. These interventions may include one-on-one individual counseling sessions and referral for professional intervention as needed. Types of interventions include the following:

a. divorce and marriage recovery
b. substance or chemical dependency
c. spousal abuse
d. grief recovery sessions.

The church family is an extension of the outpatient clinic or rehabilitation facility, although it dispenses no medication, save intimate spiritual conditioning, strength, hope, unconditional love, and a support system, addressing multiple conditions and different types of persons.

For some people, the church family is all they have. My former church, Ephesus SDA Church, in Columbus, Ohio, has so many professionals skilled in various disciplines who are equipped to conduct seminars and be mentors that most needs can be met internally. Granted, in some cases, outside referral may be necessary based on critical needs. Like the church, the family relationship must aim to build upon a solid foundation.

Last Word

Whether we admit it or not, marriage is ministry. Every challenge in marriage seems to test the core of our faith and joy. If we believe this, we will be more inclined to take our ailing hearts to God, the Great Physician, in prayer. When couples embrace the ministry of marriage as a perspective, they will spend time on their knees praying for one another instead of bickering, gossiping, judging each other, and blaming each other when things go wrong. There is no critically ill spiritual condition too hard or too complicated for Jesus to solve or heal. There are no scars so deep, or wounds so infected, or relationships so dysfunctional that He cannot mend. There is no condition, paralysis of character, devil-possessed mind, spirit of infidelity, broken heart, or disease of neglect, rejection, or betrayal that God cannot restore to 100 percent functional ability. My God is a divine heart specialist and surgeon. Our job is to ask Him to heal us. After King David sinned and planned a perfect cover-up, he offered a prayer of repentance and cried: "Create in me a clean heart, Oh God, and renew a steadfast spirit within me" (Psalm 51:10 NKJV). Later, David is described as *a man after God's own heart* (1 Samuel 13:14). Wow! Take all your cares to God in prayer. Confess your sins with a contrite heart. The core of sin is not in the act but in the failure to confess the sin, repent, and seek forgiveness. There is hope for you and me too if we confess our sins. He is faithful and just to forgive us of our sin (1 John 1:9).

$\mathcal{P}$illar # 16
$\mathcal{A}$chieving $\mathcal{G}$rowth amid $\mathcal{S}$etbacks

Foundation

The darkest hour is before dawn!

—Anonymous

All marriages, without exception, go through a season of turbulence. The issue is not whether a couple will experience a bump, turbulence, or a storm, but whether the couple is equipped to deal with the storm and emerge victorious and still united or in pieces. It does not matter whether the storm occurs as the result of our own doing, our own foolishness, or misfortune; the storm will come whether we are ready or not ready. It's a matter of when, not if, the storm will come. This section addresses some conditions that can help us deal with the impending storms of life by (1) understanding the nature of storms, (2) having the right perspective when going through the storm, (3) dealing with the aftermath, and (4) achieving growth after the setback.

Understanding the Nature of Storms

1. Storms differ in their nature, the devastation they cause, and the response they deserve.
2. Storms are unpredictable; they can be of different forms and hit different places of the world in varying degrees or magnitude.
3. Certain storms are identified by names, so we can remember and differentiate one from another and the devastating impact on each place they hit. For example, Hurricane Andrew hit Florida and devastated parts of the Caribbean. Catherine crippled Louisiana, more than other places in the United States. Sandy hit the New Jersey coast

and New York. Hurricane Demonia devastated Swaziland in Southern Africa, leaving the infrastructure debilitated and killing some people.

4. Storms are not constant; they come and go at different times. Therefore, remain joyful, knowing that this too shall pass. Likewise, Satan assails you in different forms. If he cannot bring you down through your spouse, he will try using your children, and if that fails, he will hit you with health issues. He uses anything and everything in his power to steal your joy.

5. Storms, such as a death in the family, come whether people are prepared or not.

6. Some storms are short-lived, lasting a few hours or a few days, and others seem to take forever. When you have an argument with your mate, understand that it's just a bad day, not a bad marriage.

7. Dealing with the aftermath and devastation of a storm can be overwhelming and disillusioning to the displaced inhabitants. Likewise, cleaning up after a stormy situation in a marriage can be difficult and test one's character.

Having the Right Perspective in the Storm

Dealing with the aftermath of a storm requires a perspective that helps you create an environment where healing, laughter, and love can thrive. The same applies following a setback, also addressed in this pillar. Most importantly, remember the following principles:

1. Stay on board with Jesus no matter how scary the situation. Do not jump ship and dive into the sea of the unknown.

2. Call on Jesus, the Master of storms. He will quiet the storm in His time.

3. Pray through the storm, not just before a storm. You may be in the storm, or may be heading into a storm, or may have just passed the storm. Whatever the case may be, remember that you are not alone, even if it feels like you are.

4. Storms come and go. Brace yourself and pray for strength as you prepare for another storm to hit you.

5. There is hope after a storm. Most marriages are stronger after they have been through a storm. Your storms can turn to occasions for praise.

6. Assure each other that you are in this relationship together for the long haul. Encourage one another.

7. Celebrate each other's strengths instead of dwelling on your negative or weak traits. Different temperaments can prove to be useful and play complementary roles to one another if they are viewed as strengths and channeled appropriately.

8. Stay connected to your prayer lifeline and your faith in Jesus Christ. This will pull you through hard times. Develop a slogan that will kick in when the storm hits, when things get rough, such as *Divorce is not an option!*

9. Don't leave your partner's side during the storm. This is a time when you need each other most for survival and must draw from each other's strength.

Dealing with the Aftermath

How you deal with the aftermath is a matter of perspective. If not handled appropriately, the aftermath may present a crisis that could cause a more paralyzing and a devastating effect than the storm itself. If you have the right perspective, some storms can turn out to be a blessing, leading to growth and praise. This may sound like a paradox, and yet such a thing has happened in the lives of many people amid different circumstances. For example, the story of Joseph recorded in the book of Genesis, chapter 50, is a classic example of the aftermath of a storm turning into an unfathomable blessing and praise. Joseph was sold as a slave by his jealous and resentful brothers and found himself in a strange land contending with new language and cultural mores. He was later accused by Potiphar's devious wife of attempted rape, a crime that he did not commit, and was subsequently imprisoned indefinitely. Yet God had a different plan for Joseph. He went from being a prisoner to prime minister of Egypt, and he saved his family and the people of Egypt during a severe famine. Later, reflecting on his ordeal in relation to his current station in life, Joseph declared, "You intended to harm me, but God intended it for good to accomplish what is now being done, the saving of many lives" (Genesis 50:20 NIV).

In the context of marital storms, different couples may react differently when presented with the aftermath. One couple's life may be turned upside down, shattered like glass and weathered like grass, but another couple might seize the experience as an opportunity to regroup, reflect on what needs to be done, and rebuild. The latter may expend their energy making things right, cleaning up the mess, confronting issues head-on, scraping and scratching to find amicable solutions to rebuild the marriage, and resettling, deliberately and intentionally fighting for the marriage to work and salvaging the pieces. Conversely, the former type of couple may feel a sense of hopelessness and choose to give up and/or run away from the situation by opting out of the marriage and entering other relationships, hence leaving things hanging with no solution to the current problem. A pastor once said, referring to those who go from one church to another (*church hoppers*), "When you run from a situation, you are taking the *same old unchanged* you to the new church or relationship." So, my advice to either type of couple is to call for backup—Jesus. Jesus can help you comb through the debris and pick up what can be salvaged. Pray, clean up, and rebuild your marriage. Choose to *forgive, love, and laugh* again. Rest on God's promises: "I can do all things through Christ who strengths me" (Philippians 4:13 NKJV). Yes, you can, through Christ Jesus, who enables you to fortify your mind with praise and trust in Him. He will take your marriage to new heights and help you achieve things you thought you could not do. Go for it. Your marriage is worth fighting for. Some relationships have risen to higher ground after a storm. When Jesus is invited to the marital journey, intimacy that has corroded and feelings that have decomposed can be resurrected. Indifference can turn into love, and love can be sweeter than before. Consider the miracle Jesus performed of water turning into wine at the wedding at Cana (John 2:1-11).

The main reasons for failure to deal with the aftermath of storms in a marriage are (1) an inability to navigate the bumps or weather the storms in the marriage experience because of a lack of connection with Christ; (2) failure to build an intimate relationship with Jesus, the master of storms, and the God of perfect peace; (3) failure to follow up with, reestablish friendship with, and reconnect with one's spouse after a storm; and (4) the presence of noise that makes the spouse unable to hear or see the efforts the other spouse is making to salvage the situation. The latter can take the form of stubbornness, or a quest for a new thrill (exploring green pastures), instead of expending energy to address the issues in the current marriage. If truth be told, *serial thrill-seekers* can attest to the fact that a thrill is not sustainable. It is a quick fix and temporarily lulls the mind—a pseudo peacemaker! It may work for a while, until one encounters a speed bump or turbulence occurs in the new relationship. Then what? Seeking one thrill after another gets a couple nowhere. Rather, it has devastating results that may prove worse than the initial storm in the long run.

Achieving Growth after a Setback

There is no doubt that life's storms have the potential to either make or break a marriage (the result being either posttraumatic stress or growth). At the crossroads of hardship, we are presented with a choice. One couple may choose to see a cup half full, and an opportunity to learn, grow, and rebuild a better life after a storm. Conversely, another couple may see the cup as half empty and allow the situation to destroy the relationship beyond repair. How you deal with the aftermath is a matter of perspective. Setbacks are inevitable, but misery or growth is a choice. There are several lessons to be learned about life storms, which we would never learn were it not for the situations that shake our very existence. Some of these themes are discussed by Victor E. Frankl, best-selling author of *Man's Search for Meaning*, in his book *Psychotherapy and Existentialism* (1967). The lessons relate to the following:

(a) *Paradoxical intent.* The concept is based on the notion that what one purports to do can produce an inverse or opposite energy. For example, when one plans to stay up all night and study, he or she tends to fall asleep sooner, in a heartbeat. Conversely, when one is determined to sleep longer, one finds that he or she stays awake on little or no sleep. This irony of opposing outcomes is reflected in the story of Peter's denial of Christ, three times, after he had promised never to leave or deny Him. How many spouses find themselves in the corridors of the divorce court, when they had sworn "until death do us part"? How many times do we hear people saying that if such-and-such were to happen to them, they would die? Somehow, they seem to find an enduring strength they did not even know they had to rebuild and keep going on. The apostle Paul agrees with Frankl in Romans 7:15 (NLT): "I don't really understand myself, for I want to do what is right, but I don't do it. Instead, I do what I hate." This is the reason why couples need to continuously pray and seek God's will and direction for the marriage to thrive. Jesus has power to restore a broken relationship.

(b) *Freedom to choose one's attitude toward circumstances.* According to Victor Frankl, an individual chooses his or her attitude toward life by either (1) *detaching from reality* or (2) *rejecting himself or herself* based on the awareness of who he or she really is. The person may not like what he or she sees and thus reject himself or herself. Judas, when he realized he had "sold an innocent man," Jesus Christ, instead of repenting committed suicide and ended his miserable life (Luke 21:1–6). Peter on the other hand, after realizing he betrayed his allegiance to Christ, went back to the garden of Gethsemane, prayed, confessed his sin, and sought forgiveness from God. Both men committed similarly egregious offenses against the Lord, but they had different perspectives and with different outcomes. What made the difference in these diametrically opposed outcomes? The answer is (1) freedom to choose, (2) the right attitude in dealing with the aftermath, (3) a willingness to confess sin and praying for forgiveness, (4) seeking to connect with Jesus Christ, and (5) a desire to resolve and restore a broken relationship. Thus, detaching from reality or rejecting oneself is optional. Similarly, if you as a spouse have sinned, betraying and violating your spouse's trust or boundaries, be like Peter. Confess your sin, pray, ask for forgiveness, repent, and reconnect with the Lord and your mate. "Come to Me, all you who labor and are heavy laden, and I will give you rest" (Matthew 13:28 NKJV) and the "peace that passeth understanding" (Philippians 4:7 KJV).

(c) *The ability to find meaning in life through suffering.* Frankl identifies humankind's innate ability to overcome challenges by transcending ugly or painful circumstances and achieve growth. Nevertheless, the *process* of growing or overcoming is not complete without the Lord in the mix. An individual by himself or herself cannot achieve this kind of growth without Christ. God asks, "Can an Ethiopian change the color of his skin? Can a leopard take away his spots? Neither can you start doing good for you have always done evil" (Jeremiah 13:23 NLT). *No way,* God says. Only the Lord can change bad circumstances and cause them to work for our growth. "God causes everything to work together for the good of those who love the Lord and are called according to His purpose for them" (Romans 28:3 NLT). The Holy Spirit touches our attitude, causing us to look up and seek Jesus. He teaches us, convicts us, directs us, and guides us to the path of righteousness. Jesus and only Jesus is the active agent of change in humankind's existence and circumstances. Sometimes, when we look back after the effect, we come to realize that the very painful experiences we went through were designed to make us *stronger or better individuals* and to help us learn lessons about life that we would not have learned in times of ease.

(d) *Freedom of the will to rise above adverse situations.* Adverse circumstances are inevitable, but misery is a choice. Even when we fall, we can choose to wallow in self-pity or rise. Nelson Mandela once commented, "A man should not be judged by how low he falls, but by how high he rises after he had fallen!" Michelle Obama, in her speech at the 2016 Democratic Convention in Philadelphia, said, "When critics of my husband go low, Barack goes high!" At another time, in one of her speeches, she said, "The office of the presidency does not change who you are but reveals who you are." The inherent positive effect of the storms of life is that storms tend to shine a bright spotlight on our soul, revealing what we really are. Similarly, in the context of the marital relationship, storms do not change us but reveal our character, resolve, and tenacity as manifested in the way we respond to circumstances, the way we deal with adversity, and the path we choose to follow at the crossroads. That is why in *Pillars of Joy in Marriage* I have advocated the importance of developing a Christ-centered marriage that connects us to the source of power and gives us the moral fiber to overcome adversity. Jesus gives us tenacity and endurance, including joy in tribulation. He said: "I am the way, the truth and the life" (John 14:6 NKJV). Hence, without Christ in our marriage, there is no life.

King David, following the storm of Bathsheba, plotted to kill Uriah, Bathsheba's husband, and orchestrated a cover-up, but once the prophet Nathaniel pointed out David's sin, David responded with deep sorrow for his transgression, poured his heart out to the Lord, confessed his sin, and prayed for forgiveness. God heard his prayers. Thus, he earned the esteem of God, despite his imperfections, because of his contrite heart. God hates sin, but He loves a sinner who understands that he needs a Savior, who confesses, and who repents of his sinful ways. Such should be our posture when we encounter challenges in our marital relationship.

Song

When peace like a river attendeth my way,
When sorrows like sea billows roll—
Whatever my lot, Thou hast taught me to say,
It is well, it is well with my soul.

<u>Chorus:</u>

It is well with my soul,
It is well, it is well with my soul.

—Horatio G. Spafford

My Story

Obviously, my husband and I, like any couple, have experienced storms in our fifty-year-long marriage. Some were caused by our foolishness, or poor judgment, but others were caused by unforeseen or naturally occurring circumstances. Looking back, I think the worst storm we ever experienced came as a shock. It caught us unprepared and unassuming, and rocked our existence. It left debris everywhere. We did not know what to do or where to start when cleaning up in the aftermath. We would have lost our minds were it not for our strong faith and holding on to the promises of the God of peace. "I will never leave you or forsake you." Jeremiah 33:3 (NKJV) reads, "Call me I will answer you, and show you great and mighty things which you do not know." Surely, we would have perished in the storm, or become spiritually depleted and emotionally drained. But we survived to tell the tale. (As I recount the storm, I will refrain from using real names so as to protect the integrity of the organization and the players involved in the episode.)

I had just completed my doctoral degree in educational policy and leadership, with a major in administration and a cognate area in quantitative research methodology, at the Ohio State University, which equipped me to work in institutional development. I was on cloud nine and was preparing to apply to the Immigration and Naturalization Service (INS) to convert my I-20 F1 visa to an H1 professional visa, and then embark on a career of interest.

Note: I needed to file with INS for change of status before the student visa expired. As I was contemplating filing the necessary paperwork with INS, I received a telephone call that changed my life. It was a call from a US-based organization offering me an administrative post at an affiliate college in South Africa. I requested time to think about it. I told my professor and was pleased about the prospects of being relocated, especially because he was retiring and would not be there to help me navigate the system in the United States. Obviously, I abandoned regularizing my immigration status to work in the United States, while at the same time preparing to relocate back to South Africa. I was now eager to return home and serve in my country, so I accepted the job offer. I was promised that a truck would come to pick up our belongings, and that these would be shipped for us. A hotel had been booked for an overnight stay in Washington, DC, and our airline tickets would be delivered to the hotel. We said all our goodbyes to our friends and were sitting on boxes waiting for the truck. The truck never came on the appointed date. To this day, there has been no follow-up or explanation as to why the organization reneged on its offer. All my calls were avoided. My husband and I were devastated and felt betrayed. But why had this happened?

To cut a long story short, I interviewed for an administrative job in Columbus, Ohio, and got an offer, pending the issuance of my employment visa. When I appeared before the immigration officer, he informed me that I was now out of status and facing deportation. I explained to the officer the dilemma I was facing, saying that I could not prepare to naturalize and change my immigration status to stay in the United States while simultaneously preparing to go back to South Africa, since these were two competing activities. Meanwhile, my visa had expired while I was sitting on boxes waiting to travel. The officer understood the irony but warned me *not* to take any job until I had a work permit. He then assured me that I would not be deported, because I had come to the immigration office and they did not have to go find me. He added, "Lady, it's going to be an uphill climb and a long-protracted process because your visa has fallen out of status." He advised me to find an immigration lawyer to file the initial paperwork on my behalf for the change of status, and thereafter apply for a work permit to enable me to work in the United States. The process took over a year before I finally got a work permit. I suffered an onset of high blood pressure and almost fell into depression. Prayer, and my encouraging and supportive husband and friends, spared me from that fate.

God heard and rewarded our prayers. My husband and I survived that storm. Both of us had fulfilling careers in the United States, with no regrets! We came out stronger together following that episode twenty-six years ago. No doubt, we realize now it was truly the hand of God that guided the events. The devil meant evil, but God meant good (Genesis 50:20). We are both retired and have happily relocated back home on our own terms, enjoying every minute of every day. Our families on both sides are overjoyed to have us back home. The icing on the cake was that when we were on a romantic getaway in Sandton, Johannesburg, celebrating our forty-ninth wedding anniversary, we bumped into a dear friend of ours we had not seen for over twenty-five years. She was on a business trip and had checked in to the same hotel, only to find that our suites were adjacent. Oh boy, we had a halleluiah time! She took us out for dinner, and at that time she gave us the inside scoop and shared why the deal had fallen through twenty-six years prior. I could not believe what she told us, that resistance had come from those on the South African side of the deal. The US organization really wanted the best for the institution, but the leadership at the college wanted to maintain the status quo and would not allow fresh blood, or a potential maverick who might shake things up and move things around. Wow! We finally got the clarification *in God's time*. We had closure on the matter and are now at perfect peace with all the players. So, some storms are bigger and longer-lasting than others, but with the Lord on your side, there will be no regrets because He makes your enemies your footstools, and helps you to regroup, rebuild, and come out victorious, better and stronger than you were before the storm. The onus is on you to choose to be bitter or better in the aftermath.

Last Word

My advice to the reader of this pillar is, learn from the storm. Address the aftermath and repair the infrastructure of your relationship. Do the best you can to repair the bridges of communication, confess your sins, ask for forgiveness, rebuild, and love and laugh again. The notion of seeking new thrills outside the arena of marriage, one after the other, until the marriage is crushed beyond repair, is foolish, delusionary, and a waste of time. Instead, we need to jettison any dead weight that may cause us to sink deep into a situation worse than the storm itself, especially when the storm is of our own doing. The next time you experience turbulence, call upon Jesus, the master of storms and the God of perfect peace. He and He alone can quiet the wailing winds and other noise. He can give you a spirit of forgiveness, the ability to regroup, and the ability to love and laugh again. Forget momentary pacifiers; instead, build authentic, organic spiritual intimacy with your Father God. Hold on to your Savior and your mate. You will not be sorry you did. When the storm is all over, and even if things did not turn out as you had prayed they would, stand tall and go to sleep at night with a clear conscience, knowing that you did all you could have done. Sing along with the songwriter: "It is well, it is well, with my soul!"

Pillar # 17
Revitalizing the Marriage Dream

Foundation

> You say I am rich; I have wealth and do not need anything; But, you do not realize that you are wretched, pitiful, poor, blind and naked. I counsel you to buy from Me gold refined in fire, so you can become rich.
>
> —Revelation 3:17–18

Renovations are not cheap or easy to do by any means. They come with a cost and are labor-intensive depending on the area of the house to be remodeled. But immense joy comes from just imagining the finished product. While the bulldozer rumbles and the hammer, chisel, and saw chip away, creating sawdust, the homeowner begins to salivate at the thought of a fully remodeled home, the fresh smell of paint, the new fixtures in the bathroom, the new kitchen appliances, the new drapes, and/or the new furniture. Similarly, revitalizing a marriage can be labor-intensive, and in some cases costly, but joy is inevitable when the marriage dream is realized. There are many ways to revitalize the marriage dream. Some of these are as follows:

1. *Rekindling the love flame.*

    Continue dating. Men are hunters. They like to chase a rabbit while it is running away. Once they have their kill, they do not see a need to continue chasing the dead rabbit. Well, this is the law in the jungle, but not in marriage. You ladies should put on the *whole rabbit gear* that you exhibited when you were dating to keep yourself on the move for the man to pursue the hunt. Keep the chase on, girls! This comes naturally to a woman, which I know from my own experiences.

Neither husbands nor wives can afford to take things for granted or be complacent. There are other rabbits out there in the wild! Get the point?

2. *Develop deliberate quality time together.*

Next to God, there should be nothing else competing for your attention or getting in your way of spending quality time with your mate. Remember how when you were dating you could not get enough of each other? But now that you are married, you feel you have nothing to say to each other. That is ludicrous! Come on! Yes, it can be argued that you have more responsibilities now than before. But all you need is to adjust your lens and make the commitment to give your best efforts to the one who matters most, the one who is there now and will be there for you when all other things are out of the picture, including your job. You think your job will always be there for you? *Wait until the climate changes at your job.* You will have an epiphany then and learn what really matters!

3. *Seek early intervention and counseling.*

Your marriage is worth fighting for. You cannot afford to pretend that nothing is wrong when there is a reason to be concerned. Make a deliberate resolution to seek innovative ways to make an adjustment or to rejuvenate and energize your love relationship before things get out of hand. Seek help as you do with any ailment, by going to your family practitioner for intervention. In the context of your marital relationship, attend to the following matters:

   a. restoring and repairing broken bridges of trust;
   b. restoring the sacred altar of the marriage covenant;
   c. destroying other gods, and the jezebels and the prophets of Baal in your family.

4.   *Revamp your communication pattern.*

Some of the areas to target are as follows:

     a.   Building a culture of transparency.
     b.   Establishing a safe and nonthreatening environment.
     c.   Encouraging open and honest talk.
     d.   Embracing vulnerability.
     e.   Allowing the spirit of forgiveness to rule and prevail—confessing and seeking forgiveness from your mate when you are *wrong*, and accepting an apology from your mate when you are *wronged*.
     f.   Affirming each other following a disagreement.

5.   *Evaluate and set performance measures.*

It's important to look at your marriage experiences over time and determine where you are doing well and where you not, and then redirect your attention to improving marriage performance in any areas of concern, as explained in detail under pillar #22.

6.   *Seek out and implement innovative ways to rejuvenate your marriage.*

Dr. Gary Chapman in one of his seminars suggested that couples should attend at least one marriage event or retreat a year and read a book on marriage together. He mentioned a couple in their nineties who attended one of his seminars and discovered that for the past forty-five years they had attended marriage-related events seeking innovative ways to inject life into and renovate their relationship. The old couple was committed to having the best tools to revitalize their relationship and determined not to be complacent or settle for mediocrity in their marriage. Thus, it is imperative to take a decisive stand and do something to improve the quality of your marriage. Doing nothing to revitalize the relationship should not be an option, no matter what.

The strategies couples may employ to revitalize the marriage relationship are as follows:

a. Go back to the drawing board to identify positive and negative trends and to see what is working and not working for you in the relationship.

b. Identify some *specific* things that are threatening or destructive to the marriage.

c. Take a mutually decisive stance to redirect your lives and make applicable changes.

d. Drill down to locate problem areas. It is important to keep in mind that data garnered from your experiences are meaningful and usable. So, before getting to the stage of revamping the marriage, you must drill down carefully and meticulously to find the root of the problem. A problem identified is a problem half solved. Guard against haphazard analysis and solving the wrong problem. This can prove to be evasive, or it may enable you to avoid addressing the real issue, which would be a futile waste of time and resources. Follow the outline, as suggested:

i. Take another look at your marriage experiences.

ii. Talk honestly about what is wrong in the marriage.

iii. Address how each one of you feels about the situation.

iv. Own up to the part each one of you has played in creating the mess, understanding that each one of you is responsible and accountable for positive direction and the desired outcomes.

v. Repair broken bridges in your communication.

vi. Establish the family altar and destroy other gods.

vii. Rekindle the flame, affirm each other, and resolve to laugh again.

e. Take steps to address the marriage's performance. As you try to revamp your marriage, the following things will help:

i. Speak each other's language to maintain the necessary level of fuel in the love tank.

ii. Establish a nonthreatening climate and a posture of humor to address topics that are hard to discuss.

iii. Evaluate your marriage performance and do not hesitate to redirect and make changes when data are showing a wrong trajectory.

iv. Redirect by improving positive upward trends, and vow to stop negative trends and destructive behaviors, as applicable.

v. Maintain rituals that need to be kept in good working order for you and your mate, such as praying at an altar in your home and showering each other with compliments.

vi. Seek intervention early when warranted, and if possible, consult a Christian marriage counselor consistent with your value system before problems escalate.

vii. Dig yourselves out of the ditch with the help of God—and only His help.

Use the trend analysis framework (figure 17.1) to categorize positive and negative trends based on your own experiences in your marriage walk. The diagram will guide you in sorting, labeling, and targeting critical areas that may need improvement, or exponential change, as you strive to revitalize your marriage for the collective good. The categories to address are not couple specific. It depends on what works best for you and your mate. Later, you may also refer to the redirection framework under pillar #22, and in appendices A and B.

FIGURE 17.1 Trend analysis framework

TREND ANALYSIS

	Positive	Negative
Keep	Definitely working out for the relationship	Nonthreatening (May need change downward)
Change	Maintain (May need change upward)	Critical (Must change abruptly)

EXPERIENCES

Note: One thing to remember is that for a marriage to work, both mates *must* want to revitalize the relationship and repair any broken bridges. Both must have a mutual resolve and unwavering motivation to refurbish the broken relationship. A counselor's role is that of a mentor and a coach to provide a map to point the couple in the right direction, but *not* to take a shovel and dig the marriage out of a pit. The latter is the responsibility of the two people in the relationship. Their job is to be compliant, follow through, and literally dig themselves out of the ditch they have put themselves in either by neglecting or failing to meet each other's love needs, whether unconsciously or deliberately. The counselor cannot embrace your wife or husband any more than you are willing to do so. A counselor cannot want your marriage to work more than you both want it to work or dig you out of a hole any more than you purport to do so. That is the reason you should place your marriage into the hands of a capable counselor, Jesus Christ, in the first place. He is the only way out of the woes of marriage. He alone can clean up and transform your marriage if you both so desire. Even God will not force Himself into your love affair, in either good times or bad times, unless you give Him an open invitation to tabernacle in your home. He will repair seemingly irreparably broken intimacy and restore your depleted love as He filled the empty vessels of wine at the wedding in Cana recorded in John 2:1–12. The wedding guests commented that the wine was sweeter than the one before. This narrative of the wedding in Cana attests that nothing is too hard for the Lord. He can do all things and is able to do exceedingly above all that we ask. Try Him today!

Song

A wonderful Savior is Jesus my Lord,
A wonderful Savior to me,
He hideth my soul in the cleft of the rock,
Where rivers of pleasure I see.

—Fanny J. Crosby, 1820

My Story

I remember one of my dear friends asking me the most thought-provoking question after we had shared some tough situations we had both endured. She said, "If we could wind back the hands of the clock and be young again, would you still choose the same guy as a spouse?" I said, "Without a doubt I would choose Godwin again as my husband." With a twinkle in my eyes, I asked, "What about you, girl? Would you choose your Jimmy again for a spouse?" She giggled, turning her head to the side, and said, "To tell you the honest gospel truth, I would choose someone else!" We both had a hearty laugh. But her revelation came as a shock to me. I was taken aback because I really had not assessed her marriage at that point as being that bad. Wow! I began to reflect on the relationship my husband and I have, and I had no choice but to begin praising the Lord for a mutually fulfilling relationship, despite some challenges. I realized how blessed I was. To God be the glory! Halleluiah.

When we experience a challenge or a difficult situation, I do as my husband taught me: to focus on what is wrong rather than who is wrong. We focus on the root cause, determining what is wrong and why things happened the way they did, rather than focusing on who did what. In so doing, we find ourselves teaming up to find common solutions. Teaming up together when dealing with the aftermath lightens the burden, making it easier for us to carry the load and to continue encouraging each other (instead of blaming each other). Knowing that we are a *team* allows us to a be vulnerable, agree to disagree, argue, cry, and laugh together.

Another practice, which did not come easily at first, following an argument is to try to compliment each other, reassure and reaffirm each other's love, and commit to growing together. We adopted slogans, such as "Divorce is not an option!"; "This too shall pass!"; and "We are on this journey together." At the end of the day, each one of us perfectly understands that no matter what we are going through, we are happy to be fighting on the same side. We want what's best for us. We are both fully aware that we are running this marathon together. Each one of us is committed to winning this marriage race together, as a team. It is so sweet to hear Godwin say, "I am proud I married you, my love," or "I am your partner in this dance and your teammate in this ball game!" In return, I am not shy to assure him that the feeling is mutual. I tell him that I am proud he is my soul mate in this venture and that I could not have made it without him. This has created a climate where my husband and I can talk openly and honestly about anything and tackle difficult challenges, knowing that we give each other permission to agree to disagree and to constructively criticize each other, yet we still love each other deeply, are able to laugh, and find that we are stronger after the episode.

Last Word

I am convinced that the problem we have in marriage is not the challenging circumstances we face here and there (the *what*). The problem lies in our approach, our response, or the way we deal with the problem we are facing (the *how*) and in the choice of a strategy to employ when we are faced with a crisis or conflict. I subscribe to the notion that a crisis presents both danger and opportunity. The onus is on us to welcome the opportunity to address the problem in an amicable way, rather than take a hike in the face of perceived danger. This paradigm has been explicated at length under pillar #16. Now, my husband and I begin to salivate for God's providence when we are faced with a challenge. Literally, we ask, "I wonder what God is up to this time? How is He going to solve this mess for us?" Because we know that if we present our problem before the throne of grace, prayerfully, with humility, and as a team, there is absolutely nothing God cannot do for us (Luke 1:37). It may take longer than we want, but His delay is not a denial. If He decides to say no, that is fine. We may not appreciate it at first and may be disappointed or even angry that things did not turn the way we wanted them to, but at the end of the day, once we recognize God's handiwork, we calm down. For He knows best what is good for us.

Pillar # 18
Respecting the Marriage Boundaries

Foundation

> Even so It is not the will of your father which is in
> heaven, that one of these little ones should perish.

> —Matthew 18:4

Nature Respects Property Lines

God's people perish because they lack knowledge or don't embrace wisdom
(Hosea 4:6). The story of creation in Genesis 1 informs us that God created
everything in nature to have margins or boundaries as it interacts with
the ecosystem. That is why there is abnormality when property lines are
violated. For example, the dreaded disease of cancer emanates from the
abnormal growth of cells. Once the limits are violated, disaster emerges.

Even something good like rain results in floods. Winds that carry
pollen for cross-pollination change to tornados; rivers that flow in rhythmic
poise can overflow the banks and people drown; oceans that calmly allow
gigantic ships and boats to cruise majestically become tsunamis that can
wash away an entire city, thus displacing and killing many people.

Violating Marriage's Property Lines

Couples encounter physical, emotional, and spiritual challenges or are
assailed by storms at different times in their marriage walk. These challenges
may be naturally caused or misfortunate, just one of the problems of living,
with no wrongdoing on our part. If the truth be told, most of the storms
we encounter are related to some deliberate and uncalculated choices we
have made that have adversely impacted the marriage with devastating
outcomes such as divorce, untimely death, and potentially the loss of
eternal life.

There are several strategies couples can employ to guard against the proclivity to violate marriage's property lines, as follows:

1. Be mindful of copying and impressing others.
2. Be comfortable in your own skin and love who you are.
3. Be content at every stage of life. Trust in the Lord, and know that when you encounter turbulence, this too shall pass.

Note that there are three basic guiding principles to use to prevent you from falling overboard, as follows:

1. *Respect the laws of nature.* Start by putting your marriage first. Do everything in your power to invest in your marriage by adopting a healthy lifestyle that takes care of the body God gave you. For instance, if you decide to jump from the top floor of a tall building, the law of gravity will pull you down and cause you to crash like Humpty-Dumpty no matter how much you pray. If you overeat, you will get sick, and if you go with little or no sleep, you will become sick. The laws of nature have limits that cannot be violated without serious consequences. Thus, obey the laws of nature and adhere to its limits, so you can enjoy a healthy lifestyle and be there for yourself, your spouse, and your family as discussed under pillar #13. Simply put, learn to be temperate and to discern a want from a need. Separate what is important and essential from what you only feel you must have, and choose wisdom to be your guiding light rather than what feels good.
2. *Uphold the laws of God.* Adhere to the Ten Commandments as a moral standard to guide, define, and explain marital boundaries. For instance, God instructs us not to covet others, not to steal from others, not to commit adultery or have hanky-panky relationships outside the confines of the marriage. You must love your neighbor as you love yourself, and love and honoring God as demonstrated by your sole allegiance to Him. Forsaking all other gods is a sign that you are on the right track and are unlikely to violate the boundaries God put in place. Remember Sampson. He chose

what pleased him rather than what God prescribed and ordained for him.

3. *Abide by the law of the land.* Be a law-abiding citizen and do not try to cut corners or beat the system. Once you understand that the laws of the land were meant to protect us all, it makes it easier to uphold and adhere to those laws. For instance, each time I am tempted to go over the speed limit or run a red light, I think about what might happen if I foolishly speed. I might injure myself or kill innocent people. Fortunately, the law has a strong arm to grab you, throw you into jail, and prosecute you in a heartbeat for violating certain laws. Unfortunately, you will not be prosecuted for breaking God's law, overindulging, overeating, or satisfying your sexual appetite in such a way that violates the limits of marriage, such as by having extramarital affairs, unless your actions have an adverse impact on others. Thus, the test of character for couples is to understand the limits of each law and to respect the boundaries defined by each law (the law of nature, the law of God, and the law of the land).

Some techniques to employ are as follows:

i. *Guard your family name and reputation.* Before engaging in any sleazy deals, think about your spouse and family, rather than doing so after the event. God designed you and your spouse to be partners with different foresight and intuition. In most cases, women can smell a rat from far away. They are a ready resource for an impulsive husband. God did not ordain women to be helpmates for nothing. In His divine wisdom, He knew that women would play an integral part in ensuring the head of the household remained moderate and temperate. Women, also, consult your husbands before making uncalculated purchases or falling prey to sharks who take advantage of innocent or naïve women.

ii. *Respect and protect your children's dignity.* If couples would think seriously of the impact of their actions on their children and how it will break their hearts when they hear how Dad or Mom did such-and-such, they would think again before they engaged in foolishness. Unfortunately, the reality sets in only after the news appear in the gossip columns of the newspapers or on the evening news. Respect for your children and your family name goes a long way. See, money cannot buy happiness in a marriage. If you doubt that, ask the megastars of Hollywood. By the same token, a parent should avoid teaching a child anything he or she will have to spend years trying to undo later. Being a parent is not easy; you make unpopular decisions, but they will be appreciated long after you are gone.

iii. *Avoid using kids as shields.* Please do not put your children in the middle of the boxing ring, directly or indirectly, or have them fight your battles against your spouse. This stance violates the boundaries or property lines. Keep your children's innocence protected at all costs. Remember, God designed both you and your spouse to nurture and groom your children. Avoid favoritism and scapegoating of your children. Good or bad, they are all yours. Also, do not seek sympathy or favor from your children against your spouse. You are not the only good parent. You are both in this together. Instead, stand behind your spouse.

My mum was a master teacher on this one; she protected Dad against us children. She would make statements such as, "Hey, your dad does not have money," or when it is convenient, she would say, "Ask your dad, and whatever he says is okay with me!" Because of that, we respected both parents and never tried to divide and conquer them.

Respect In-Laws as Family Too

We should be grateful for in-laws for three reasons: (1) Without them your spouse would not exist. (Amen to that!) (2) They are your kinsmen and an extension of your lineage. (3) They bring joy to the family and are a support system in various ways. But bear in mind that in-laws are a necessary good and an evil at the same time. Granted, some in-laws can be nightmares and busybodies, meddling in the affairs of the nuclear family to the demise of the relationship. But on the other hand, they can make or form a beautiful tapestry of kinsmanship.

There is a popular opinion that in-laws are off-limits. There seems to be a misunderstanding or misinterpretation of the Bible: "Man shall leave and cleave to his wife and be one" refers to Eros-type love, bonding and cleaving together, but does not mean that a husband should cast away his family of origin and have nothing to do with them anymore. The problem is that the interpretation of that Bible verse is not what God intended. It means that the husband's first responsibility and consideration is his wife, and that all others are considered on a secondary basis, but *not* neglected or cast away. The fact is, when one gets married to Prince Charming or Ladylove, she or he is espoused to the groom or bridegroom but married into the larger clan. Unfortunately, some parents-in-law, especially on the male spouse's side, feel threatened by the new daughter-in-law and perceive her as stealing the love or loyalty their son had for them, rather than seeing that they are gaining a daughter.

Oh, come on now, it's a matter of perspective! How about looking at it instead as gaining a son or daughter rather than as having to contend with an intruder? See, when the clan begins to compete for attention or resources, they engage in a tug-of-war with the other spouse. Such a spirit of selfishness tends to violate the boundaries or property lines, and breeds animosity and "busybody third-party syndrome," which in turn tends to suffocate and threaten the unity and the relationship of the new nuclear family. Nevertheless, as a wife or husband who is also a child of God, you need to keep a level head and learn to operate within a toxic environment sometimes. Pray for the spirit of Christ to shine through you and enable you to love your in-laws despite the prevailing animosity. Pastor Goodman Pilane made a remark at his youngest sister's wedding: "Natural love shall fall or crumble under pressure, but what is of God cannot; instead it shines brighter under pressure!" God is awesome in that He is an enabling power. He instituted the matrimonial relationship, and only He can sustain it, not you on your own power, but through His omnipotent power!

Song

Not I, but Christ, be honored and exalted;
Not I, but Christ, be seen, be known, be heard;

Not I, but Christ, in every look and action;
Not I, but Christ, in every thought and word.
Not I, but Chris, my every need supplying,
Not I, but Christ, my strength and health to be;
Christ, only Christ, for body soul and spirit;
Christ only Christ, here and eternally.

—Fannie E. Bolton

My Story

I remember in the early years of our marriage my husband would share with me things that a member of his family did that hurt him. Although I was young and naïve, I could smell a rat. I knew that he was telling me these things because he wanted me to chime in and take the responsibility of addressing it somehow. See, Godwin is an introvert and does not like controversy and strife, especially with his family members. Now, looking back on my marriage journey, I am convinced that he would share some of his frustration with me deliberately or unconsciously hoping that I would chime in and tell the party in question to back off. Granted, as an extrovert, I have no problem giving someone some straight talk, saying what I think and feel, but this is not the case with in-laws. It would have been a violation of the boundaries if I had chosen to confront them. I subscribed to the belief that one catches more flies (in this case, in-laws) with honey than vinegar. I was determined not to meddle in my in-laws' business, as it did not concern me.

Early in my marriage, my mom had warned me, among other things, that as a wife I was called not to tear down bridges but to build them. I really did not grasp what Mother meant until I was facing a certain crossroads. I prayed about it and God impressed on me to respect the property lines or family boundaries, to be cautious of what I said, to whom I said it, and how I said it, and which battles to fight and which to walk away from. He, gave me wisdom to push back nicely, by hitting the ball back into my husband's court. As a spouse, if you are not careful and you put your nose in to family feuds, you become the bad guy, fast, and your in-laws' son or daughter will come out smelling like a rose!

So, drawing from my experiences, I say that if your spouse is trying to use you as a shield, telling you how bad Auntie Sue and Uncle Bill are, heating you up to the boiling point so that you will pick the fight with his or her side of the family, hold your horses! Establish property lines and determine the battles you need to be involved in or that are worth fighting for. How do you do that? I am glad you asked. First, acknowledge that your mate is hurting, and empathize with him or her. Do not trivialize how your mate feels. After calming your mate down with concern and grace, just politely say to him or her, "Honey-bunch, do your uncle and auntie know how you feel about this? It would be good, dear, for you to let them know how [x, y, or z] hurt you. I know they love you very much and have your best interests at heart. Once you address the issue and they realize how much you are hurting because of them, the matter will be history." Be assuring to your mate and mean what you say.

Please, do not be shocked when you follow up later to find out that your mate has not addressed the issue with his or her relatives. You will discover that Prince Charming or Ladylove has forgotten and cannot even remember what you had talked about in the first place. Your spouse may even say, "What was I supposed to say to So-and-So, by the way?" Please do not be mad! Just say to your heart, *"Holy moly! Wow! Really?"* Just gather up the courage and say politely, "Oh, dear, don't sweat it. You will remember when you feel the sting again the next time around." Duh! When I followed this rule, I had joy at the end of the day because I had not compromised the integrity of the relationship and at the same time, with grace and poise, I had withdrawn from the gaming table, thereby avoiding being rolled and tossed as dice to score points for my mate by entangling myself in his people's mess.

Last Word

What I have learned about life in general is that we all are different when it comes to our personality traits, tastes, interests, and physical and emotional makeup. However, we are all children of the King. We are brothers and sisters in Christ, made from one blood by one God, whose blood was shared for all of us, regardless of nationality or culture (Acts 17:26). What I am trying to emphasize here is that we have more in common than we do things that separate us, for example, the color of our skin. I have friends on both sides of the aisle, brown-skinned and white-skinned alike, and have found that we all want the same things in life, such as respect, achievement, and success. We all laugh, cry, and bleed. For instance, if a Caucasian is involved in a car accident and needs a blood transfusion, the issue that matters is his or her blood type, not the color of his or her skin. If the person has blood type B+, he or she will be administered B or O-positive blood without a label indicating race or skin color or religion, such as African, Caucasian, Asian, Jewish, or Muslim. At a time such as this one, the common goal or interest is to save the life of the injured. Why can't we apply the same paradigm in relationships?

Similarly, difference of opinion is inevitable, but respect is a choice. My mother, used to say, "Embrace all people and do not engage in class distinction. Classify what you are talking about, but don't classify the person." Wow! Such wisdom has kept me going through my life and career. Now, looking back, I see that is what kept me sane when dealing with family members, friends, and professional colleagues. I embraced them all regardless of how they treated me or how I felt about them. But one thing is for certain, I knew what I must not share with or say to So-and So. Another strategy that has helped me not to go overboard in dealing with some people is creating an illusion of invisibility but ensuring that I am available when it counts.

Last, I offer a word of caution: beware of the people who pretend to love you but who mean you no good, encouraging you to violate your moral integrity, your boundaries, your limits, or the property lines in your marriage. They are not your true friends! Gain the courage to weed them out of your garden of friends quickly. True friends will want and support what's best for you all the time. Remember that!

Pillar #19
Inspiring Optimum Potential

Foundation

> If you cannot fly, drive; if you cannot drive, run; if
> you cannot run, walk; if you cannot walk, crawl.
> But keep moving. Keep moving forward.

> —Dr. Martin Luther King

Seeking to *inspire* your mate to excel is one of the best investments a spouse can make in the marriage. Notice that I did not say *change* your mate but *inspire* your mate by being a positive influence. However, a spouse needs to know which areas to expend energy on. Figure 19.1 explains the personality domains or spheres you should target to reach optimum potential.

FIGURE 19.1 Johari window

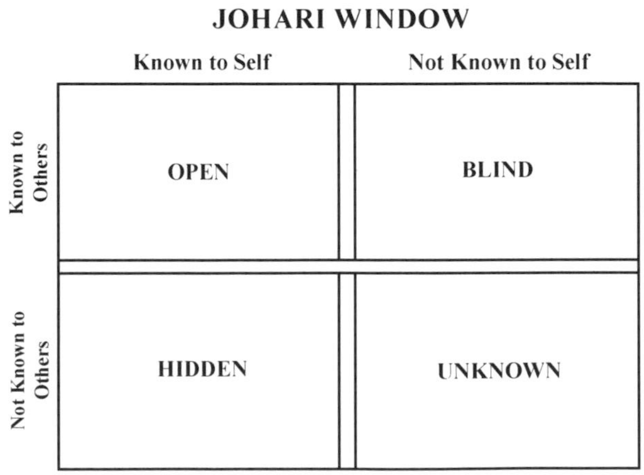

JOHARI WINDOW

	Known to Self	Not Known to Self
Known to Others	OPEN	BLIND
Not Known to Others	HIDDEN	UNKNOWN

Adapted diagram. Concept developed by psychologists Joseph Luft and Harry Ingham of UCLA in 1955. Free diagram available at Businessball.com.

The Johari window was developed in 1955 by American psychologists Joseph Luft and Harry Ingham, of UCLA, to improve self-awareness and group relations. According to the Johari paradigm, we all have open spots and blind spots when it comes to our character development, capability, and elasticity to grow. Once we understand and put in perspective all these domains, we begin to have self-awareness. I have adapted the Johari domains to assess and target potential areas we can work on to achieve optimal growth.

A. *Open*—This spot is an open book to both you and your spouse. When you point out something to your mate, he or she readily understands where you are coming from. To use colloquial English, your mate *feels you*. This area is crystal clear, allowing your spouse to see the where he or she can improve or excel. Here there is no second-guessing of his or her limits or potential, and what he or she can do to achieve optimal growth. This is the easiest domain to work with on both sides. There is no faking and no blind spot here.

B. *Blind*—In this the domain, you have a blind spot, but your spouse can perceive what is going on. Thus, it is very tricky and frustrating for your mate to inspire you to reach your maximum potential with your cooperation. This means that your mate can see your potential for growth that you do not see yourself. Instead, you feel like saying, *What the heck is going on here, and what is she [or he] talking about?* The problem in this domain is that you tend to second-guess your spouse's motives for pushing you to excel. Furthermore, in this domain, there is plenty of room for *denial*, taking your mate for granted, and seeing him or her as demanding or pushy. Thus, when your mate points out something to you, you do not readily understand where he or she is coming from. Things are not crystal clear and you do not see the potential to improve or excel. Similarly, you may not appreciate your spouse's efforts to inspire excellence in you.

C. *Hidden*—This domain is opposite to the open domain in that it indicates a spot that is hidden or blind to your mate but open to you. This means your mate cannot see the potential for growth that you plainly see. The problem with this domain is that your spouse may think you are delusional or that you have grandiose ideas that are not attainable. You may hear things like, *Where in the world did you get that crazy idea? How are you going to finance that?* And so forth. You need to exercise patience; don't take the ball and run with it. Think things through, sell your ideas with love, explain what you plan to do step by step, and refrain from giving directives and ultimatums. At first you spouse may not appreciate your efforts to inspire excellence, so give him or her time to buy into your plan. If he or she eventually comes to believe in you and understand where you want to go with your ideas, you will be surprised to find that your mate is your best ally in achieving excellence.

D. *Unknown*—On one hand, this domain is a dark or blind spot, closed to both of you. On the other hand, this domain is a sphere packed with possibilities for unleashed or untapped potential that can be realized to achieve optimum potential and, as a result, great things. Now, since both of you are oblivious to what is going on, who can provide the spark to make both of you realize things that are not readily apparent? This is where leaning on divine guidance comes in. This domain is open to Jesus, and only the Holy Spirit can impress upon you and your mate that you are to excel beyond imagination. The Bible states that the Holy Spirit, in addition to doing other things, inspires, teaches, convicts, and leads us to all truth (John 16:12–15). The saga of Phillip with the Ethiopian eunuch, in Acts 8:26–40, is a classic example of what God can do to guide us to inspire others whom we do not even know. How much more can He do to help us to inspire our mates? Phillip was inspired by the Holy Spirit to teach the eunuch and lead him to salvation through baptism (Acts 8:26–40). When we pray, the Lord can reveal to us things we do not know and inspire us to help our mates reach their optimal potential and thereby achieve excellence.

There are several conclusions that can be drawn from the discussion of the Unknown domain, as follows:

1. *The Visionary Developer's Urge*

This is predicated on the psychological notion of the "vacant lot" concept, which basically asserts that sometimes we have the capability to see potential through an imaginary picture or vision that is not apparent to others. That sounds like faith to me. Sometimes when you share with others your dream or aspiration, they crack up and say, "Really? Are you kidding?" Or perhaps they roll their eyes and say, "There you go again!" This very thing happened to Walt Disney, who as a developer exhibited heart and enthusiasm. He envisioned a resort and a castle being built on obscured swampland in Florida. He also envisioned an amusement park built on that swampland. He went ahead and purchased the humongous tract of swampland and developed what we know today as Disney World, one of the most lucrative amusement parks in the world that attracts the young and the young at heart. There are several conclusions that can be drawn from the "vacant lot" concept. So, not everyone can handle your inspiration or dream. Sad to say, even your mate cannot sometimes.

2. *Surprise, Surprise Syndrome*

It can be argued that the unknown sphere has many surprises. In the unknown sphere, we may find ourselves in deep trouble and be unable even to figure out how we got there. I am sure you are familiar with statements such as, "I cannot believe So-and-So would do that, or even that he [or she] could be capable of doing [x, y, or z]." A spouse can even say: "How did I not see it coming?" Well, surprise, surprise, it did happen. Your child, your spouse, or even you did it without even knowing that you could do such a thing or even had the capability. That is why it is crucial to surrender our will to the unfailing hand of God, as He will guide us and protect us, even from ourselves. Because of this, the unknown sphere is *prime real estate* to be surrendered to God. We should intentionally and constantly present ourselves before the

Lord and ask Him to occupy our hearts and minds, asking that He use them according to His will by doing the following things:

i. Creating in us a new heart and a right spirit (Psalm 51:10).
ii. Making us a new creature in the Lord (2 Corinthians 5:17).
iii. Establishing in us a mind like Jesus's (Philippians 2:5).
iv. Keeping our bodies pure as the temple of the Lord (1 Corinthians 6:19).
v. Transforming us from sinners into saints by helping others turn away from sin and inspiring them to partake of this marvelous light (James 5:19–20).

3.   Be Energized through Imperfection

The virtue of imperfection involves accepting your limitations and presenting them before the Lord. Imperfections keep us real, humble, and tolerant of other people's weaknesses, knowing that we cannot do much on our own. We need the Lord! There is abundance in emptiness, for God does not call the prepared but instead prepares those He has called. Sometimes, God strips us of self and casts away the crutches we depend on, so we can develop trust in and dependence on Him, knowing that we do not have all the answers and sometimes cannot even explain what we experience. In our weakness, we are made strong through Christ, our Lord (2 Corinthians 12:9–11).

4.   Melting Pot or Salad Bowl?

Marriage is not a melting pot of personalities but a salad bowl. Each person has his or her own identity and personality type. That's why I have argued in *Pillars of Joy in Marriage* that the key to having joy in marriage is to embrace and celebrate the differences. Can you imagine that you've invested $100,000 in your portfolio and then, when you try to withdraw money, the bank manager weakly explains, "Sir, I am sorry, the bank cannot distinguish your account from those of our other clients because we put all the accounts into one big melting pot." Boy, you would go crazy!

Marriage is like an investment. Each spouse works on his or her own *character and personality portfolio*. Your identities, or who you are, have a big role to play in your relationship portfolio. You are different so that you may complete each other. Your personalities are not enmeshed. Each of you has a unique identity and character, but you are one in spirit and when agreeing how you will run your marriage business. If this were not the case, then God would not have talked about submission, because there would be no need to submit to your spouse. He instructed men to love their wives *as they love their own bodies*, because women are delicate vessels and need to be handled with care. Think about that!

Song

Nearer, still nearer, close to Thy heart,
Draw me, my Savior, so precious Thou art;
Fold me, O fold me close to Thy breast,
Shelter me safe in that haven of rest,
Shelter me safe in that haven of rest.

—C. M. Morris

My Story

The story I am going to share in this pillar is bittersweet and very dear to my heart. Looking back, I see that it shaped who I have become as matriarch of the Nxumalo household. At first things were not great between my mother-in-law and me. I am from South Africa, and my husband is from Swaziland. This is a huge difference in terms of customs and traditions. There were cultural differences that impacted our relationship in ways that are too painful to recall and share. All I can say is that I felt deficient and could not measure up to my mother-in-law's demands as her daughter-in-law and wife of her firstborn son. To add insult to injury, I did not bear a child for seven years and all her other sons' wives had conceived and had children at that point. I cried and prayed a lot. Like Hannah in the Bible, I began to look at things differently. Instead of focusing on things that hurt me, I focused on the experiences that brought me joy, my husband's love for me, and the assurances he gave me through it all. I felt an abundance of blessings in my emptiness. I returned the love I felt from my husband's baby sister (Jill), the only girl among six brothers (a rose among thorns). Most importantly, I forgave my mother-in-law for things she put me through and I was at peace with her. God heard my prayers. In His time, I conceived and bore a son, the prince of the Ndwandwe clan. About fifteen years into my marriage, my mother-in-law asked me to forgive her. She confessed and apologized for all she had put me through. I was shocked, and I did forgive her. In fact, I told her that I had already forgiven her.

Just before my husband and I came over to the USA to study, the boys and their wives were all visiting Mama's house. As we were bracing to leave and return to our respective homes, Mama ordered all of us to sit and said that she had an announcement to make. Without further ado, she came over to where I was sitting, pulled a set of keys from her pocket, placed them in my hand, and said, "Let it be known today that La-Kheswa [the surname of my clan of origin] has been promoted to the status of my sister. She is no longer considered a daughter-in-law to me, but a matriarch of the family. She will be mother of the Ndwandwe clan when I pass on. Whatever you want or need, let her be the one who deals with that. I am confident that she will do right in this role. Respect her as your mother. These keys are a symbol of *respect, honor, and promotion* to a higher calling."

When Mama passed away, I was a doctoral student at the Ohio State University. I could not go to her burial, but I was at peace with her. I have no residual anger toward her whatsoever. Instead, I received the trust she had invested in me. If truth be told, she is the main reason why I decided to leave the United States and return home to be closer to the family. She instructed me to be a surrogate mom to her boys and to look after them. They are all professionals, but they still need a mother's wisdom and guidance here and there. They still love me dearly, and I love them too. They were so happy to see us back home. They are my family now in the true sense. Thank you, Mama. May you rest in peace! So, couples, when you encounter a turbulent period in your marriage, stay the course, stay on board, and do not jump ship. Do not whine or adopt the "why me?" syndrome. Change your perspective and pursue growth in the aftermath of trouble, and things will be all right in time. Who knows, the same frustrating situation may be a double blessing in the long run.

Last Word

If you are not willing to make long-term investments in your marriage relationship, you are not ready to be married. Part of making a genuine commitment to each other is being patient with each other's development and growth as you pass through the different seasons of your marriage. The next time you are frustrated with your own imperfections, remember that the Lord is not finished with you yet! When you feel like complaining about your spouse's imperfections or when you are having difficulty inspiring your mate to reach greater heights, remember that if he or she really was as good as you wanted him or her to be, he or she would have married someone other than you. Think about that!

Pillar #20
Adopting an Attitude of Gratitude

Foundation

Speaking to yourselves in psalms, and hymns, and spiritual
songs, singing and making melody in your heart and the
Lord; Giving thanks always For all things unto God And
the Father In the name of our Lord Jesus Christ.

—Ephesians 4:19–20 (KJV)

Building Block of Joy

Adopting an attitude of gratitude is the *building block* of a joyous marital
relationship. In all things give thanks (1 Thessalonians 5:18). Let's go back
one more time and revisit the garden of Eden, the illustrious home of the
first couple, Adam and Eve. In the book of Genesis, chapter 1, when God
created the earth and fullness thereof, He punctuated each day of creation
with "It is good!" God said, "Let us make man to reflect our image," and
on the sixth day, He created Adam, holy and perfect, stately, tall, and
handsome, but not a happy camper. That moved God to say something
that changed the trajectory of His order: "It is not good for Adam to be
alone" (Genesis 1:18). See, elephants and zebras could not turn Adam on,
so God made Eve from Adam's rib, near the heart, as his companion, soul
mate, and helpmate. Without Eve, Adam was not complete.

Once Adam woke up from the "heavenly anesthesia" and God presented
Eve to him, his first impression *Wow!* Adam exhibited an attitude of praise
and gratitude to God. He philosophized: "This now is bone of my bones
and flesh of my flesh: she shall be called *woman*, because she was taken
out of a man. Therefore, shall a man leave his father, and shall *cleave* unto
his wife; and they shall be and mother" (Genesis 2:23–24 KJV, emphasis

added). There are several conclusions for couples that can be drawn from the Adam–Eve marital relationship, as follows:

1. God is the source of a good marital relationship. God instituted marriage because it was good.

2. God knows what is good for you more than you imagine He does. Adam was not even aware that something was missing, and he would have not filled his void without God's ingenious intervention.

3. God is the one who said it was not good for man to be alone, and it was God Himself who declared, "He who finds a wife finds a good thing and obtains favor from the Lord" (Proverbs 18:22 NKJV).

4. God plucked the left rib to remind a man to keep his wife close to his heart as his confidant, soul mate, lover, and helpmate. That is why God has commissioned men to love their wives as the Lord loves and makes sacrifices for the church (Ephesians 5:25).

5. God could have created Eve from a *head bone* to symbolize that the wife is the ruler, the head of something, but He did not. Instead, God commissions wives to submit to their husbands as unto the Lord (Ephesians 5:22).

6. God could have made Eve from a foot bone, implying that a man is licensed to trample on his wife, stalling, impeding, and suffocating her development, but God did not.

7. God could have taken Eve from the shoulder bone to make the statement that the woman has sole responsibility for carrying the weight of the household, but He did not.

8. God could have created Eve from the neck bones to symbolize that wives are justified to control the movements of the head of the household, the husband, or exhibit a stiff neck posture, stalling and halting the husband's progress, but God did not.

9. God could have taken a face bone to create Eve to make the statement that the wife is the face or spokesperson of the household, the go-to person for the affairs of the house, but God did not.

10. But what God did was to make Eve as Adam's soul mate and helper, a woman to stand side by side with him, submitting to him as head of the household and supporting him with love and

wisdom. That is why God says a man who finds a wife has favor from God.

Thank God for Things You Do Not Understand

The verse that expresses and supports the notion of adopting an attitude of gratitude even when you do not understand God's agenda, and when circumstances are puzzling or make no sense whatsoever, is Romans 8:28, which states, "All things work together for good to those who love God and are called according to his purpose" (Romans 8:28 KJV). All things work together for good—really?! To me this is one of the most difficult and challenging Bible verses to comprehend! But if you believe in and trust the God who said it, you will be at peace with yourself and others, knowing that the Lord will work all things in your favor, and give you courage and resolve to forge ahead through difficult circumstances. Instead of grumbling and murmuring, you will begin to praise and worship Him for who He is, not for what He has done. This is an attitude of joy despite your circumstances.

Achieve Spiritual Growth in Adversity

The Bible has long established the virtue of joy amid trials (1 Peter 1:6–9; Romans 5:13, 12:12). The psychological view of achieving growth after adversity or a setback is a new phenomenon that seems to compete with the notion of posttraumatic stress. So, it can be argued that psychology is beginning to catch up with the long-established biblical view of rejoicing in tribulation. Deriving joy from adversity indicates a high level of maturity and growth. Friedrich Nietzsche, a German philosopher, discovered that "what does not kill us makes us stronger," which helps us develop a new perspective or positive outlook on life, people, and circumstances. Lorna Collier has cited the positive signs of transformation exhibited by some people following traumatic experience. These are as follows:

- appreciation of life
- relationship with others
- new possibilities in life
- personal strength
- spiritual change.

The Adversity in Life Compass blog has identified some helpful steps to guide an individual in the face of challenges, such as the following:

- welcoming and embracing obstacles as opportunities for growth;
- making a list of opportunities that may arise from these obstacles;
- identifying individuals who may help in your situation;
- developing action steps to take and follow through on.

Hence, adversities have the potential to help individuals develop a new perspective on and appreciation of life and people. They also help to cultivate character, resilience, and experience, building better-valued relationships.

Pray for Courage in the Face of Challenges

Shelly Queen, of 3ABN, in one of her sermons once said, "Courage is worry bathed in prayer!" Prayer conquers fears and worry. Dr. Barry Black once said, "Prayer is the most powerful arsenal in the artillery of a Christian and is the most underestimated and underused." There can be no worry when we pray. Worrying and praying are opposite constructs, like light and darkness. One occurs in the absence of the other, and the other cannot occur in the presence of the other. The implications here are as follows:

1. When challenges assail you, pray.
2. Suffocate worries with prayer. No prayer, more worries; much prayer, no worries. A friend once said to me, "If you pray, you stand, but if you fast and pray, you last!"
3. An attitude of gratitude changes your perspective and the world around you. You begin to see the cup half full, rather than half empty.
4. Prayer builds your courage and changes your view of life, even though the present circumstances have not changed.
5. Gratitude lifts you up to God and helps you rise above difficult situations.
6. Gratitude conquers fear and helps you begin to count your blessings. Thus, other things diminish and become insignificant at best.

7. An attitude of gratitude promotes an understanding of your own limitations and an acceptance of others' struggles and sacrifices. You feel motivated and want to reciprocate the good deeds by helping someone else in your predicament. You begin to reflect, *If others can do x, y, or z for me, why can I not do the same for them? I have no excuse. Why can't I bless someone else by returning the favor, doing the same thing, or even more, for others?*

Song

O for a thousand tongues to sing
My great Redeemer's praise,
The glories of my God and King,
The triumphs of His grace!

Hear Him, ye deaf; His praise, ye dumb,
Your loosened tongues employ;
Ye blind, behold your Savior come;
And leap, ye lame, for joy.

—Charles Wesley

My Story

This is the shortest story in *Pillars of Joy in Marriage*, but it is the most profound. If the spirit of gratitude and giving to others made one poor, then some people I know would be indigent, broke, or penniless today, but such is not the case. God seems to bless them abundantly. This holds true for several individuals I know who seem to enjoy giving to others more than they enjoy receiving. Right now, I can think of several people who have enriched my life without even knowing it. They have a spiritual love language of giving to others. But God seems to bless them even more. They are selfless and seem to enjoy giving to others until it hurts. These are, to name a few, Grace Brown, Marjorie Cooper, Babsie Ndlela, and Dr. Michele Oyortey. If I could enumerate the many ways in which these individuals have blessed me and my family when we lived in the United States, through different seasons of my life, *Pillars of Joy in Marriage* would not be able to contain the material. All I can say to these individuals is "Thank you, and I promise to be like you to others when I grow up! May God richly bless you in all spheres of your life!"

Last Word

God has clearly indicated that it is more blessed to give than to receive (Acts 20:35). Make sure you become a blessing to others, as God has blessed you. It does not make you less than anyone else when you say thank you. But most of all, understand that God is a giver of all good things and that He can use other people to bless you, as He sees fit. Acknowledge Him and thank Him for the friends you have who seem willing to go the extra mile for you. Showing gratitude and blessing others in your path generates a ripple effect! You may never be able to bless or return the favor to those who bless you, but you can sure be a blessing to others in your path by duplicating the good things you see in others and by choosing to be on the giving side of the fence. So, strive to make the world better than you found it. God will honor that! A Bible story that has always touched me is the healing of the ten lepers, with *only one* of them coming back to Jesus to say, "Thank You." The rest went on their way, thinking about the possibility of a living a new life without the deadly disease. Unfortunately, the nine missed the most lasting blessing, salvation. All ten were cleansed of the grievous illness, *but only one was saved*, because he came back to Jesus and said thank you. Likewise, being grateful does not make a mate weak or less than, but instead it saves or improves the relationship!

Pillar #21
God-Driven Marriage

Foundation

A journey of a 1000 miles begins with just one step!

—Chinese proverb

Installing God's Peace and Security System (GPS)
God's peace and security system (GPS) is compatible with the model of marriage you have. Just plug it in. It is predicated on acknowledging God as the driver, with you and your spouse being willing passengers enjoying the scenic view. He negotiates the twists and turns of your life. May I take the liberty to relate the foregoing Chinese proverb to the marriage journey? The long journey to eternity begins with God as the driver of our existence. If we accept this, then we will sit back, relax, and allow God to pilot this ship of marriage to Zion, the land of glory! As we embark on our marriage journey, we, whether we admit it or not, all drive under the influence (DUI) of something or someone. The questions couples need to ask themselves are: Who really drives our marriage when we find ourselves on the complex highway of life, in an unsafe neighborhood, at a frightening corner, or at an uncertain crossroads? Really, who is our guide, our peace, our security system, our GPS? Without a doubt, God is the clear choice to guide me. He has been my faithful GPS through the complex maze of my marriage for over forty years. He can be yours too if you invite Him into your marriage.

Provision and Survival Kit for Your Marriage
As you do for long drive, in marriage you need to pack some provisions and a survival kit in case of emergency. Scriptures confirm that God is love and the giver of the many blessings and gifts we enjoy, as all good things come

from Him (James 1:17). Before we continue with this line of reasoning, we need to understand and internalize a few important things, as follows:

1. *Understanding who God is.* God is love. He is a loving Father and the perfect lover. He is all-powerful, all-knowing, and omnipresent at all times. He is a faithful guide, the God of peace, the King of Kings, and the Lords of Lords. He is the Word. He is larger than life itself. No human mind can comprehend or explain God in His entirety. Ravi Zacharias, one of the greatest Christian apologists of our time, once said, "God created Himself within Himself by Himself."

2. *Accept Jesus as your brother.* In one of his sermons, Dr. Calvin Rock said, "Jesus is God, and yet Jesus is man. God cannot die, but through Jesus God could die. Mankind, in their sinful nature cannot see the face of God and live, but Jesus inherited human elements, so the God of justice can empathize with the apathetic sinner like me and you. Now, if you attempt to quantify God mathematically, what fraction of God is human and how much of God died you will lose your mind. But at the same time, if you do not believe this gospel you will lose your soul." Any effort to measure God is futile (C. E. Bradford). Thus, we should accept God and who He is by faith. "The *deep calls to deep* in the roar of your waterfalls of troubles, uncertainty, waves of your unbelief and when breakers of doubt are sweeping over you" (Psalm 42:7 NIV, emphasis added).

3. *Understand the one thing God is not.* God is not a liar. The Bible tells us that "God is not human, that He should lie" (Numbers 23:19 NKJV). He did not create us as robots but as moral agents with the free will to choose or reject Him. If God is not a liar, usurper, or hijacker, He will not force Himself on us. So, do not be presumptuous and assume that God will hijack your marriage willy-nilly or take control of the steering wheel. You must invite Him willingly and with a full understanding of what He can do in your marriage. Hand over the keys, take a back seat, and enjoy the ride. You cannot fake God's companionship. The invitation must be real! Without Christ at the center of a marriage, *power, fame, or riches* cannot do it!

4. *Acknowledge that God created marriage to make us holy.* Before sin, Adam and Eve were perfectly happy and carefree. But sin intruded and changed the perspective of humankind, distorting humankind's allegiance to God and ushering in misery and death. Thus, humankind lost true happiness and holiness. Dr. Gary Thomas in his book *The Sacred Marriage* poses a question: "What if God designed marriage to make us holy instead of to make us happy?" He observed that marriage is a training ground for Christian couples to achieve holiness. Hence, a marriage journey founded and propelled by God is the key to experiencing a mutually fulfilling relationship. God, and only God, is the guarantor and the fundamental ingredient to the art of loving and finding joy in marriage. Indeed, the Lord is the perfect insurance policy and the ultimate heavenly security system to protect our relationship, more than ADT, AT&T, and the like. There is nothing that catches Him off guard because He does not sleep or slumber (Psalm 121:4).

5. *Know that God's foolishness is wisdom to us.* The Bible tells us that all wisdom comes from God, "for the Lord gives wisdom; from His mouth come knowledge and understanding; He stores up sound wisdom for the upright" (Proverbs 2:6–7 NKJV). God's inspired wisdom helps us navigate rough terrain and the crossroads of life and supplies us with the stamina to climb or descend the ups and down of married life. God has proven to be a faithful guide. Nothing surprises the Lord or derails His course. Thus, He admonishes us not to lean on our own understanding, but to acknowledge Him in all our undertakings (Proverbs 3:6). Why? Because human intelligence is limited at best and can only explain what it knows, sees, studies, and experiences, but God's wisdom is foreknowledge and instructs us in what He knows will work. Well, it is easier said than done to convince oneself and profess that marriage is guided by the Lord. But is it really? That is the test of character, for the steps of a good person are directed by the Lord (Psalm 37:23).

If you subscribe to this view, look at yourself, your choices, your decisions, and how you govern your marriage to determine whether you are a faithful steward. Answers to the following questions indicate your level of integrity and help you see who really drives your marriage journey.

a. Who defines your values or morality?
b. Who establishes your ethical principles?
c. Who is your hero and the model of your love relationship? Is it God or Hollywood?

Principles of a God-Led Marriage

The principles of a God-led marriage as derived from the discussions within *Pillars of Joy in Marriage* are as follows:

- A God-led marriage derives joy in giving.
- A God-led marriage displays selfless service.
- A God-led marriage creates a culture of prayer.
- A God-led marriage exhibits unconditional love.
- A God-led marriage develops the right perspective.
- A God-led marriage puts trust in God's divine wisdom.
- A God-led marriage demonstrates submission to God's ordained will.
- A God led marriage manifests an attitude of gratitude.
- A God-led marriage seeks God's intended plan over the plan of either spouse.
- A God-led marriage responds to a need despite the other's faults.
- A God-led marriage understands the power of a forgiving spirit.
- A God-led marriage yields to the guidance of the Holy Spirit.
- A God-led marriage experiences joy when waiting for His direction, in His time.

These principles attest to the fact that marriage is not as easy as it appears to be. A God-led marriage establishes an organic unadulterated intimate spiritual relationship as the core ingredient for mutually satisfying sensual intimacy. Without an intimate connection with God in our marriage, we cannot be successful in this journey. He is the founder of the institution of marriage and knows how we can navigate the terrain, the crossroads, and the intricacies of married life. If we surrender our hearts to His mighty plan for each one of us and rely on His divine wisdom to lead us at every step along the way of the marriage journey, His Word assures us that we need not worry. We may take all our cares to Him, including the challenges present in our marriage. In so doing, we will be successful. Listen to God's promises. They have assured me to trust in Him implicitly with my own marriage and have strengthened me beyond measure.

Specific promises that have sustained me in difficult times are listed below:

1. When I am stressed with problems with life, my spouse, my children, or my work, God comforts me and says, "Be anxious for nothing, but in everything by prayer and supplication, with thanks giving, let your requests be made known to God" (Philippians 4:6 NKJV).

2. When I am not sure if I can accomplish anything, He assures me that "I can do all things through Christ who strengthens me" (Philippians 4:13 NKJV).

3. When I am faced with an impossible task and do not know what to do, He says to trust in Him because "with men, it is impossible, but not with God; for with God all things are possible" (Mark 10:27 NKJV).

4. When I am facing mighty challenges and doubts, He says, "Call me in time of trouble, I will deliver you and show you great and mighty things you know not of" (Jeremiah 33:3 NKJV).

5. When I am afraid of the twists and turns of life and do not know how things will turn out, God assures me, "Fear not, for I am with you; be not dismayed, for I am your God; I will strengthen you, Yes, I will uphold you with My righteous right hand" (Isaiah 41:10 NKJV).

6. When the going is tough and I encounter obstacles, God assures me that He will turn the situation around in my favor and turn my obstacles into stepping stones. "All things work out together for good to those who love God, who are called according to His purpose" (Romans 8:28 NKJV).

7. When I am scared, and the future seems uncertain, I rest assured that God is dreaming about me and planning for my future. He

says, "For I know the thoughts I think for you ... thoughts of peace and not evil, to give you a future and a hope" (Jeremiah 29:11 NKJV).

8. When my financial resources are depleted, He assures me thus: "Now to Him who is able to do exceedingly abundantly above all that we ask or think, according to the power that works in us" (Ephesians 3:20 NKJV). He places His resources at our disposal not based on our needs but according to His riches in glory (Philippians 4:19).

9. When an enemy rises up and the devil and the principalities of darkness seem to be hanging around and appear to have the long end of the stick, God says, "Put the whole armor of God that you may be able to stand the wiles of the devil ... girded your waist with truth; taking the shield of faith with which you will be able to quench all the fiery darts of the wicked one ... take the helmet of salvation and the sword of the spirit, which is the Word of God; praying always with all prayer and supplication in the Spirit, being watchful *to the end* with all perseverance" (Ephesians 6:11–18 NKJV, emphasis added).

10. Now that I am in my autumn years, with the greed of my fellows abounding, and even governmental policies seem ineffective and unresponsive to my needs as a senior citizen, I sing and shout with the psalmist, "I have been young, and now I am old; yet I have not seen the righteous forsaken, nor his descendants begging bread" (Psalm 37:25 KJV).

There is unspeakable joy, and no need to fear or worry at all, when you have aligned your relationship to heaven's model governing the marriage institution. The Lord has promised never to leave you or forsake you. He has given the assurance that He will lead you through greener pastures, even at the twilight of your life. God will take care of you and continue to be with you. Even as you walk through the valley of the shadow of death (Psalm 23), He will be with you!

Song

Guide me, O Thou great Jehovah,
Pilgrim through this barren land;
I am weak, but Thou art mighty;
Hold me with Thy powerful hand;
Bread of heaven, bread of heaven,
Feed me till I want no more,
Feed me till I want no more.

—William Williams

My Story

Throughout the many years we spent in the United States, Godwin and I prayed that we could one day relocate and settle back home in the land of our fathers. Both of us understood that we had to go to the United States to get the education and technology skills necessary to be able to give back to society. We continued with our careers and were at peace with the thought that God would lead us at an opportune time following my retirement from the Ohio Department of Education. I had a push to start on writing my book, but I was ambivalent about doing so, since I was not sure if it would be feasible to endure the stress of winding up thirty-five years of our life in the United States, packing, and embarking on writing at the same time. We intensified our praying and God guided us step by step.

I remember listening to LeBron James's rebuttal of his critics when he returned to Cleveland after he had left the Cleveland Cavaliers to play for the Miami Heat. He said something like, "I had to leave and get the preparation I needed so that I could return home to Cleveland well prepared to win championship for my home team!" Indeed, he did win the NBA championship, 2015–16, and beat the renowned and talented Golden State basketball team. LeBron's sentiment quickened our resolve to pack and go back home. In 2016 God nudged us, indicating that it was time for us to go back home to Southern Africa. We started packing and preparing to ship our belongings, but we had a setback in May 2016; my husband had a minor stroke and was hospitalized. His doctors said that he should not travel for six months. In November 2016, he was given a clean bill of health. We were cleared to travel in December 2016 to enjoy Christmas with our loved ones. Halleluiah!

When we landed at the O. R. Tambo International Airport in Johannesburg, tears ran down my cheeks as I reminisced about the goodness and mercies of the Almighty God, who guided us through all the years in the United States and through our plans to relocate and settle back home. The setback we'd experienced was divinely orchestrated by our heavenly Father to allow my husband to receive the best treatment in the United States and heal before coming home. I began to praise God for allowing me to land with Godwin instead of having to leave him in a graveyard somewhere in Columbus, Ohio, or having his body flown home in the cargo hold. Oh Lord, what would I have told his family? Our God is awesome, and His love and mercies endure forever. I have not stopped praising Him! He is awesome. Godwin is doing well and is looking good, even more handsome than before, halleluiah! And I did get the rest and peace I needed to embark on my book.

Last Word

One of my favorite hymns is "Great Is Thy Faithfulness," particularly the chorus, "Morning by morning new mercies I see, all I have needed thy hand has provided, great is Thy faithfulness, Lord unto me!" God provides a fresh supply of blessings for us every day—no leftovers! Our job is to look up and put our trust in God when things go wrong in our marriage. We need not fear, or turn to other gods for answers, or be tempted to consult sorcerers or fortune-tellers, or experiment with alcohol, drugs, or related chemical substances because there is *no answer at the end of the bottle*. Rather, let us be deliberate and resolve to press onward and upward, seeking to stand on higher ground. With Jesus on our side, the view below is different. Trust Him even if you cannot trace Him. Let's trust His love and promises. All things will be all right if you follow God's agenda! You will never go wrong with God on your side! Questions to ask yourself are as follows:

a. Whom do you turn to when circumstances in your household seem dark and gloomy?
b. Where do you seek consolation when you experience betrayal?
c. How do you bounce back after a devastating loss or setback?

Pillar #22
Evaluating Your Marriage Performance

Foundation

> And behold I am coming quickly and My reward is
> with me, to give everyone according to his work.

—Revelation 22:12 (NKJV)

A conscious evaluation of marriage performance is crucial if couples are to maintain a mutually fulfilling relationship. As can be expected, couples have many things to deal with, and the tendency is to run and rarely stop to look at what we are doing and how we are faring in this marriage marathon. Performing a self-evaluation of your marriage is like taking your pulse. Now, having read all the pillars of joy that have been discussed in *Pillars of Joy in Marriage*, you no doubt have a sense of the level at which your relationship stands. Additionally, if by chance you are experiencing some heavy-duty bumps in your relationship and are thinking of a divorce, please watch the movie *Fireproof* before you move forward with your plan. If you've already seen it, please take some time to relax and watch it again. I suggest also that you do the following things:

1. Take notes and critically analyze how the dynamics resemble your situation.
2. Identify to what extent your marriage relationship differs from the marriage of Caleb and Catherine in the movie. Try the strategy prescribed in this video, the part called "Love Dare," on your spouse for forty days.
3. After you have completed the Love Dare, evaluate your marriage performance to see where it stands.

4. As a couple, you may elect to do something different to evaluate your marriage performance. For your convenience, I have also developed and included (in appendix A) a questionnaire you may utilize. Furthermore, I have included an accompanying plan of corrective action in appendix B, to guide you as illustrated below.

Analysis and Corrective Action Plan Model

1. *Identify the mission for your marriage relationship*—The mission should express your heartfelt desire of what you would like to see as a couple and be all about. For instance, when people look at you, what do you think they say about your relationship, what you represent as a couple, your values and behavior, and what is important to you.

2. *Determine the end sought or set the desired goal(s)*—Address what you would like to see your marriage be and what you want to achieve as a couple. Be honest, truthful, serious, and vulnerable. Fakeness or superficiality will not get you anywhere.

3. *Establish specific benchmarks*—Identify a yardstick or specific themes to determine if you have reached your targets. These themes should answer the question "How will we know that we are on the right track and meeting our short- and long-term goals?"

4. *Observe*—Make day-to-day observations through honest and open discussion.

5. *Perform data analysis*—Analyze the performance of your marriage to determine if your targets are being met or not. Data are meaningful when usable. Introspection is necessary here as you look at what is wrong (and not at who is wrong), what contributed to your success, and what the stumbling blocks are.

6. *Decide*—You must have an honest and serious discussion, but avoid making accusations, assigning blame, and finger-pointing. The disposition should be deliberate and decisive: "We are in this together. What can we do to change the negative trends?" A truthful discussion should lead to three plausible decisions, once the analysis is completed: (1) whether to redirect upward, (2) whether to redirect downward exponentially, or (3) whether to

maintain what seems to be working experientially, as illustrated in figure 22.1, below:

FIGURE 22.1. Redirection model to guide decision-making

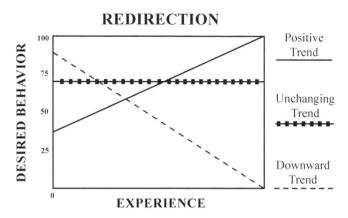

Diagram developed by Nozipho N. Nxumalo

Figure 22.1 illustrates three possible choices a couple can make to address the improvements needed to achieve a mutually rewarding marital relationship. Targeted areas will vary from couple to couple, depending on goals the couple wants to achieve.

Decision Framework

After collecting at least three pieces of information related to the desired goal you want to achieve, examine the trends carefully and decide whether you need to redirect. There are three plausible decisions to make, as follows:

1. *Redirect upward.*

    If the data analysis of your experiences reflects consistent negative trends, you may want to change the related behavior. Adopt strategies to improve the undesirable situation. This will be reflected by an upward trajectory, as illustrated by figure 22.1. For example, a couple may decide to implement innovative strategies that elevate the *level of the love tank* or to meet *unmet love needs* over time. A couple may target any condition they want to improve, depending on the results of an evaluation, the goal, and the plan of corrective action.

2. *Redirect downward.*

When the data analysis of your experiences reflects an unacceptable behavior, you may want to address the problem immediately by adopting tough measures to cut off the undesirable behavior abruptly, especially if the trend proves to be costly, destructive, and/or detrimental to core of the relationship—such as a *spouse having an affair*. Once the couple comes to terms and agrees that a destructive or egregious behavior should stop, they need to apply deliberate strategies and measures to change such behavior. This will be accompanied by an immediate decline or downward curve, as illustrated in figure 22.1, depending on the desired goal and corrective plan of action to address that behavior.

Example: Let's use a scenario whereby a spouse is having an extramarital affair. There are practical, tangible, and measurable steps that a spouse in question can follow to redirect, as identified by Mashudu Ravhengani in his book *Unleashing the Marriage Potential*, p. 131. These are (1) cutting the ties and bringing the relationship to an end by deleting phone numbers, removing email addresses, and removing the party from friends lists in social media; (2) changing jobs or offices or churches as applicable; and (3) ignoring the person completely. And if he or she seems stubborn and won't take no for an answer, "be a Joseph—run for your life!" There is a saying that there is power in numbers, but there is more power in "e-x-o-d-u-s." Simply flee from fornication (1 Corinthians 6:18). Above all, I may add, is that you confess your sin to God and seek forgiveness from your mate. Pray a lot and strive to regain your mate's trust and confidence. Avoid situations that will lead you to the same trap. Philippians 4:13 assures us that we can do all things through Christ who strengthens us. Stay the course!

3. *Maintain the current trend.*

Maintaining the current trend, or keeping the status quo, may not be a bad idea if the analysis of experiences or trends show desirable results consistent with the expected end. Thus, the couple needs to maintain the trends that do not warrant change or drastic innovative strategies. In this case, simply use resources to maintain the situation, as things seem to be working for your marriage. As Americans say, "If it's not broken, don't fix it!"

Creating and maintaining a joyous marriage is a heavy-duty task, but it pays great dividends. It is rewarding, but not easy by any means. It requires (a) intentional and reflective introspection, (b) deliberate and constant evaluation, and (c) a mutually developed plan of action to address or correct the problems threating to spoil or steal the joy in the marriage. (See appendices A and B, where you will find guidance for doing a self-assessment and making a corrective plan of action to help you address things that are not working out in your marriage walk or to find deficits getting in the way of a joyful, mutually fulfilling marital relationship.)

Song

Breathe on me, Breath of God,
Fill me with life a new,
That I may love what Thou dost love,
And do what Thou wouldst do.

Breathe on me, Breath of God,
Until my heart is pure,
Until with Thee I will one will,
To do and to endure.

—Edwin Hatch

My Story

When I married my husband, he was a devout Catholic, and I was a staunch Adventist. We loved each other very much, but we were not equally yoked spiritually speaking. Because of this, we could not have a sound discussion about spiritual matters. Each time I talked to him about the Sabbath and told him to remember the seventh day and keep it holy, it would remind him to polish his shoes and attend a 6:00 a.m. Mass. He wanted us to attend a soccer game on the Sabbath and do other such kinds of activities. This was beginning to take a toll on our relationship, so I decided to pray about the matter and fast. God answered my prayers in three ways: First, my father-in-law, a preacher for the African Methodist Episcopal (AME) Church, called us and told us that he was not pleased to see us worship on separate days. He added that couples who worship together usually stay together. What helped and worked in my favor was not what he said but what he did not say. See, according to African culture, the word of the patriarch is law. Based on the African ethos, my father-in-law, the patriarch of the Nxumalo clan, could have easily mandated that I stop the nonsense and join my husband's church, case closed! But he did not say that. Instead, he counseled me and my husband to talk openly and review the fundamental biblical truths of the two churches, the reasons for our belief, and related doctrine from both churches, and then choose which was best for us from among the following options: (1) the Catholic Church, (2) the Seventh-day Adventist Church, (3) the AME Church, his home faith, or (4) any neutral denomination of our choice other than these three. He stressed that being of *one faith* was the major requirement and that we must not take it lightly. He then gave us six months to deliberate, explore, and come back to him with a decision. We both understood that attending *two separate churches* was not an acceptable option to my father-in-law.

My husband received a scholarship to study industrial relations in London. I prayed and fasted for God to lead the way. While Godwin was in the United Kingdom, he started attending a Seventh-day Adventist church. The rest is history. He accepted the Adventist faith, and all his brothers joined one by one, eventually marrying Adventist women. Now, their offspring are Adventists, and almost the entire Nxumalo clan. Please note that this experience left a lasting impression on me and has become a building block for me and Godwin and part of the framework for evaluating what is not going well in our marriage. We talk openly about issues, and once we identify the root cause, we conduct an analysis, redirect, and look at options, solutions, and a course of action prayerfully. But what is most important to us is finding a mutually satisfactory solution that will work for us as a couple. Once we take a course of action, there is no assigning of blame when things fall apart because we are both in this marriage marathon for the long haul. We rise or sink together!

Last Word

Finally, please remember that problems are inevitable in any marriage, but misery is optional. Joy can be experienced regardless of setbacks. Choose joy over misery. Joy is an attitude or state of mind that prevails even in the face of difficult circumstances. Joy is lasting and is internally determined. Joy is constant and unshaken by situations, whereas happiness is circumstantial, short-lived, and manipulated by external factors. Count it a joy to be able to identify what is wrong or not working well in your relationship. Redirect and apply strategies that will help your marriage be successful and bring mutually satisfying intimacy in all dimensions, *physical, emotional, spiritual, and intellectual.* May God bless your efforts.

Summary

I am Alpha and Omega the beginning and
the End, the First and the Last.

—Revelation 22:11 (NKJV)

It is puzzling that an institution as old as marriage, which predates the church establishment, is so misunderstood and unappreciated by many. Some fear it and are paralyzed by the thought of being married, and others take it too lightly and for granted. Whatever camp you fall in, the reason lies in the lack of a prescribed life curriculum to teach to those planning to enter into matrimony, leading them to understand what marriage really is or what it is not. For many, the only frame of reference they have is to draw from the life experiences of relationships preceding theirs. But the question is, was that the best environment to learn how to be married? I guess in most cases, the answer would be no.

We all walk the same matrimonial path, but unfortunately some are unprepared for the task at hand. Meanwhile, we pride ourselves on possessing bogus credentials, a certificate and license, say, without formal training for real marriage life. For some of us, this has created the illusion of preparedness. When life's pop quizzes, tests, and exams come our way, we fail dismally. We then realize how unprepared we are for the reality of marriage. Once we have this epiphany, it may be too late to mend the damage. There is no accredited institution that will issue a diploma and license to practice to any person who does not have the requisite training and a qualifying exam score in the discipline of interest, but the institution of marriage requires no such credentials. We forget that the first couple, Adam and Eve, were under the tutorage of God Himself. But in the realm of marriage, we take our chances and issue credentials without training. Then we wonder why there are so many casualties along the way of the marriage marathon.

It is my desire and hope that through the twenty-two pillars of joy in marriage, as addressed in *Pillars of Joy in Marriage*, couples will gain the perspective to help them (a) take another look at marriage, (b) perceive the union through heaven's lens, (c) find some tools to sustain their love relationship, (d) exercise wisdom in navigating the rough terrain and the heat of the marriage "welding process" as the two different lives are welded into one piece of art and the two souls are knitted into one beautiful tapestry, (e) embrace and celebrate each other's personality differences as strengths to complement the other's weaknesses, (f) derive joy from the marital relationship, even in the face of imperfection and life's challenges, and (g) invite Jesus Christ to be the center of the marriage, to rule and guide the marriage ship to its hopeful eternal destination.

The twenty-two pillars of joy in marriage, as explicated in *Pillars of Joy in Marriage*, affirm the notion that the marriage disposition model for God's children should strive to develop spiritual intimacy and instill in the couple the desire to reflect the character of God. Encourage Christians to anticipate, prepare, and wait for the marriage of the Lamb, our Lord Jesus Christ, the true Prince Charming, with His beloved—the church! He promised that He will come back again for His church, adorned as a bride and ready to meet Him at the altar in the sky, without sin, blemish, or wrinkles, to spend eternity with Him (Revelation 21:2–3, 22:2; Ephesians 5:24–27).

Let us all therefore hold on, because Jesus, our true Prince Charming, has assured us that He has prepared many rooms in His mansion for His bride in heaven (John 14:1–3), a getaway place for an eternal honeymoon with His beloved, where there will be organic spiritual intimacy and fellowship through everlasting eternity. "And it shall come to pass that from one New Moon to another, and from one Sabbath to another, all flesh shall come to worship before Me, says the Lord" (Isaiah 66:23 KJV). Let us remember also that sin deformed us, and because of this, our true Prince Charming has promised His bride the following:

1. That He is coming again to take us to an eternal reunion, never to be separated again.
2. Access to the tree of life—an everlasting healing therapy and an ageless diet that will reinstate us to the pre-sin physical condition and flawless stature experienced by Adam and Eve in the garden of Eden.
3. Transformation of our mortal bodies to a state of immortality. "When this corruptible has put on incorruption, this mortal must

put on immortality …. 'Death is swallowed up in victory'" (1 Corinthians 15:54 NKJV).

4. Restoration of spiritual and intellectual capacity, experienced by Adam and Eve in the pre-sin condition, characterized by perfect holiness and perfect happiness in an environment free of curses, evil, and sorrow. Yes, "there will be no more death or mourning or crying or pain, for the former things have passed away" (Revelation 21:4 NKJV). Surely, we will live happily ever after, and enjoy the pre-sin condition as articulated in the introduction to *Pillars of Joy in Marriage.*

In our sinful state, our carnal minds are limited and have difficulty trying to fathom a place of perfect happiness and everlasting joy without crime, sickness, and graveyards. That is why the apostle Paul exclaimed, "No eye has seen, no ear has heard, and no mind has imagined what God has prepared for those who love Him" (1 Corinthians 2:9 NLT).

In sum, whether we like it or not, all of us are driving our marriage under the influence of either someone or something. Nevertheless, there are choices to be made in shaping our marriage for eternity. Moving forward, the questions to ponder are as follows:

1. Whom do I want to govern my marriage relationship?
2. What model of the marriage institution do I want for me and my spouse?
3. Who determines the moral values in my house? Do I follow God's ordained will, and do I walk and do as God says?
4. Do I want to follow the crowd and do what others do, despite what God wants for my marriage?
5. Or do I want, like Samson in Judges 14:3, to follow my own will and do what pleases me, regardless of what God has ordained for my marriage and the institution of holy matrimony?

May I remind you that God did not design human beings to be robots. He made us to be free moral agents, with a choice to obey Him or not to obey Him. He will not force Himself into our homes to guide our marriages. He must be invited to do so. However, we need to be mindful of making a definitive choice about where we would like to spend eternity because God will not force that experience upon us either. Still, the question remains, on that great Judgment Day, which side of the fence would you like to be on? Do you prefer to be inside heaven looking out or, alternatively, to be outside heaven looking in? Luke 13:27 (NIV) tells us that outside heaven "there will be *weeping and gnashing of teeth*, when you see Abraham, Isaac and Jacob and all the prophets in the kingdom of God, but you yourself, thrown out" (emphasis added)! But inside heaven, there will be joy, unspeakable joy, full of glory, shouting, and praising for eternity. As a trusted steward of the ordained marriage institution, what would you prefer the Bridegroom to say to you as He opens the heavenly gates to welcome His bride, the saints, into the joy of eternal life? The Bible is unequivocal about the fate of those who have an organic and intimate spiritual relationship with the Bridegroom. The Lord shall declare to them: "Well done good and faithful servant; thou hast been faithful over a few things, I will make thee ruler over many things, enter thou into the joy of thy Lord" (Matthew 25:23 KJV).

Song

I cannot think of any song other than this wonderful piece by Fanny J. Cosby that describes the light of the blessed hope of the coming of Jesus Christ, to restore a better world made new, and to praise Him for all that He has done for His children, and what He has in store for us in His kingdom.

To God be the Glory, great things He hath done'
So, loved He the world that he gave us His Son,
Who yielded His life an attornment for sin,
And opened the life gate that all may go in.

Chorus:

Praise the Lord, praise the Lord, let the earth hear His voice
Praise the Lord, praise the Lord, let people rejoice;
Oh, come to the Father, through Jesus the Son,
And give him the glory, great things He hath done.

My Story

My story is one of praise, awe, and wonder as I reflect on the mercies of God toward His people, even toward a wretched sinner like me. Let me confess, I did not want to write *Pillars of Joy in Marriage*. I was hesitant to do so and felt a sense of inadequacy. I could have written and completed it two years ago, but I did everything in my power to avoid writing it. The reason I was afraid is that I felt God had impressed on me that I should write a how-to book on marriage that would also appeal to and tap into the conscience of specific target groups: the well-educated, the wealthy, and the worldly. Then I was really scared. I started doing what I know best, seeking clarification from God Himself through intense prayer, asking for His guidance and direction. I began to reflect on some of my friends, relatives, and associates whose lives represent those three categories and whose marriages were falling apart. It dawned on me that all three components, *education, wealth, and worldly lifestyle*, standing alone fail to sustain a marriage, although the union might have been founded on true love in the first place. Thus, I realized that being in love alone cannot sustain the marital relationship because love is fragile and easily bruised, but a marriage founded on God as the architect and central pillar can survive the turbulence of life, as reflected in my own marriage journey shared in *Pillars of Joy in Marriage*.

Now, the underlying challenge I had was to author an integrated how-to book founded on sound biblical principles yet garnished with scholarly or scientific flavor that might appeal to a variety of readers. It is easier to say to others "do this" or "do not do that," but to write a how-to book proved to be a challenge for me. I could not grasp how I would rise to the occasion of scripting material that appeals to the conscience of people in all three categories aforementioned. I began to claim the promises of God that have proven to sustain my own marriage through the years. Hence, I inquired of the Lord in prayer how I might achieve the task at hand.

First, regarding the educated audience, I reflected on the verse "the fear of the Lord is the beginning of wisdom" (Proverbs 9:10 KJV). God impressed on me that He does not depend on our academic preparation for Him to achieve His purpose, as He does not call those who are prepared but those whom He will prepare and who are willing to depend on His guidance. I reflected on the story of Jonah. He did not want to go to Nineveh, but God redirected him in nontraditional ways to land in the place where God had wanted him to be in the first place. I took comfort in Dr. William Cox's statement "If you do what God has commissioned you to do, He will make Himself personally responsible for your success."

Second, there was the challenge of also reaching the rich. I was concerned because I do not have material wealth, so how in the world could I tap into the conscience of the wealthy? Again, He impressed on me that I do not need to have riches to reach or appeal to the wealthy, because my God is rich, and I am His daughter. I reflected on His riches in glory as expressed in Haggai 2:8, which tells us that silver and gold are His. He owns cattle upon a thousand hills (Psalm 50:10). And the earth is the Lord's, as is everything in it (1 Corinthians 10:26). I then understood that my responsibility was to depend on Him as His faithful steward.

Third, I said in my heart, *Okay, Lord, I get it, but what about this worldly thing now?* As I continued meditating on my challenge, the Holy Spirit reminded me that I am not better off than the ordinary Jane Doe. I myself come a long way in my Christian walk. I was not always doing the right thing. The Lord found me in a dark pit of this earth, but He called me to the marvelous light by His grace and by the love of His Son, who died for me, which gave me the privilege of calling myself His child.

Marriage is a serious institution. God likens marriage to His relationship with His people—the church. He is the author of the marriage institution from the beginning of the world, so no one would understand the marriage institution more or better than God Himself.

I reflected on and found comfort in several stories in the Bible where individuals dared to do incredible things that sometimes seemingly appeared scary, stupid, or uncalculated. I thought of Jochebed, Moses's mother, who feared the decree issued by Pharaoh to kill all the Hebrew baby boys, but who was impressed to save baby Moses by wrapping him in a blanket, putting him in a basket, and dropping him in the wild Nile River. Certain things could have thwarted or aborted the ordained plan. For example, rain could have saturated the basket and sunk it. Poisonous creatures or river snakes could have bitten and killed the baby. Perhaps a crocodile could have gobbled up the baby, or the basket could have gone down the river out of control and disappeared. But instead, the Holy Spirit guided the basket to the feet of the princess of Egypt. Moses instantly became royalty and later led the children of Israel from bondage to freedom. At that point I was convinced that the Lord understood my dilemma and had heard my prayers. I remember mumbling to myself something like, "Now, Lord, I will write this book." I felt peace in my soul and was settled about writing the book, with no doubt in my mind that God had heard my plea and that He would guide me through it all as He did with baby Moses. Sure enough, He did.

But let me be honest. While I had no doubt in my mind that He was leading me, I did not believe I was ready for His agenda, because He literary controlled what I wrote and when I would write *Pillars of Joy in Marriage.* I was busy packing and jumping over bubble wrap and the like, preparing to ship our belongings home to South Africa, when he impressed on me to start writing the outline of *Pillars of Joy in Marriage.* After I completed the outline, my husband felt sick and was admitted to the hospital. I took that as a sign to stop focusing on the book for a while and pick it up again in South Africa, after we were settled into a home. I put together a collection of books on marriage written by big-name authors to take with me. I donated the rest of my library to friends, charitable organizations, and a neighborhood church, only to find that I still had too much luggage and all my suitcases were overweight. None of the books I thought I would take with me made it to Johannesburg, South Africa. The attendant at the airport pulled out even the books I had tried to squeeze in my luggage, to keep my bags within the weight limit. I was very upset, but I quickly returned to my senses and took this as a sign that the Lord really wanted me to depend on Him to pen my story and would lead me to nontraditional references I would not have considered otherwise. I rehearsed the promises of God and remembered His assurances: "Be strong and of good courage, do not fear nor be afraid …; for the Lord your God, He is the one who goes with you. He will never leave you nor forsake you" (Deuteronomy 31:6–8 NKJV). "And we know all things work for the good of those who love Him, who have been called according to His purpose" (Romans 8:28 NIV). "Trust in the Lord with all your heart; do not depend on your own understanding" (Proverbs 3:5 NIV). "But they that wait upon the Lord shall renew their strength; they shall mount up with wings as eagles; they shall run and not be weary; and they shall walk, and not faint" (Isaiah 40:31 KJV).

Finally, I began to ask myself, *Now what's the problem? Didn't the Lord and I settle this? Nozipho, learn to depend on Him and you will be fine. If He gives you a task, He will enable you to accomplish His design. Have faith, be obedient, and enjoy the ride.* I bowed my head in silent prayer, asking God to forgive me for my lack of faith. I asked Him to guide me and help me write *Pillars of Joy in Marriage* and achieve His plan for me. I promised to be obedient and not to trust in my own understanding or educational preparation. I felt a resurgence of courage and peace. Ten months later, *Pillars of Joy in Marriage* was completed and ready to be uploaded to the press.

Now, looking back at my writing journey, I realize that the Lord led me to read a variety of books that were not even related to marriage but that had a significant impact on shaping some of the pillars addressed in my manuscript. Surely, God wanted me to write my own story. For example, Dr. Calvin B. Rock's book *Something Better: God's Gracious Provision for Our Daily Decision* inspired me to see nuances in the marital relationship resembling the struggles of ministry, whereby the church contends with overcoming sin and desires to reflect the character of God in a sin-sick world while preparing for His coming. Dr. Ravi Zacharias's book *Why Jesus?* discussed human existence in the new age of mass-marketed spirituality. This confirmed to me the need for married couples to intentionally rediscover and embrace Jesus as the central pillar of their relationship if the marriage institution and family are to survive the onslaught of humanity's archenemy, the devil. Dr. Barry Black's book *The Blessing of Adversity: Finding God's Given Purpose in Your Life's Troubles* was very helpful in making me realize that couples can survive the turbulent times and vicissitudes of life when they are totally submitted to God and trust in His power to turn painful circumstances around. Dr. Jim Sharps' *Health Quotient*, on basic principles of health, inspired my view of marriage as an investment and taught me that a healthy lifestyle is one among numerous viable assets that is helpful in achieving a sound marriage investment portfolio with substantial dividends, now and later in life. I am pleased with how *Pillars of Joy in Marriage* turned out, and I have no doubt that God inspired and guided me in my writing. Indeed, God keeps His word!

Last Word

The prophet Isaiah has warned us that "the redeemed of the Lord shall return and come with singing unto Zion; and everlasting *joy* shall be upon their land: they shall obtain gladness and *joy*" (Isaiah 51:11 NKJV, emphasis added). Through the twenty-two pillars, *Pillars of Joy in Marriage* has articulated how couples can obtain joy in marriage, even in the absence of true happiness and holiness on this earth, which is colored by sin. In various ways, *Pillars of Joy in Marriage* has argued that a joyous marriage does not come by chance or happenstance but is predicated on developing the right perspective and an organic relationship with Christ, which includes an understanding of our existence on this earth as we deliberately prepare for the coming of Jesus Christ, our true Prince Charming!

The choice is clear for me. I liken myself to Joshua, who was faced with similar circumstances and choices, such as whether to serve the Lord or other gods of the land. He chose to serve the Lord (Joshua 24:14–15). I declare, without a doubt in my mind, "As for me and my house, I choose God's prescribed moral imperative to shape my marriage union for eternity." What about you? Perhaps you would not mind our Lord Jesus Christ, the true Prince of Peace, painfully rejecting you, saying, "Depart from me I never knew you; you workers of iniquity" (Matthew 7:21–23, 25:12, 21)! Or perhaps, like me, you would prefer to fall within the group mentioned in Revelation 22:15 and hear the Lord welcoming you, saying, "Good and faithful servant, welcome to the joy of salvation and enjoy eternal life forever more." The choice is yours! You still have time to redirect your life and change your perspective so that it is consistent with the original design for humankind's existence, to reflect the character of God and inherit eternal joy! "A good name is to be chosen over great wealth; favor is better than silver and gold" (Proverbs 22:1 NLT).

Oh, what a day of rejoicing it will be when we join a multitude of believers in that sea of glass, singing the song of Moses and the Lamb! In my imagination, I see us joining hands, worshipping and praising, shouting and singing.

> Holy, holy, holy! Lord God Almighty;
> Early in the morning our songs shall rise to Thee;
> Holy, holy, holy, merciful and mighty;
> God over all who rules eternity.
> Holy, holy, holy! Angels adore Thee,

Casting down their bright crowns around the glassy sea;
Thousands and thousands worship low before Thee,
Which wert and evermore shall be!

—Reginald Heber

I plan to be there in our eternal home at last. Will you be in that number?

Appendix A

Marriage Self-Assessment

Ten Critical Questions to Reflect On

1. Who taught me how to be married? _____ Where? _____

    _____

    _____

2. Looking back, was this an ideal environment in which to learn how to be married? _____

    _____

3. What is keeping me married to my spouse now? _____

    _____

    _____

4. What is currently threatening to destroy the joy in our marriage? _____

    _____

    _____

5. What things do I wish I could change about our relationship? _____

    _____

    _____

6. What is the #1 thing that must change for me and my spouse to experience full joy in our marriage? _____

_____

_____

7. What do I consider to be unchangeable assets in our marriage? _____

_____

_____

8. I believe my spouse and I experience greater joy in the following areas of our marriage: _____

_____

_____

9. If we decide not to take any steps to change, what would happen? _____

_____

_____

10. I believe that improving the following areas would enhance the joy in our marriage: _____

_____

_____

Appendix B

Corrective Action Plan Framework for Married Couples

Looking at your marriage journey (per your responses to the questions in appendix A), write a corrective action plan to remodel your marriage. You may also incorporate your responses to the self-assessment questions in appendix C. (*Note:* You and your spouse should write your answers independently, and then compare your responses to ensure you are in sync.) The key is to help you define the root cause of any problems and arrive at mutually fulfilling solutions. Choose the areas you need to address using the framework described under pillar #22, and then develop an action plan as follows:

Vision statement for our marriage _____

_____

Long-term goal _____

_____

Short-term goal(s) _____

_____

Benchmarks _____

_____

My responsibility _____

_____

My spouse's responsibility _____

_____

Evaluation *(establish indicators to determine when you have met your goals [performance measures])* _____

_____

_____

_____

_____

_____

Decision to redirect *(refer to figure 22.1)* _____

_____

_____

_____

_____

_____

Appendix C

Revitalizing Marriage Intimacy Self-Assessment

This instrument is designed to help married couples evaluate their intimacy and identify areas that need attention in meeting each other's needs. The results will provide an opportunity for open dialogue, a decision to redirect, and the resolve to fill each other's love tank levels, thereby revitalizing intimacy and infusing the marriage with joy moving forward.

(Respond to statements *alone*, prayerfully, and with introspection, and be as honest as possible.)

1. On a scale of 1 to 10, how much do you really know your mate's likes and dislikes?

Check   (Wife's)   Check   (Husband's)

----   _____   ----   _____

2. On a scale of 1 to 10, how much do you really know your mate's love needs?

Check   (Wife's)   Check   (Husband's)

----   _____   ----   _____

A. Dr. Gary and Barbara Rosberg have identified five love needs of men and women, as listed below. Please select your needs and rate each one you selected on a scale of 1 to 10 to indicate how well your mate is meeting your love needs.

Check and select only five love needs: (Wife's)   Check   (Husband's)

---- Companionship   _____   ----   _____

---- Encouragement and affirmation   _____   ----   _____

---- Sexual intimacy   _____   ----   _____

---- Communication and emotional   _____   ----   _____
intimacy

---- Spiritual intimacy   _____   ----   _____

----   Unconditional   love   and   _____   ----   _____
acceptance

B. Dr. Gary Chapman identified five love languages. Select what you consider to be your primary or major love language(s) from these: (1) quality time, (2) words of affirmation, (3) giving and receiving gifts, (4) acts of service, and (5) physical touch. Then, using a scale of 1 to 10, rate your love language to the degree or level at which your spouse is meeting your love language needs or is filling your love tank.

Quality time (e.g., commitment to filling up the void or loneliness; spark; joy of togetherness; fun and laughter):

Wife _____   _____ Husband

Words of affirmation (e.g., commitment to marriage permanence; engaging in healthy talk and positive communication; resolving conflict / working things out):

Wife _____   _____ Husband

Acts of service (e.g., doing, serving, and ministering to my mate and striving to meet my mate's needs):

Wife _____   _____ Husband

Giving and receiving gifts (loving unconditionally, and giving practical gifts, time, talent, and treasure):

Wife _____   _____ Husband

Physical touch (e.g., a mutually fulfilling relationship at all levels of intimacy, as it relates to the following things):

- Physical intimacy: Wife: _____   _____ Husband
- Emotional intimacy   Wife: _____   _____ Husband
- Spiritual intimacy: Wife: _____   _____ Husband
- Intellectual intimacy   Wife: _____   _____ Husband

Scoring: highest possible score is 150; average score is 75; lowest possible score is 15

Tally and total your scores. Have an honest discussion with your mate to decide which areas of intimacy you need to work on or make some changes to. The results mirror how fulfilled you are overall by your marriage.

Note: Problematic situations in marriage are inevitable, but misery is optional. If mediocrity is not an option for you, then choose *joy*, not misery, by working on the problematic situations you have identified in your marriage.

Redirecting: There are three possible choices to make: (1) *improve* what is not working well, (2) *maintain* what seems to work for you, or (3) *stop doing* whatever seems detrimental or is not helping.

Appendix D

Health Quotient

A Simple Health Evaluation Tool

For each item, indicate how often you do the thing mentioned. If never or rarely (1 to 3 times a month), **enter a 0**; if sometimes (1 to 2 days a week), **enter a 3**; if most of the time (4 or more times a week), **enter a 6**; if daily (6 or 7 days a week), **enter a 10**. Total both scores and subtract the *factors minimizing health* from the *factors maximizing health*. **The result is your HQ.**

A maximum HQ of 150 *indicates superior health*. A score of 100 to 125 is a *good intermediary goal for most of us*. A score of 60 to 100 represents *suboptimal health*, even though there may be no current symptoms. A score of 60 is problematic for most people and requires improvement. By looking at both the positive and negative elements relating to health, you can make some practical adjustments to meet your personal health objectives.

Scoring	Points
Never or rarely	0
Sometimes	3
Most of the time	6
Daily	10

This is just a simple HQ applying a simple formula
to basic health and wellness principles. Try it, apply
it, have fun with it, and enjoy good health.

Factors maximizing health		Score	Factors minimizing health	Score
1	Plant foods (fruits, vegetables, nuts, seeds)		Meat	
2	Chew food slowly and thoroughly		Meat substitutes	
3	Avoid liquids with meals		Fried foods	
4	Wait four to six hours between meals		Recreational drugs	
5	Eat a small supper at least three hours before bed		Prescription drugs	
6	Drink sufficient water		Dairy products	
7	Deep breathing		Alcoholic beverages	
8	Exercise		Tobacco	
9	Sufficient sunlight when available		Caffeine or chocolate	
10	Sufficient rest (six to nine hours a day)		Excessive work or exercise	
11	Positive attitude and emotions		Air pollution	
12	Safe and clean environment		Soda or store-bought juices	
13	Meditation/prayer life		Snacks between meals	
14	Purpose for life		Processed or junk foods	
15	Personal responsibility for health		Excessive TV (> 10 hours per week)	
Total maximizing factors			**Total minimizing factors**	

Column 1 _____ – Column 2 _____ = _____ (My HQ score) Scoring	Points
Radiant Health—Optimal	125–150
Health—Suboptimal	100–125
Suboptimal Health	60–100
Needs Improvement	< 60
Disclaimer: This HQ instrument was adapted from the original developed by the International Institute of Original Medicine (IIOM). Copyright © 2012 by the International Institute of Original Medicine, and posted by Marvin Marshall. Used with permission of Dr. Jim Sharps. All rights reserved.	

Appendix E

New Start toward Healthful Living

You Can Do It!

Whether rich or poor, we do have a choice and the ability to decide the investment we will make in our health. We all have the innate attributes or basic initial value of assets in our health investment account bestowed by God. These are available to all of us equally, at no cost, only if we would take advantage of these gifts and add them to our health investment portfolios. All we need is a conscious resolve to follow through, receive the gifts, and make a *new start* by maximizing the capital obtained from the following:

> **N**—Nutrition capital. Investing in nutrition is a choice and an indirect commitment to the body to keep it healthy and sound, so your spouse may enjoy you for the rest of your life. Dr. Jim Sharps suggests a vitality diet consisting mostly of fruits, vegetables, grains, and nuts, from which we derive natural nutrients. According to Sam Davis, "we are what we eat and we derive better health benefits from food when we consume nutrients in their natural state closer from the tree and ground, such as fruits, grains, vegetables and nuts; and the better they are for our system than when they have been processed and loaded with chemicals."

> **E**—Exercise capital. We need at least fifteen to thirty minutes of moderate exercise daily. Inactivity is a killer in many ways! I was taken aback when I heard in a Sam Davis seminar that an overwhelming majority of chronic diseases are lifestyle based, and that at least 80 percent of these diseases can be reversed with intentional lifestyle changes.

> **W**—Water capital. Blood is made up of 80 percent water. The vital benefits of water are widely publicized, from maintaining the elasticity of our skin, to excreting and flushing toxins from our system, to

lubricating the eyes. We need to drink at least six to eight eight-ounce glasses of water a day. One of my friends shared with me that she does not drink water but instead relies on sodas—Coke and the like. But the turnaround for her was when she developed serious health problems and the doctor attributed her condition to water deficiency. I now understand a statement Sam Davis made: "80 percent or more of chronic conditions can be reversed by making simple lifestyle changes, such as intentional choices and commitment to good nutrition, water, exercise and the like."

S—Sunshine capital. The sun is a source of energy. Other than the fact that it warms us, we derive vitamin D to dissolve calcium from the sun. With our sedentary lifestyle and our rarely walking outside to breathe the fresh air and bask in the sun, we have come to rely on supplements to make up for the deficiency in natural nutrients. I can attest to the value of vitamin D. One time I was very sick and weak, and a doctor diagnosed me with a gross deficiency of vitamin D. I know firsthand the value of sunshine capital. It is a health investment.

T—Temperance capital. Overindulgence, even in a good thing, such as food, is detrimental to our system and alters the mood. Imbibing intoxicating drinks and doing recreational drugs adds insults to injury. Sometimes, using common sense, which is no longer common, is a virtue. Knowing when to stop or disengage from adverse behavior is a test of character. This is where the guiding hand of the Lord is a plus. Our bodies are the temple of the Lord, and whatsoever we eat or drink we should have glorifying the Lord on our minds. According to Sam Davis, "Anything we put in our mouths, eat or drink, has a potential to build or kill our body." Think about this!

A—Air capital. Fresh air invigorates the body, gives clarity of mind, and leads to a sweeter disposition. Unfortunately, we are stifled by sitting constantly at work. We are bombarded with environmental pollution and chemicals in the air that take away from the benefits of walking in open air. A brisk walk in an open space early in the morning at a park or around the neighborhood is beneficial.

R—Rest capital. We need at least six to eight hours of quality sleep daily for renewal and vitality. Sometimes, given the necessity of just making ends meet, we are overworked, and sometimes we work too much to keep up with the Joneses. In the long run, this type of lifestyle has negative consequences and breaks down our immune system. What's the point of gaining financial rewards and losing your health and enjoyment of life? Some illnesses that could be prevented by simple lifestyle changes are very expensive to contend with and can wipe out all your cash savings in an instant. You worked hard for the money, but it is worthless if it is at the expense of your health.

T—Trust capital. We need to trust in divine power. One thing is for sure: faith and worry do not go together. We cannot be stressed and trust in the Lord at the same time. These are diametrically opposed constructs and one must supersede the other. You have a right to choose which one of the two rules should be dominant in your life. When we pray and have faith in the Divine Power to lead us and solve our situation, we develop positive energy and have a resurgence of hope and peace from knowing that our situation is in the capable hands of God. At that point, there is no need to worry and stress. Trusting the Lord through prayer, and having faith in God's GPS and guidance, is an intentional lifestyle. So, choose *trust*. The assurance is our Father's words: "Anyone who comes to me, I will by no means cast out" (John 6:37 NKJV).

References

Adventist Hymnal. South African Union Conference, 1960.

Banschick, Mark. "The High Failure Rate of Second and Third Marriages." *The Intelligent Divorce* (blog). *Psychology Today*, February 6, 2012, https://www.psychologytoday.com/blog/the-intelligent-divorce/201202/the-high-failure-rate-second-and-third-marriages.

Black, Barry. *The Blessing of Adversity: Finding Your God-Given Purpose in Life's Troubles.* Carrol Spring, IL: Tyndale House, 2011.

———. "Higher Ground: Improving Your Prayer Life" (sermon), September 23, 2011. Normandie Avenue SDA Church.

Bonham, Tal D. *Humor: God's Gift.* Baptist Sunday School Board, 1987.

Bradford, Charles E. *Find Out about Prayer: An Urgent Call to Rediscover the Secret of Spiritual Power.* Fallbrook, CA: Hart Research Center, 1993.

Brown, Brené. *The Gift of Imperfection.* Center City, MN: Hazelden, 2010.

Brown, Marvin C. Remarks at a renewal of wedding vows ceremony. Cape Town, South Africa, 2013.

Chapman, Gary. *The Four Seasons of Marriage: Which Season of Marriage Are You In?* Wheaton, IL: Tyndale House, 2005.

Chapman, Gary. *The Five Love Languages.* Chicago: Northfield Publishers, 1995. (For the official online version of the Love Languages Quiz, see www.5lovelanguages.com.)

Cleveland, E. E. Class lecture. Huntsville, AL: Oakwood College, 1982.

Colliers, Lorna. "Growth after Trauma: Why Are Some People More Resilient Than Others?" *American Psychological Association*, http://www.apa.org/monitor/2016.

Cole, Steven. "Focus on the Family: Issues on Marriage." stevencolesermons.org/sermons.

Cox, W. T. Sermons. Columbus, OH: Ephesus Seventh-day Adventist Church, 2009.

Davis, Sam. Lectures on healthy lifestyles. Sandton, Johannesburg, South Africa: Metro Mission SDA Church, May 2017.

Doherty, William H. "How Common Is Divorce and What Are the Reasons? Should I Keep Trying to Work It Out?" Utah State University Extension. https://divorce.usu.edu/files-ou/Lesson3.pdf.

Eib, Lyn. *Finding the Light in Cancer's Shadows*. Carol Stream, IL: Tyndale House, 2006.

Eysenck, Hans J., and M. W. Eysenck. *Personality and Individual Differences: A Natural Science Approach*. New York: Springer/Plenum, 1985.

Frankl, Victor. *Psychotherapy and Existentialism: Selected Papers on Logotherapy*. New York: Pocket Books, 1967.

Fuller, Jean. "Shekinah Glory Intimacy: What Does Shekinah Glory Have to Do with Sex?" *Christian Intimacy Experts*. https://www.christianintimacyexperts.com.

Gibson, Ty. *Sermons at Light Bearers*. Eugene, OR: Storyline SDA Church.

Goodall, Wayde. "Healthy Marriages." FamilyRelationships.com. https://family-relationships.com/videos/healthy-marriages.

Goyer, Tricia. "Physical Intimacy in Marriage: Sex Can Be an Oasis in Your Marriage." www.triciagoyer.com.

Gray, John. *Men Are from Mars, Women Are from Venus: The Classic Guide to Understanding the Opposite Sex*. New York: Harper Collins, 2007.

Hale, Frank W. Jr. Family Life Marriage Symposium. Columbus, OH: Ephesus SDA Church, 2009.

Hasel, Frank M. *Adult Sabbath School Bible Study Guide: The Holy Spirit and Spirituality*. Silver Springs, MD: Pacific Press, 2017.

"The Health Benefits of Laughter." *Whole Health Insider* (July 2012): 1–6.

Hunter, Charles, and Frances Hunter. *Healing through Humor: Keep the Doctor Away with a Giggle a Day*. Lake Mary, FL: Creation House, 2003.

Johari Window Communication Model of Self-Disclosure and Personality Development, 1995. UCLA. http://communicationtheory.org/the-johari-window-model.

Kot, Linda. Sabbath Fellowship Discussions. Metro-Mission Seventh-day Adventist Church. Sandton, Johannesburg, May 2017.

La Haye, Tim. *Your Temperament: Discover Its Potential*. Carol Stream, IL: Tyndale House, 1984.

Life Compass blog. "Overcoming Obstacles and Adversities in Life," December 2011. http://www.lifecompassblog.com/overcoming-obstacles-adversity.

Maxwell, Randy. *Love Strong: Break through to Your Dream Relationship*. Chicago: College Press, 2016.

Moya, E. S. Sermons in Mbabane Seventh-day Adventist Church. Swaziland, Southern Africa.

Nxumalo, Nozipho. Family Life Marriage Symposia. Columbus, OH: Ephesus SDA Church, 2008, 2009.

Rock, Calvin B. *Something Better: God's Gracious Provision for Our Daily Decisions*. Hagerstown, MD: Review and Heralds, 2016.

Rogers, Adrian. "Your Sense of Humor: A Gift from God," September 14, 2011. *Love Worth Finding*. http://www.christianity.com/devotionals/love-worth-finding.

Rosberg, Gary, and Barbara Rosberg. *The Five Love Needs of Men and Women: Groundbreaking Research That Will Change Your Marriage*. Carol Stream, IL: Tyndale House, 2000.

Ravhengani, Mashudu M. J. *Unleashing the Marriage Potential: Proven Principles for Building, Restoring, and Sustaining Marriage in the 21st Century*. Irene Glen, Gauteng, South Africa: Living Power Books, 2014.

Sigl-Davis, Donna. "Pillow Talk" (presentation). Columbus, OH: Ephesus SDA Church, 2004.

Spalding Colbum, Carol. *A Touch of Joy: Devotional Thoughts for Women by Women*. Hagerstown, MD: Review and Heralds Publishing Association, 1995.

Thomas, Gary L. *The Sacred Marriage: What if Marriage Was Designed to Make Us Holy More Than to Make Us Happy?* Grand Rapids, MI: Zondervan, 2007.

Van Pelt, Nancy. *Keys to Happiness Character-Building Library: A Guide to Successful Marriage, Highly Effective Workbook*. Portland, TN: Wilks Publications, 1990.

Walsh, Brenda. *Moments with God: One-Minute Devotions to Encourage, Inspire, and Spiritually Change Your Life*. Nampa, ID: Pacific Press, 2017.

Webster's Online Dictionary with Multiple Thesaurus. https://groups.google.com/forum/.

White, Ellen G. *Christ Object Lessons: The Ellen White Publications.* Hagerstown, MD: Review and Heralds, 1941.

————. *Steps to Christ.* Mountain View, CA: Pacific Press Publishing Association, 1892.

Willschiebe, Charles E. *God Invented Sex.* Nashville: Southern Publishers Association, 1974.

Wilson, P. B. *Liberation through Submission: The Ultimate Paradox.* Eugene, OR: Harvest House, 1990.

Wright, Henry. "Here Comes Jesus" (sermon). Washington, DC: Tacoma SDA Church, 2015.

Zacharias, Ravi. *Why Jesus? Discovering His Truth in an Age of Mass Market Spirituality.* Nashville: Faith Words, 2012.

Songs Referenced

Category 1—Hymnal Sacred Songs

Seventh-day Adventist Hymnal. Hagerstown, MD: Review and Heralds Publishing Association, 1985, 2008

Belden, F. E., "We Know Not the Hour"

Bolton, Fannie E., "Not I but Christ"

Chisholm, Thomas O., "Great Is Thy Faithfulness"

Crosby, J. Fanny, "He Hideth My Soul" (1820)

———, "Blessed Assurance, Jesus Is Mine" (1873)

———, "To God Be the Glory" (1875)

Davis, Frank M., "Lord, I Care Not for Riches"

Graeff, Frank E., "Does Jesus Care?"

Hatch, Edwin, "Breathe on Me, Breath of God"

Heber, Reginald, "Holy, Holy, Holy, Lord God Almighty"

Morris, C. H., "Nearer Still Near"

Mote, Edward, "My Hope Is Built on Nothing Else"

Osterman, Eurydice, "God, Who Stretched the Spangled Heavens" (1984)

———, "I Want Jesus to Walk with Me" (1984)

Shorey, Marry Ann, "My Lord and I"

Spafford, Horatio G., "It Is Well with My Soul"

Stead, Louis, "'Tis So Sweet to Trust in Jesus"

Stebbins, George, "Have Thine Own Way, Lord"

Stuttle, Avery L. D., "Oh, Let Me Walk with Thee"

Walford, William, "Sweet Hour of Prayer"

Watts, Isaac, "Lord in the Morning"

Wesley, Charles, "Oh, for a Thousand Tongues"

Williams, William, "Guide Me O Great Jehovah"

Category 2—Other Sacred Songs

Rambo, Dottie, "He Looked beyond My Faults"

Smallwood, Richard, "Jesus Is the Center of My Joy"

Category 3—Secular Love Songs and Blues

Benton, Brook, "Looking Back Over My Life"

Cole, Nat King, "When I Fall in Love"

Printed in the United States
By Bookmasters